Economics

Economics

Stephen Ison

Senior Lecturer in Economics, Department of European Business Economics,
Anglia Business School, Anglia Polytechnic University

THE M & E HANDBOOK SERIES

Pitman Publishing
128 Long Acre, London WC2E 9AN

A Division of Longman Group UK Limited

© Longman Group UK Limited 1993

First published in Great Britain 1993

A catalogue record for this book is available from the British Library.

ISBN 0 7121 0845 9

Founding Editor P.W.D. Redmond

Printed and bound in Singapore

Contents

Part two   Macroeconomics

Preface

This book has been specifically written for those students who want a clear and concise reference book which is an up-to-date introduction to the fundamental principles of economics.

It is clearly structured for ease of use and is ideal for students of 'A' level economics and professional courses who are studying economics for the first time and who want to quickly grasp the essentials. The topics covered in the 18 chapters are common to most 'A' level and professional syllabuses. Students will find also this book excellent for revision.

The book is split into two parts and progresses from microeconomics covered in Chapters 2-9, to macroeconomics covered in Chapters 10-18. There is a frequent cross-referencing throughout the book which the reader will find helpful, either to remind the reader of areas already covered in previous chapters or to refer to topic areas which will be covered in more detail later in the book. At the end of each chapter there are progress tests in order for the student to check their understanding. Each question is cross-referenced to the appropriate section in the chapter.

In writing this text, I would like to thank, first, the Controller of Her Majesty's Stationery Office, the Central Statistical Office and the Bank of England for granting permission to reproduce a number of their tables and figures. Second, I am grateful to Jennifer Mair, Soraya Romano and Catriona King at Pitman for their patience and flexible attitudes throughout the production of this book; and third, I would like to thank my wife and children, Susanna, James and Naomi, for putting up with me spending long periods of time in my study in front of a PC. Finally, I am grateful to Harry Zavros, Alan Griffiths and Ross Catteral for reading many of the chapters and making useful comments and observations. However, I bear full responsibility for any errors and omissions.

Stephen Ison
Cambridge
December 1992

1

The nature of economics

The subject matter of economics

1. Introduction

What causes unemployment? What determines the wage level? What is the role of money in the economy? What causes inflation? Is there a need for government intervention in the economy? These are the types of questions economists are interested in and around which theories have been developed in order to aid our understanding.

This chapter aims to introduce a number of the basic concepts which you will find useful as you progress through the book. The economic problem of scarcity and choice is central to economics and will be covered in this chapter, together with the economic systems which attempt to deal with the economic problem.

2. Defining economics

There is no one definition of economics, although a useful starting point is the well established definition provided by Lord Robbins as long ago as 1932. He defined *economics* as '*the science which studies human behaviour as a relationship between ends and scarce means which have alternative uses*'. At first reading this may appear a difficult definition to understand, however, if it is studied in more detail it can be seen to offer a useful insight. We can dissect the definition as follows:

(a) Economics is a '*social science*' in that it uses scientific methods to study human behaviour.
(b) Human needs are unlimited whereas resources are in limited supply, hence the problem of *scarcity*.
(c) The resources can be put to *alternative uses* in order to meet certain *ends*, such as the building of a power station or a railway line. Since resources are scarce, *choices* have to be made as to how resources are utilised.

3. The economic problem

Economics studies the allocation, distribution and utilisation of resources to meet human needs. A central element in the economic problem, then, is the allocation of scarce resources among alternative uses. *Resources* (human, physical and financial) are *limited* in supply while human needs and desires are infinite. These needs are usually called '*wants*'. Some of the wants are *necessities* such as basic food, clothing and housing but there are also desires for other items such as CD players, video recorders or even a night at the opera. Probably at the level of the individual and certainly for human kind as a whole, human wants are *unlimited*. If you think about your own situation some of the goods and services you require you will be able to obtain with the scarce resources, i.e. income, available to you. There are likely, however, to be other items you would like to have but are unable to obtain because of limited resources. The same economic problem faces all individuals, organisations and societies — limited wants, unlimited resources.

The resources an economy has at its disposal are used to satisfy the unlimited wants. These are often termed by economists *inputs* or *factors of production*. They are the means of producing the goods and services society requires to meet human needs and can be divided into four main categories:

(a) *land*, which is the natural resource;
(b) *labour*, which is the human resource;
(c) *capital*, the man-made resource;
(d) *enterprise*, the resource which organises the other factors of production and takes the risks.

The factors of production will be dealt with in more detail in Chapter 5: **9-13**.

Since the resources are limited in supply (i.e., scarce) and there is the existence of unlimited wants, *choices* have to be made — choices involving the allocation of scarce resources among alternative uses to achieve given ends. Economics is also concerned with the *distribution* of resources between different groups in society. So in addition to the problem of *what* gets produced (allocation), there is the problem of *who* gets what is produced (*see* Chapters 8 and 9). Moreover, there is the problem of resource *utilisation*, ensuring that all the available resources are used effectively. This is the subject matter of *macroeconomics* and is dealt with in Part two.

4.   Opportunity cost

As stated, resources are limited in supply and have alternative uses. However, if they are used in the production of, say, hi fi equipment then they cannot be used in the production of video recorders. So if society chooses to produce more hi fi equipment it would have to forego a certain quantity of video recorders which those same resources could have produced. In other words, the *opportunity cost* of producing more of the former is less of the latter. This concept is central to the study of economics at a number of levels:

(a) *At the individual level*, if one decides to grow more potatoes in the garden then one has to reduce the production of, say, carrots. The limited space in the garden can be viewed as the scarce resource and one cannot produce more of one good, potatoes, and still produce the same amount of another, carrots.

(b) *At the level of the firm* the resources currently used to produce, say, milk chocolate can only be used to produce plain chocolate if they are diverted to it.

(c) *At government level*, a decision to build two new schools may be at the expense of the alternative option of building a new hospital.

When considering opportunity cost it is important to note that such choices are only required if all existing resources are being fully used. If this were not the case the idle resources, in our examples, garden space, machinery and taxation revenue, could be used instead.

Society has to decide what goods and services it is going to produce. This will involve choices because producing more of one good or service will normally mean producing less of another if all existing resources are being fully utilised.

5. The production possibility frontier (PPF)

The central problem in economics of scarcity, choice, opportunity cost and resource allocation can be analysed by using a production possibility frontier or curve as shown in Figure 1.1.

Figure 1.1 represents a hypothetical production possibility frontier AF for an economy producing two products: food and clothing. The PPF shows the alternative combinations of the two products that the country can produce if it fully utilises all of its resources. For example, if all the country's resources were used in the production of clothing then the total output would be 30 units of clothing and there would be no food production. This is represented by point A. If, however, all the resources were devoted to the production of food, the economy would be at point F with 25 units of food produced but zero clothing. Alternatively, the economy could be at any point on the PPF producing a certain amount of food and clothing. However, if the economy were at point G it would signify that the economy was

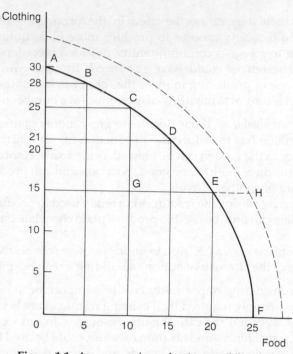

Figure 1.1 *An economy's production possibility frontier.*

under-utilising its resources. There would be unemployed resources and by bringing those resources into use the economy could move to a position on the curve such as point D, where more clothing and food could be produced.

It is clearly sensible for an economy to be on the PPF rather than inside it since at point G the economy is producing 15 units of clothing and 10 units of food, whereas at point D the economy is producing 21 units of clothing and 15 units of food. Once on the PPF it is not possible to increase the production of one of the two products without reducing the production of the other product. So, for example, if the economy were at point D a movement along the frontier to point E would involve a reallocation of resources. Hence an increase in food production of 5 units would require a reduction in clothing production of 6 units.

Points outside the frontier such as H, representing other combinations of food and clothing output, are unattainable – given the existing resource availability and the state of technology. A shift outwards in the PPF represents *economic growth*, which means the ability to produce more goods which in the example used means more food and clothing. This can be brought about either by technological change, i.e. new and better ways of producing the goods and services, or through an increase in the economy's productive capacity, achieved through an increase in the supply of the factors of production.

6. The PPF and opportunity cost

The frontier can be viewed in terms of opportunity cost since to produce more units of one product needs resources to be taken from the production of the other. In Figure 1.1 the frontier is *concave* to the origin and this means that the opportunity cost will change as we move along the frontier. If we start at point A and move down the curve we can see how the opportunity cost changes (*see* Table 1.1).

Table 1.1 The opportunity cost of food

Movement along the curve	Change in food	Change in clothing	Opportunity cost $\dfrac{\Delta \ in \ clothing}{\Delta \ in \ food} X - 1$
From A to B	+5	−2	0.4
From B to C	+5	−3	0.6
From C to D	+5	−4	0.8
From D to E	+5	−6	1.2
From E to F	+5	−15	3.0

A movement from A to B involving the production of 5 units of food requires a reduction of 2 units in the production of cloth. So the opportunity cost of 5 units of food is 2 units of clothing, with an opportunity cost of 0.4. (One unit of food has been gained at the expense of 0.4 units of clothing.) The opportunity cost is initially small as the resources better suited to the production of food move from the production of clothing.

As more food is produced, it is necessary to reallocate resources which are less suited to the production of food. In moving from B to C an extra 5 units of food production will involve a reduction in clothing production of 3 units, with a resulting opportunity cost of 0.6. A movement from C to D will require a loss in clothing production of 4 units (an opportunity cost of 0.8) and from D to E a loss of 6 units of clothing (an opportunity cost of 1.2). Finally a movement from E to F, again with an extra 5 units of food production, will require foregoing 15 units of clothing with an opportunity cost of 3.0.

The production possibility frontier provides an insight into the issues of scarcity and choice which an economy faces when deciding what goods and services to produce.

Economic systems

7.   Introduction

Although all countries throughout the world have to face similar economic problems, the economic system they adopt as a means of dealing with them will differ. Essentially there are two approaches to tackling the economic problem of allocation, distribution and utilisation of resources:

(a) A *market* economy allocates resources through the forces of demand and supply with prices being determined by the market.

(b) A *planned* economy allocates resources through administrative decisions.

A *mixed* economy contains features of both the market and planned economic systems

8.   The market economy

In a 'pure' free market economy there would be no government intervention and decisions as to the allocation of resources would be taken by individual producers and consumers, through a system known as the *price mechanism*.

The market or price mechanism is a central feature of a market economy. An outline of how the market mechanism works can be seen in Figure 1.2.

Throughout the economy millions of consumers are making decisions as to how to spend their income. By changing their preferences from good A to good B they are sending a signal to the producers of these goods. As the demand for good B increases and that of good A declines the prices of the two products will change and, *other things being equal*, the profit obtained from the two products will change. Profit is the key motivator in the market economy and the producers will reallocate their scarce resources to those goods and services which will yield the most profit.

One can see why this process is called the 'free' market because the allocation of resources occurs without government intervention — reallocation of resources is 'automatic'. The consumer has an important role to play in the market economy for it has been their

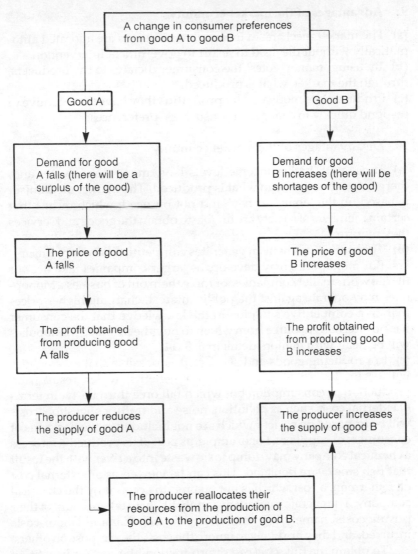

Figure 1.2 *The market mechanism.*

change in tastes which has ultimately led to a change in what is produced. The scale of the influence depends on the level of income the consumer has. When consumers spend on a particular product, they are essentially voting for that product. The more income they have, the more 'money votes' they can cast and, therefore, the greater their influence on what is produced.

9.   Advantages of the market economy

(a) The market mechanism means that resources are allocated automatically without the need to resort to government intervention.
(b) By using 'money votes' the consumer dictates to the producers, through the market, what is produced.
(c) Producers are motivated by profit thus they have the incentive to respond quickly to changes in consumers' preferences.

10.   Disadvantages of the market economy

(a) Those with higher income levels have more money votes and, therefore, a greater say in what is produced. The market mechanism is based on the 'ability to pay' and not on need, which means that certain members of society are unable to obtain the goods and services they require.
(b) The market mechanism generates competition between consumers. But monopolies may develop, as larger companies take over or merge with smaller companies, or force them out of business. Monopolies may operate against the public interest, charging higher prices than in a competitive situation in the knowledge that the consumer has no alternative source from which to buy the product. Monopolies will be dealt with in more detail in 6: **8–14**.
(c) In producing goods and services it is possible that externalities will occur. Externalities are costs (or benefits) which result from production or consumption but which fall on a third party. In terms of external costs such as pollution, noise and traffic congestion, costs will be imposed on society which are not included in the decisions of consumers or suppliers. For example, as part of its productive process a chemical company may dump toxic waste into a river with the result that fish stocks are depleted. This can be viewed as an external cost on fishermen, a cost which is not taken into account by the chemical company. The chemical company is only likely to take account of their private costs, namely the rent, rates, raw material and labour costs incurred, and they are likely to ignore the costs they impose on others.
   To obtain the full *social cost* of production, the cost (or benefit) of externalities should be added to the private cost. The external costs are likely to continue unchecked if left to the free market and are one of the reasons for government intervention.
(d) Certain goods, namely *public goods* and *merit goods*, may be underprovided or not provided at all in a market economy. Public goods can be defined as those goods which when consumed by one individual can still be consumed by others. Examples include defence and

flood control and if they were paid for by one individual then others would be able to obtain a 'free ride'. Merit goods are goods which the government feels would be under-consumed if they did not provide them. They are, therefore, subsidised or provided free by the government. Neither would be adequately provided if left to the market mechanism. Public goods and merit goods are dealt with in more detail in 15: **2**.

11. The planned economy

In a planned economy the government makes all the decisions about what is produced, how resources are allocated and at certain times, through rationing, how the finished products are distributed. A government planning office decides on the allocation of resources, estimating the types of products it considers individuals to want.

12. Advantages of the planned economy

(a) The planning office decides what goods and services are produced which means that any wasteful competition is avoided.

(b) Since the planning office controls production it is in a position to deal with the externalities, such as pollution, when deciding what goods and services to produce. A planned economy is better placed, theoretically, to deal with the harmful effects of the productive process.

(c) It has been argued that a planned economy can lead to a more equal distribution of income and wealth since the factors of production (excluding labour) are controlled by the state.

(d) The planning office administers the prices of products and can, therefore, effectively control inflation. The result is that when shortages occur in the economy they manifest themselves in queues, rationing and the black market rather than in increased prices.

13. Disadvantages of the planned economy

(a) Since the allocation of resources is undertaken by the planning authority, they may misjudge the preferences of the consumers. This means there may be an over-production of certain products and an under-production of others. The shortages will result in long queues and rationing, whereas the over-production of goods will lead to large stockpiles of unwanted products.

(b) As the state owns the assets of the economy it will mean that there is a reduced incentive to work harder. There can be a lack of motivation among management and workers since individuals do not own businesses or benefit directly from the profit those businesses earn.

(c) With business being organised as a state monopoly there is a lack of competition between companies, and a resulting lack of variety and quality of products. In fact, products tend to be rather standardised with the absence of product differentiation.

(d) In the market economy resources are allocated automatically via the market mechanism whereas in the planned economy a large bureaucracy has developed to administer the system. This bureaucracy can be viewed as a misuse of resources.

It is because of the failings of the planned economy that in recent years countries throughout Eastern Europe have moved towards a market economy system — in fact becoming more mixed economic systems.

14. The mixed economy

As the name suggests, this type of economic system aims to combine the merits of both the free market and the planned economies. The main advantage of the market economy is the automatic working of the market mechanism. The mixed economy aims to allow the market to operate, with government intervening in the economy only where the market fails. This means providing those goods and services such as law and order, education and health services, which would have been under-provided if left to the market. The free market economy is also susceptible to:

(a) *Booms and slumps* in the level of economic activity. In this area government intervention is geared towards creating a stable economic environment.

(b) *Monopoly power*. There is, therefore, a role for government to monitor and control the activities or potential activities of monopolies — through the Monopolies and Mergers Commission in the UK.

(c) *Inequalities*, for example in the distribution of income and wealth. This is something that government can attempt to correct through the taxation system (*see* 15: **5-8**) and through its expenditure.

(d) *Externalities*. It is also possible for the government to make sure that companies take account of the externalities they create, e.g. by the Environmental Protection Act 1990.

In reality most economies throughout the world are mixed economies.

15. Positive and normative economics

At this point it is useful to distinguish between *positive* and *normative* economics. Positive economics is concerned with issues such as how individuals behave in trying to maximise their satisfaction from a given income level or how firms behave in maximising their profits. Positive statements deal with *what is* or *what will be* — statements that can be empirically tested. For example, 'if the government increases income tax it will lead to a fall in the level of consumer expenditure' is a positive statement because it can be checked against the evidence and proved correct or incorrect. One of the main aims of economics has been to develop theories which could help explain economic behaviour and deal with positive statements.

Normative economics deals more with value judgements, statements which include the words *should* or *ought*. For example, 'income should be distributed more equally' is a normative statement. Unlike a positive statement, there is no way of proving it correct or incorrect.

16. Micro and macroeconomics

It is important to distinguish between micro and macroeconomics. Microeconomics deals with the decision making of individuals and firms, and how particular markets work. Macroeconomics studies the operation of the economy as a whole, covering areas such as unemployment, inflation and aggregate demand. Part one of *Economics* will deal with microeconomics and Part two with macroeconomics.

Progress test 1

1. What is the economic problem? (3)

2. Outline what is meant by the production possibility frontier and show how useful it is when analysing opportunity cost. (5, 6)

3. What are the economic merits and weaknesses of the market economy? (8, 9, 10)

4. Distinguish between public goods and merit goods. (10)

5. Outline the differences between a market economy and a planned economy. (7, 8, 11)

6. Define a mixed economy. (14)

7. Distinguish between positive and normative economics. (15)

8. How would you distinguish between microeconomics and macroeconomics? (16)

Part one

Microeconomics

2

Demand, supply and market equilibrium

1. Introduction

The aim of this chapter is to explain clearly the factors which influence the demand for and supply of a particular good or service, and how the interaction of demand and supply determines the market price.

2. The market

The market can be defined as any situation in which the buyer and seller of a product communicate with each other for the purpose of exchange. The collective action of the buyers in the market determine the market demand for a particular product while the collective actions of the sellers determine the market supply. It is the interaction of these two forces (known as *market forces*) which determines the market price for the product.

The existence of a market does not mean that the buyer and seller have to meet although that may be the case. The market may in fact have no exact location, as is the case with the foreign exchange market, where the buyers and sellers of foreign currencies are in contact with each other by telephone. Alternatively the buyer and seller may be in contact with each other through a third party, such as an estate agent or a stock broker.

The market may be *local* such as that of a fish and chip shop, *regional* as with a newspaper such as the *East Anglian Daily Times*, *national* such as the housing market which consists of many estate agents operating throughout the country, or *international* as is the market for oil. A market can take a number of different forms; it could be a product market such as that for chocolate bars or it could be a labour market where those individuals with particular skills supply their services to firms who demand those skills. In the latter case the demand is called *derived demand* because the labour demanded is determined by the demand for the product which that labour produces.

Demand

3. What is demand?

You may want a particular product but not have the money to pay for it or you may have the money to buy a product but not desire it. Neither situation constitutes *effective demand*. Effective demand means there has to be the ability and willingness to buy a product.

In terms of demand it is not sufficient to say 'the demand for a good or service is 50 units' for it is also important to know at what price 50 units would be demanded and over what period of time. If the product is chocolate then in terms of the total market it might be 2 million bars demanded per week at 30 pence each. For newspapers it could be 5 million demanded per day at 35 pence each and for shoes it could be 2,000 pairs per month at £50 per pair.

When you think of demand it is natural simply to consider an individual's demand but, although this is important, it is the market demand for the product which is of greater concern. We will deal with the relationship between individual and market demand later but for now we will simply consider the market demand for a product, which means the total amount that consumers demand at a particular price over a period of time.

The demand for a product, for example chocolate bars, depends upon a number of factors which can be expressed in the form of a *demand function*:

$$qdx = f(Px, Y, P1 \dots Pn{-}1, T, A)$$

where:

qdx	refers to the quantity of product x demanded, i.e. chocolate bars
Px	refers to the price of product x
Y	refers to the level of household income
P1 … Pn–1	refers to the prices of all the other 'related' products in the economy
T	refers to the tastes of the consumer
A	refers to advertising

It is not possible to study at the same time, all of the factors which influence demand so the economist makes use of *ceteris paribus*, which means 'other things remaining unchanged'. It is, therefore, possible to study the relationship between demand and each of the variables in turn, assuming the other factors remain constant.

Table 2.1 The demand schedule for chocolate bars (showing the relationship between the quantity demanded and price)

Price (pence per bar)	Quantity demanded (million bars per week)
0	12
10	10
20	8
30	6
40	4
50	2
60	0
70	0

4. Factors influencing demand

This section outlines the factors which influence the demand for a product, as given in the demand function in **(3)**. The example of chocolate is used.

(a) *The price of the product (Px).* A change in the quantity of chocolate bars demanded is caused by a change in its price. The relationship between the quantity demanded and price can be shown in the form of a *demand schedule* such as in Table 2.1. It is possible to present the information given in Table 2.1 in the form of a graph showing the *demand curve*, as in Figure 2.1.

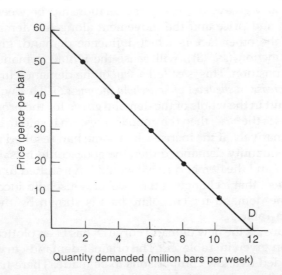

Figure 2.1 *The market demand curve for chocolate bars.*

This is a more convenient means of presenting the information and a number of important points can be noted:

(i)   Price is on the vertical axis and the quantity demanded over a time period on the horizontal axis.

(ii)   Demand is a *flow* concept which means that it is measured over a period of time.

(iii)   The demand curve will normally slope down from left to right (a negative relationship). This is because the lower the price, the greater the quantity demanded and vice versa.

(iv)   In Figure 2.1 the demand curve is a straight line although this does not necessarily have to be the case.

(v)   At a price of 60 pence the quantity demanded by the market is zero.

(vi)   While considering the relationship between the quantity demanded and price we have assumed *ceteris paribus*, which you will remember means all other factors remaining unchanged.

(vii)   A change in price will lead to a movement *along* the demand curve. For example, as the price increases from 20 to 30 pence the quantity demanded falls from 8 to 6 million bars per week. This is sometimes called a *contraction* of demand. If the movement had been in the opposite direction it would have been called an *extension* of demand.

It is most important that the difference between a movement along a demand curve and a shift in a demand curve is fully understood. So far we have discussed the relationship between quantity demanded and price and the movement along the demand curve. However, the other factors which influence demand, given in the demand function (*see* **(3)**), will cause the whole demand curve to change its position. This is called a *shift* of the demand curve.

(b)   *An increase in the level of household income (Y).* This will *normally* lead to a shift in the whole of the demand curve for the product to the right. If this is the case, then the good in question is said to be a *normal good.* Alternatively, if the increase in income had resulted in a reduction in the quantity demanded then the good could be said to be an *inferior good* and the demand curve would have shifted to the left.

The effect that a change in the level of household income might have on the demand for chocolate bars is shown by the demand schedule in Table 2.2

In Figure 2.2 the new demand curve D_1 has been plotted from the information given in Table 2.2. The original demand curve has also been included to allow comparisons to be made. There has been an increase in the quantity of chocolate bars demanded *at each price*, so

Table 2.2 The demand schedule for chocolate
bars following an increase in household income

Price (pence per unit)	Quantity demanded following an increase in household income (million bars per week)
0	16
10	14
20	12
30	10
40	8
50	6
60	4
70	2
80	0

whereas at a price of 20 pence 8 million bars per week were initially demanded now 12 million bars per week are demanded. There has been a *shift* in the demand curve to the right. It can also be seen that, whereas initially demand was zero at a price of 60 pence, it is now 80 pence before demand is zero.

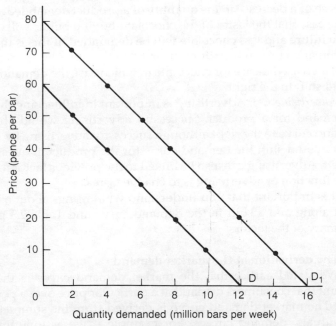

Figure 2.2 *A shift in the demand curve to D1 following an increase in household income.*

(c)   *A change in the price of other related products in the economy (P1 ... . Pn–1).* This would affect the demand for chocolate bars in one of two ways. If the product in question was a *substitute* product for chocolate, such as crisps, and its price rose relative to that of chocolate, then the demand for chocolate bars would rise at every price. This would lead to a shift in the demand curve for chocolate bars to the right and in terms of Figure 2.2 could be represented as a shift in demand from D to D_1. On the other hand, if the price of the substitute product was to fall then this could lead to a decrease in the quantity of chocolate bars demanded and, therefore, a shift to the left in the demand curve.

Alternatively, the product whose price changed could be a *complementary* product, for example cars and petrol, video recorders and video cassettes. In the above example it could be chocolate bars and cups of tea (which may be consumed together), although you may not see them as complements, for products which are complementary products are normally purchased together. If the price of the complementary product tea fell, it would lead to an increase in the demand for chocolate bars and a shift in the demand curve to the right.

(d)   *Changes in tastes (T).* A change in tastes will bring about an increase or a decrease in the quantity of a product demanded. It may be the case that the tastes of the chocolate-buying public will change in the future and less chocolate will be demanded. If this is the case, the demand curve will shift to the left. On the other hand there may be an increased desire for chocolate in which case the demand curve would shift to the right.

(e)   *Advertising (A).* Advertising is important in influencing the level of demand for a product. Successful advertising would shift the demand curve to the right although successful advertising by a competitor could shift the demand curve for the product in question to the left. Advertising can also be linked to the previous factor in that a main function of advertising is to change tastes.

It is important that you understand what brings about a movement along and a shift in the demand curve and Table 2.3 gives a summary of the factors.

5.   The derivation of the market demand

We stated earlier that the market demand curve is the total amount that consumers demand at a particular price over a period of time. The market demand curve is derived from the summation of individuals' demand curves. For example if we assume just two individuals, A and B, then summing their demand curves horizon-

Table 2.3 The factors leading to a movement along and a shift in the demand curve

A movement along the demand curve for chocolate bars	
The quantity of chocolate bars demanded	
falls if:	rises if:
• the price increases	• the price falls

A shift of the demand curve	
The quantity of chocolate bars demanded	
falls (shifts to the left) if:	rises (shifts to the right) if:
• there is an increase in household income and the product is an inferior good	• there is an increase in household income and the product is a normal good
• there is a fall in the price of a related product (a substitute)	• there is a rise in the price of a related product (a substitute)
• there is an increase in the price of a complementary product	• there is a decrease in the price of a complementary product
• there is a change in tastes away from the product	• there is a change in tastes towards the product
• a competitor has a successful advertising campaign	• there is a successful advertising campaign

tally would produce the market demand curve as shown in Figure 2.3. Obviously in the real world the market is made up of more than two individuals, but the way to calculate the market demand curve is just the same no matter how many individuals are involved.

Supply

6. What is supply?

The market supply of a product is the total quantity that individual firms together are willing and able to put onto the market at a particular price over a particular period of time. We will assume that the prime motive for supplying a product is to make a *profit* and that supply is the market supply rather than an individual firm's supply. The factors which influence the quantity supplied can be expressed in the form of a *supply function*:

$$qsx = f(Px, P1 \ldots Pn\text{-}1, F1 \ldots Fm, Te, Z)$$

where:

qsx   refers to the quantity supplied of product x, i.e. chocolate bars

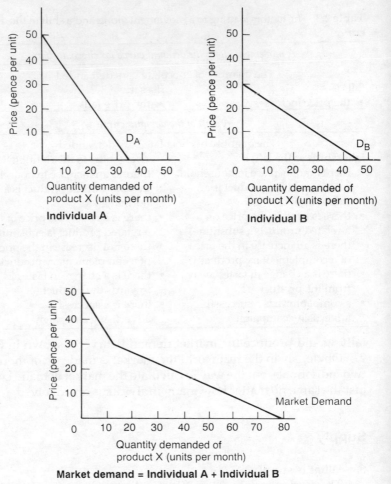

Figure 2.3 *The derivation of the market demand curve.*

Px	refers to the price of product x
P1 ... Pn–1	refers to the prices of all the other products in the economy
F1 ... Fm	refers to the cost of the factors of production
Te	refers to the state of technology
Z	refers to all the other factors which might influence the quantity supplied.

When considering the above equation it is necessary, as with demand, to make use of *ceteris paribus*.

Table 2.4 The supply schedule for chocolate bars

Price (pence per bar)	Quantity supplied (million bars per week)
0	0
10	0
20	2
30	4
40	6
50	8
60	10
70	12

7. Factors influencing supply

This section outlines the factors which influence the supply of a product, as given in the supply function.

(a) *A change in the price of the product (Px)*. This is likely to have an important influence on the amount of a product supplied to the market. If we assume *ceteris paribus*, an increase in the price of the product will mean that it is more profitable to produce and thus there will be an incentive for the producers in the market to increase the quantity supplied. The relationship between the quantity supplied and the price can be presented in the form of a *supply schedule* (*see* Table 2.4).

From the information given in Table 2.4 it is possible to produce a graph showing the *supply curve* (*see* Figure 2.4).

As with demand it is important that the difference between a movement along and a shift in the supply curve is fully understood. A change in the price of the product will lead to a movement along the supply curve. However, the other factors which influence supply, as given in the supply function (*see* **6**), will cause the whole supply curve to *shift* its position. These factors are discussed below.

(b) *A change in the price of other products (P1 ... Pn–1)*. This is likely to influence the quantity of a product (in our case chocolate bars) supplied. If the price of, say, boxed chocolates or candy bars fell, then assuming *ceteris paribus* these products would be less profitable to produce when compared to the chocolate bar. If this was the case then the quantity of chocolate bars supplied would increase at each and every price. In other words, resources would be reallocated from the production of boxed chocolates to chocolate bars.

The information given in Table 2.5, which shows the new quantity

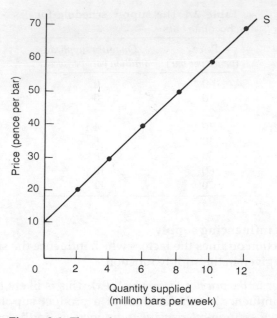

Figure 2.4 *The market supply curve for chocolate bars.*

supplied following a reduction in the price of another product such as boxed chocolates, can be plotted as in Figure 2.5. The initial supply curve has also been plotted so that a comparison can be made. It should now be possible to see how a *shift* in the supply curve has taken place from, say, 4 million bars supplied per week at a price of 30 pence to 6 million bars supplied per week at a price of 30 pence. In other words, the supply curve has shifted to the right from S to S_1. If, instead of a reduction in the price of boxed chocolates or candy bars, their price had increased then *ceteris paribus* the supply curve for chocolate bars would have shifted to the left.

(c) *An increase in the price of the factors of production (F1 ... Fm).* An increase, for example, in the price of labour used in the production of chocolate bars would make that product less profitable to produce and would lead to a shift in the supply curve to the left. If, however, there was a fall in the price of a factor of production used it would lead to a shift in the supply curve to the right (*see* Figure 2.5).

(d) *A change in the state of technology (Te).* This would influence supply in that if there was an improvement in the technology used to produce chocolate, it would lead to an increase in the profitability of that product and, therefore, more would be supplied. This means that

Table 2.5 The supply schedule for chocolate bars following a reduction in the price of another product

Price (pence per bar)	Quantity supplied following a reduction in the price of another product (million bars per week)
0	0
10	2
20	4
30	6
40	8
50	10
60	12
70	14

there would be a shift in the supply curve to the right.

(e) *All other factors which might influence the quantity supplied (Z).* This refers to such factors as the weather conditions. Weather only affects particular products such as agricultural output. Changes in government policy, such as the introduction of a tax on the product or a

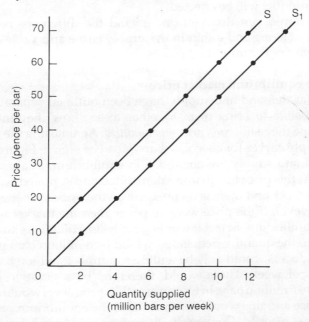

Figure 2.5 *A shift in the supply curve to S₁ following a reduction in the price of a related product.*

Table 2.6 The factors leading to a movement along and a shift in the supply curve

A movement along the supply curve for chocolate bars	
The quantity of chocolate bars supplied will	
fall if:	rise if:
• The price falls	• The price rises

A shift of the supply curve for chocolate bars	
The quantity of chocolate bars supplied will	
fall (shift to the left) if:	rise (shift to the right) if:
• there is an increase in the price of another product	• there is a reduction in the price of another product
• there is an increase in the price of a factor of production	• there is a reduction in the price of a factor of production
• there is a deterioration in the technology used in the production of chocolate	• there is an improvement in the technology used to produce chocolate
• there is the introduction of a tax on the product	• there is the introduction of a subsidy on the product

subsidy, will also influence supply because the level of profit made on that product will be affected.

It is important that you understand the difference between a movement along and a shift in the supply curve and Table 2.6 gives a summary of the important points.

8.   The equilibrium market price

So far demand and supply have been outlined separately. It is now possible to bring them together to see how they interact to determine the *equilibrium price and quantity*. Again using the demand and supply curves for chocolate bars, it can be seen in Figure 2.6 that demand and supply are equal, i.e. in equilibrium, at a price of 35 pence. At this price the quantity demanded and supplied is 5 million bars per week and there is no pressure on the price to change.

However, if the price were 20 pence then the market would be out of equilibrium, in fact it would be in a *disequilibrium* situation. At this price the quantity demanded would be 8 million bars per week but, producers would only be willing to supply 2 million bars to the market per week. There would, therefore, be a situation of *excess demand* of 6 million bars. In response to this, producers would increase their price and this would continue until the equilibrium price of 35 pence was reached. Conversely, the price could have been 50 pence per bar. Here the quantity demanded would have been 2 million and

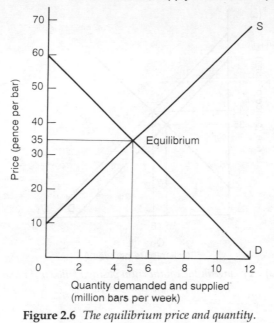

Figure 2.6 *The equilibrium price and quantity.*

8 million would have been supplied. In other words there would have been *excess supply* of 6 million bars. Again the market would be in a disequilibrium situation and the price would fall in response to the excess stocks held by the producers until the equilibrium price was reached.

9. Changes in the market equilibrium price

Once in equilibrium it is only possible for that equilibrium to change if there is a change in one of the demand or supply factors. For example in Figure 2.7(a) the market is initially in an equilibrium situation at a price of 35 pence and a quantity of 5 million bars. If there is then a change in tastes and more of the product is demanded, the demand curve will shift to the right from D to D_1. Initially there will be a shortage of 2 million units (shown by the dotted line). This will lead to an increase in price which will stimulate producers to supply more and will also 'choke off' some of the demand, until the new equilibrium is reached at a price of 40 pence and a quantity of 6 million bars.

In Figure 2.7(b) the initial equilibrium is the same as in the previous example with a price of 35 pence and a quantity of 5 million bars. If there is then a reduction in the price of labour used in the

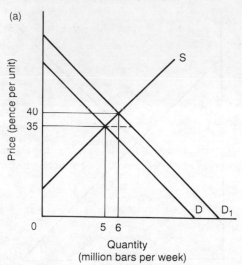

Figure 2.7(a) *A change in the equilibrium position following a change in tastes by the consumer.*

production of the product, it is more profitable to produce (assuming *ceteris paribus*). The result would be a shift in the supply curve to the right and, although there would initially be an excess supply of 2 million units (shown by the dotted line), the price would fall until the

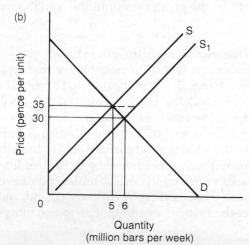

Figure 2.7(b) *A change in the equilibrium position following a reduction in the price of labour.*

new equilibrium is reached. This would be at a price of 30 pence and a quantity of 6 million bars.

Progress test 2

1. What is meant by 'the market'? **(2)**

2. Outline the factors which would bring about a movement along and a shift in the demand curve for an economics textbook. **(4)**

3. With the aid of a demand and supply diagram, show the effect on the market for dishwashers if there is an increase in income (dishwashers being a normal good) while at the same time the manufacturer of dishwashers has introduced a new technique of production which significantly reduces the cost of production. **(4, 7)**

4. Using demand and supply diagrams outline the main factors which could affect the price of houses in the UK. **(4, 7)**

5. What is meant by the equilibrium market price? **(8)**

6. The following demand and supply schedules for good X are:

Px (£)	Quantity demanded	Quantity supplied
1	120	0
2	100	20
3	80	40
4	60	60
5	40	80
6	20	100

(a) What is the equilibrium price and quantity? **(8, 9)**
(b) What would be the excess demand or supply if the price were:
(i) £2?
(ii) £6? **(8)**
(c) If there was an increase in income and the product was an inferior good what would be the new equilibrium price and quantity if 20 units less were demanded at each and every price? **(8, 9)**

3

Elasticity

1. Introduction

In Chapter 2 demand and supply curves were introduced. It was shown how, among other things, the demand for a product could be affected by a change in its price, a change in household income and a change in the price of other products (*see* 2: **4**). It was also demonstrated how supply was, among other things, affected by a change in price (2: **7**).

The ways in which demand and supply respond to the above changes are important and can be measured by the use of a concept known as *elasticity*. The aim of this chapter is to deal with the four types of elasticity:

(a) price elasticity of demand;
(b) income elasticity of demand;
(c) cross elasticity of demand;
(d) price elasticity of supply.

Price elasticity of demand

2. Price elasticity of demand

It is possible to measure how the demand for a good responds to a price change by using the concept of price elasticity of demand. The relationship can be presented as a formula:

$$\text{Price elasticity of demand (ed)} = \frac{\text{Percentage change in the quantity demanded}}{\text{Percentage change in the price}}$$

This can be rewritten as:

$$\frac{\frac{\Delta q}{q} \times 100}{\frac{\Delta P}{P} \times 100} = \frac{\Delta q}{\Delta P} \times \frac{P}{q}$$

where:

q = the original quantity
P = the original price
Δq = the change in quantity
ΔP = the change in price

For example, in Figure 3.1 a price increase from 10 pence to 20 pence causes the quantity demanded to fall from 10m to 8m per week.

This means that a 100 per cent increase in price leads to a 20 per cent fall in the quantity demanded, which will produce a price elasticity of demand (ed) equal to 0.2 or, to be absolutely correct, –0.2. The reason for the negative sign is because of the negative slope of a normal demand curve (*see* Figures 3.1 and 3.2). However, it is normally the convention to omit the negative sign. The elasticity of demand obtained is less than 1, i.e. demand is *inelastic*. This is because the percentage change in the quantity demanded is *less* than the percentage change in the price and demand is, therefore, not very responsive to a price change. The lower the elasticity of demand the less responsive is demand to a change in price. This has obvious implications for firms making their pricing decisions, as will be seen later in the chapter.

When the percentage change in the quantity demanded is greater than the percentage change in price then demand is said to be *elastic*.

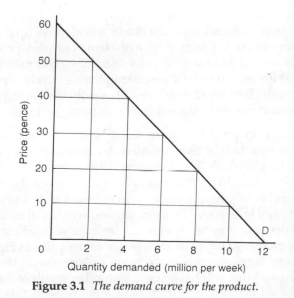

Figure 3.1 *The demand curve for the product.*

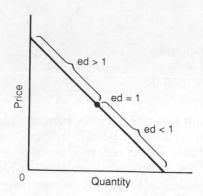

Figure 3.2 *Price elasticity of demand (ed) varies along the length of a demand curve.*

That means that demand is responsive to a price change. If the ratio is equal to 1, then the percentage change in the quantity demanded and the percentage change in price are equal. Here the elasticity is said to be *unity*. So the greater the elasticity value the more responsive demand is to a price change either up or down.

Normally the elasticity of demand for a product will vary along the length of the demand curve. Again taking Figure 3.1, as the price increases from 20 pence to 30 pence demand falls from 8m to 6m per week and the ed is 0.5 (inelastic). A price increase from 30 pence to 40 pence causes demand to fall from 6m to 4m per week resulting in an ed of 1 (unity). A price increase from 40 pence to 50 pence results in a fall in demand from 4m to 2m per week and the ed is 2 (elastic). The demand curve is, therefore, more elastic as we move up the demand curve from right to left, from a price of 0 to a price of 60 pence. Figure 3.2 is a graphical summary of price elasticity of demand (ed) and shows that the ed is unity halfway along the demand curve.

Although elasticity of demand will usually vary along the length of the demand curve there are three exceptions (*see* Figure 3.3):

(a) A change in price in Figure 3.3(a) will have no effect on the quantity demanded. In this situation demand is perfectly inelastic along the length of the demand curve with a value of 0. No matter what price is charged for this good demand does not change.
(b) Demand is infinite at a price Po in Figure 3.3(b). If price were to increase to any level above Po then demand would fall to zero. In this situation demand is perfectly elastic with a value of infinity (∞).
(c) Any percentage increase or decrease in the price in Figure 3.3(c) leads to the same percentage decrease or increase in the quantity demanded and this will be the case along the length of the demand curve. The ed is, therefore, unity and a curve with this particular quality is called a *rectangular hyperbola*.

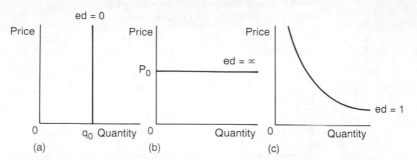

Figure 3.3 *Three demand curves with constant price elasticity of demand.*

3. Price elasticity of demand and total revenue

The elasticity of demand of a good is important in relation to its effect on suppliers' total revenue (TR). Total revenue will be covered in more detail in Chapter 6 but for the purposes of this section it can be defined as the total amount that is earned by a firm from the sale of a product. Total revenue is, therefore, the price of the product (P) multiplied by the total quantity sold (q).

$$TR = P \times q$$

As can be seen in Figure 3.4(a), as the price falls from P_1 to P_2 the total revenue increases as the loss in revenue (–) is outweighed by the gain (+). This arises because the elasticity of demand is elastic. Note that the shaded area is 'common' both before and after the price fall.

In Figure 3.4(b) a fall in the price from P_3 to P_4 leaves total revenue unchanged as the revenue lost (–) is equal to the revenue gained (+). In this situation we have unit elasticity of demand.

In Figure 3.4(c) a fall in the firm's price from P_5 to P_6 leads to a

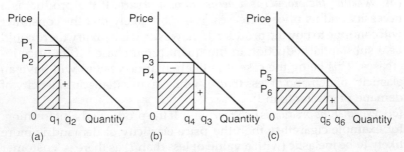

Figure 3.4 *Price elasticity of demand and total revenue.*

Table 3.1 The relationship between price elasticity of demand and total revenue

Price elasticity of demand	Price	Effect on total revenue
Elastic >1	fall	rise
	rise	fall
Unity = 1	fall	no change
	rise	no change
Inelastic <1	fall	fall
	rise	rise

reduction in total revenue with the loss (–) being greater than the gain (+). In this situation the elasticity of demand is inelastic.

The possible effects of a change in price on the total revenue earned by a firm and the resulting elasticity are summarised in Table 3.1.

4. Factors determining price elasticity of demand

There are a number of factors which together determine the value of the price elasticity of demand for a given product.

(a) *Whether close substitutes are available.* If a product has a close substitute then it is likely that the demand for that product will fall if its price increases. The closer the substitute, the greater the fall. If this is the case then demand will be elastic. The reason for this is that consumers, faced with a price increase, will switch their expenditure to the close substitute. For example, a product like petrol has a relatively inelastic demand since there are no close substitutes available, whereas particular brands of petrol have a much more elastic demand, as each brand is a more or less perfect substitute for each other.

(b) *Whether the product is a necessity or a luxury.* If the product is a necessity and its price increases, it is more likely that the consumer will continue to buy the product. If, however, it is a luxury there could be a substantial reduction in the quantity purchased if its price increases. This being the case it is likely that necessities will have an elasticity of demand of less than 1, while luxury items an elasticity of demand of greater than 1.

(c) *Whether the product is habit forming.* If the product is habit forming, for example cigarettes, then the price elasticity of demand is more likely to be inelastic (with a value of less than 1) as there is 'customer resistance' to price changes.

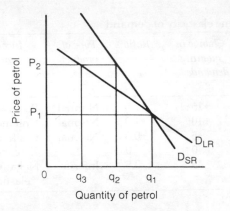

Figure 3.5 *The change in the price elasticity of demand over time.*

(d) *Time period*. The demand for certain products is likely to be relatively more responsive to a price change in the long run than in the short run.

Example
Figure 3.5 relates to the demand for petrol. Following a price increase from P_1 to P_2 the demand in the short run may fall from q_1 to q_2 along DSR as consumers use their cars less. In the long run, however, the consumer may purchase cars which have smaller engines, using less petrol. So, in the long run, demand is likely to fall to q_3 along DLR, with demand being relatively more elastic.

Income elasticity of demand

5. What is income elasticity of demand?

Whereas price elasticity of demand measures the responsiveness of demand for a product to a change in its price, income elasticity of demand (YED) measures how the demand for a product responds to a change in income. The formula for YED is:

$$YED = \frac{\text{Percentage change in quantity demanded}}{\text{Percentage change in income}}$$

This can be rewritten as:

$$\frac{\frac{\Delta q}{q} \times 100}{\frac{\Delta Y}{Y} \times 100} = \frac{\Delta q}{\Delta Y} \times \frac{Y}{q}$$

Table 3.2 Income elasticity of demand

	Income increase %	Change in quantity demanded %	Ratio	Type of product	Income elasticity of demand
a	10	+15	+1.5	Normal	Positive income elastic
b	10	+10	+1.0	Normal	Unit income elasticity
c	10	+5	+0.5	Normal	Positive income inelastic
d	10	0	0		Zero income elastic
e	10	−5	−0.5	Inferior	Negative income elasticity

where:

q = the original quantity
Y = the original income
Δq = the change in quantity
ΔY = the change in income

Table 3.2 displays a number of examples of the response in demand to an increase in income. The following situations can be noted:

(a) The percentage increase in the quantity demanded outweighs the percentage increase in income, and the resulting ratio is positive, a normal product and, greater than 1, income elastic. This would suggest that the product could be a consumer durable such as a CD player where the demand increases rapidly as income increases.

(b) The percentage increase in income leads to the same percentage increase in quantity demanded and this can be seen as unit income elasticity of demand.

(c) Demand increases as income increases but by a smaller percentage. The elasticity is less than 1 but greater than zero and is, therefore, income inelastic. The type of product which could result in this response is basic foodstuffs. In general, one would not expect a substantial increase in the quantity of basic food purchased as income increases.

(d) It may be the case that an increase in income has no effect on the quantity demanded. Here there is zero income elasticity of demand.

(e) In general with price elasticity of demand we ignore the positive/negative sign; however, with income elasticity of demand the sign attached to the ratio is all important. A plus sign (+) signifies a so-called normal good, whereas a minus sign (−) reveals the product

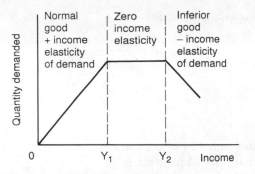

Figure 3.6 *The relationship between the quantity of a good demanded and income.*

to be an 'inferior' good. An inferior good is one where the quantity demanded *falls* as income increases.

The relationship between the quantity demanded of a product and income can be understood further by studying Figure 3.6.

With no income there is zero demand for the product; however, as income increases (up to Y_1) demand for the product increases. The product, up to an income level of Y_1 is a normal good with a positive income elasticity. As income rises from Y_1 to Y_2 there is no extra demand for the product because the household may have reached their saturation level and the income elasticity of demand is zero. As income increases above Y_2 then the quantity demanded actually falls, indicating that the product is now perceived by consumers as an inferior good and thus has a negative income elasticity of demand.

Although Figure 3.6 has given the three possible situations relating to income elasticity of demand, all products may not follow the pattern outlined and in fact the income elasticity of demand may be positive at all income levels.

Cross elasticity of demand

6. What is cross elasticity of demand?

Cross elasticity of demand refers to the response of demand for one product to the change in the price of another product. The formula is:

$$\text{Cross elasticity of demand} =$$

$$\frac{\text{Percentage change in the quantity demanded of product A}}{\text{Percentage change in the price of product B}}$$

This can be rewritten as:

$$\frac{\dfrac{\Delta q_A}{q_A} \times 100}{\dfrac{\Delta P_B}{P_B} \times 100} = \frac{\Delta q_A}{\Delta P_B} \times \frac{\Delta P_B}{q_A}$$

where:

q = the original quantity of product A
P = the original price of product B
Δq = the change in the quantity of product A
ΔP = the change in the price of product B

Three possible outcomes are shown in Figure 3.7:

(a) *In situation (1)* as the price of B increases the quantity demanded of A increases. The cross elasticity of demand is therefore positive and the two products concerned are substitutes. For example, as the price of carrots increases the quantity of peas demanded may increase since they are often seen as substitutes for each other.
(b) *Situation (2)* relates to complementary products, for as the price of product B increases (for example petrol), the quantity of product A demanded (for example cars) declines.
(c) *Situation (3)* refers to two products which are totally unrelated. So if for example the price of soap increased it is unlikely to result in a change in the quantity of ballpoint pens demanded.

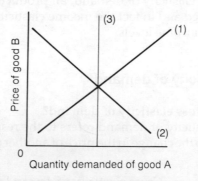

Figure 3.7 *A diagram to show the relationship between the price of product B and the quantity demanded of product A.*

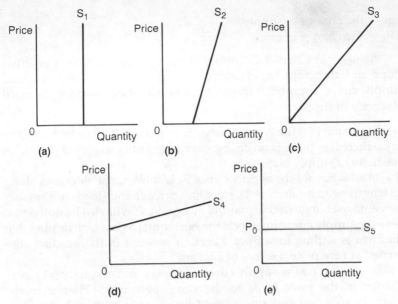

Figure 3.8 *The supply curve and the price elasticity of supply.*

Price elasticity of supply

7. What is price elasticity of supply?

Whereas the study of price elasticity of demand refers to the responsiveness of demand to a change in price, price elasticity of supply refers to how supply responds to a price change.

The relationship can be presented as a formula:

Price elasticity of supply (es) =

$$\frac{\text{The percentage change in the quantity supplied}}{\text{The percentage change in price}}$$

This can be rewritten as:

$$\frac{\frac{\Delta qs}{qs} \times 100}{\frac{\Delta P}{P} \times 100} = \frac{\Delta qs}{\Delta P} \times \frac{P}{qs}$$

where:

qs = the original supply
P = the original price

Δqs = the change in supply
ΔP = the change in price

As seen in Chapter 2, supply curves generally have a positive slope and, therefore, the elasticity of supply is positive for a normal supply curve. Figure 3.8 illustrates five situations relating to price elasticity of supply.

(a) *In situation (a)* the supply curve S_1 is perfectly inelastic for as the price increases there is no change in the quantity supplied (the price elasticity of supply is zero).

(b) *In situation (b)* the supply curve S_2 is inelastic at all points along its length (with a value of <1). Here any price change leads to a smaller percentage change in the quantity supplied. It will also be noted that here the supply curve intersects the horizontal axis which implies that the firm is willing to supply a certain amount of the product concerned at zero price, i.e. free of charge.

(c) *In situation (c)* the supply curve S_3 shows unit elasticity (=1). Any change in the price leads to the same percentage change in the quantity supplied and any straight line supply curve which passes through the origin has a price elasticity of supply equal to 1 at all points along its length.

(d) *In situation (d)* the supply curve S_4, which intersects the vertical axis, is elastic (value >1) at all points along its length. Any change in price will lead to a greater percentage change in the quantity supplied.

(e) *In situation (e)* the supply curve S_5 is perfectly elastic with an elasticity of supply equal to infinity. Suppliers in this situation would be willing to supply an infinite amount of the product at a price of P_0. However, in this situation a small fall in the price would lead to the quantity supplied falling to zero.

8.   Factors determining price elasticity of supply
The following factors determine the price elasticity of supply.

(a) *The existence of spare capacity.* Even if the price of the product increases a firm may not be able to increase supply if they do not have spare, unused or surplus capacity. They may, in fact, be operating at full capacity so that, in the short run at least, supply may be perfectly inelastic. On the other hand, if the firm has spare capacity and a plentiful supply of land and raw materials it could respond to the price change by increasing output in which case supply will be more elastic.

(b) *The availability of stocks.* The firm may have accumulated a large

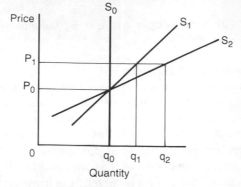

Figure 3.9 *The supply curve over a time period.*

quantity of unsold stocks which can be quickly supplied to the market. If this is the case then supply will tend to be more elastic.

(c) *Mobility of the factors of production.* If the firm can easily reallocate its resources, namely its labour and its productive capacity, from one type of production to another then the supply for that product will tend to be more elastic. However, the labour force employed by a firm may be highly skilled in the production of a particular product and the capital equipment highly specialist. If this is the case then it may be difficult to shift resources from one use to another. In this situation the factors of production are said to be immobile and supply is relatively inelastic.

(d) *The time period.* It will take time for a firm to adjust to a change in a product's price, assuming other things remain constant, and from the above points it should be clear that supply is likely to be more elastic in the long run. In fact the time period can be divided into three periods (*see* Figure 3.9).

The momentary period is where supply will be restricted to the amount currently on the market. Here the price elasticity of supply will be zero, shown by the supply curve S_0. In this case a price increase from P_0 to P_1 has no effect on the quantity supplied.

In the *short run period* the firm may be able to transfer (reallocate) some of its resources to the production of the product in question, in which case supply will increase from q_0 to q_1 (*see* Figure 3.9). The workforce could be persuaded to work overtime and thus the short run curve could be represented by S_1.

In *the long run* it is possible for the firm to expand the factory and purchase more machinery in which case the firm's productive capacity has been increased. Supply will then increase to q_2 as price rises from P_o to P_1, giving a supply curve of S_2, i.e. a more elastic supply curve.

9/ The importance of elasticity

Many firms find it important to obtain detailed estimates of the price elasticity of demand and supply for their products. Reliable information on the price elasticity of demand, i.e. how sensitive demand is to a price change, will allow the firm to be more confident about the effect on its revenue (and possibly its profit) when considering a price increase or decrease. If a firm considers its demand curve to be elastic around the price it is currently charging, then a reduction in price would allow the firm to increase its total revenue. If the demand was inelastic then a price increase would also have the desired result of increasing total revenue. For example, in Figure 3.1 a price increase from 10 pence to 20 pence (ed= 0.2) will increase total revenue from £1m to £1.6m.,

In terms of income changes in the economy, information on the income elasticity of demand will be vital for firms, for, if they are producing what can be classed as 'inferior goods', they are likely to find the demand for their product declining as incomes increase. If incomes are increasing then normal products with a high income elasticity of demand, such as luxury goods, would merit the firm's attention as possible items to produce.

Cross elasticity of demand will be of importance for companies such as tyre producers because a change in the price of motor cars or petrol will have implications for the tyre industry.

10. Applications of demand and supply

Having worked through Chapters 2 and 3, it is possible to introduce the applications of demand and supply. There are numerous applications but this section will concentrate on just two, namely maximum price legislation and the introduction of a tax on the sales of a commodity.

(a) *Maximum price legislation.* In Figure 3.10 the equilibrium price for, say, chocolate bars is 35 pence and the equilibrium quantity is 5 million. If a maximum price of 25 pence were then to be introduced by the government through legislation it would lead to an excess demand of 4 million bars. At a price of 25 pence producers of chocolate bars would be willing to supply only 3 million bars to the market and, if it were possible for *black marketeers* to obtain that total supply, they could sell it illegally on the *black market* at a price of 45 pence per bar. This would mean that they would make a profit of £600,000 (the

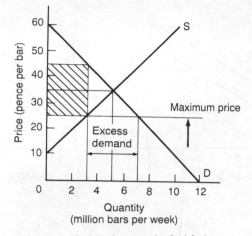

Figure 3.10 *Maximum price legislation.*

shaded area). Again using Figure 3.10, if the government were to introduce a minimum price of say 45 pence per bar the result would be an excess supply of 4 million bars and thus there would be a glut of the product on the market. Given this situation the government could purchase the excess and *stockpile* it.

(b) *Introduction of a tax on the sales of a commodity.* In Figure 3.11 a tax of 10 pence per unit is placed on a product. This would have the effect of reducing the profitability of that product and therefore the supply curve would shift to the left, i.e. to S+t. The tax per unit is the vertical

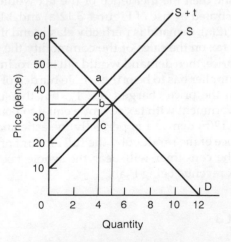

Figure 3.11 *Introduction of a tax of 10 pence per unit.*

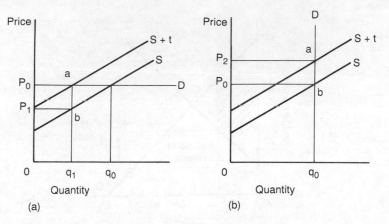

Figure 3.12 *The incidence of a tax.*

distance, ac, between the old and the new supply curve (*see* Figure 3.11). The *incidence of the tax* which measures the relative burden of the tax on the consumer and the producer are the same in this example, i.e. the consumer pays 5 pence per unit in tax (ab) and the producer pays 5 pence per unit in tax (bc). Overall then the taxation revenue to the government is £400,000, of which the consumer and producer both pay £200,000. After the tax has been paid, the producer is left with £1,200,000.

If, however, demand for the product were perfectly elastic or perfectly inelastic then the incidence of the tax would be different. This can be illustrated by use of Figures 3.12(a) and 3.12(b).

In Figure 3.12(a), demand is perfectly elastic and if following the imposition of a tax on the sales of the commodity the supplier were to increase the price, then demand would fall to zero. In this situation, therefore, the supplier has to bear the whole burden of the tax. There is no change in the price charged, i.e. P_o, but the supplier has to provide the government with tax revenue equal to $P_o abP_1$.

In Figure 3.12(b) demand is perfectly inelastic and the supplier can raise the price of the product by the full amount of the tax, ab. In this situation the consumer will bear the whole tax burden, with government tax revenue being $P_2 abP_o$.

Progress test 3

1. What is meant by price elasticity of demand ? **(2)**

2. Distinguish between a demand curve which is perfectly elastic, perfectly inelastic and unit elasticity. **(2)**

3. If the demand for a product is inelastic what will be the effect on total revenue if the price of the product falls ? **(3)**

4. Outline the factors which influence price elasticity of demand. **(4)**

5. In terms of income elasticity of demand what is the difference between a normal and an inferior good? **(5)**

6.

	Beef and veal	Potatoes	All food
Price elasticity of demand	(−) 1.25	(−) 0.21	−
Income elasticity of demand	(+) 0.08	(−) 0.48	(+) 0.01

Explain how the theory of demand would account for these estimates of elasticities and how the values might be of use to the agricultural industry. **(2, 4, 5)**

7.

Price £	Quantity demanded per week	Quantity supplied per week
20	20	0
40	16	4
60	12	8
80	8	12
100	4	16

(a) What is the price elasticity of demand when the price increases from £40 to £60? **(2)**
(b) What is the effect of a price increase from £40 to £60 on the total revenue? **(3)**
(c) Calculate the price elasticity of supply following a price increase from £60 to £80. **(7)**

8. Outline the factors which influence price elasticity of supply. **(8)**

9. What is meant by 'the incidence of a tax' and how is the incidence affected by demand elasticity? **(10)**

4

Consumer theory

1. Introduction

This chapter looks more closely at what lies behind the demand curve. We are interested in why consumers behave the way they do and why it is that the consumer will normally buy more of a good when its price falls. Consumer behaviour can be explained using two main approaches, namely marginal *utility theory* and *indifference curve analysis*. The theory of consumer behaviour will be used to determine the shape of a demand curve for a single good.

Marginal utility theory (the cardinalist approach)

2. What is marginal utility theory?

This theory is based on the premise that the amount of satisfaction or *utility* obtained from the consumption of a particular product can be measured in the same way that physical units can be measured. The theory was developed by Alfred Marshall who introduced an imaginary unit called the *util* as a means of measuring utility. Hence, if an individual consumed a bar of chocolate which resulted in him deriving 30 utils and a packet of crisps which resulted in 15 utils, then comparisons between the different levels of satisfaction could be made and a measure of the overall level of satisfaction could be obtained. This approach was termed cardinal since cardinal numbers could be used to measure utility.

3. Total utility

Total utility is the total satisfaction obtained from all the units of a particular product consumed over a period of time. If we take an example of a particular product, product x consumed over a period of time, say one week, then as the quantity consumed increases, the total utility will increase (*see* Table 4.1). There will, however, be a point at which total utility will begin to fall and in the example given this is after the fourth unit of the product is consumed.

Table 4.1 Total and marginal utility illustrating the principle of diminishing marginal utility

Quantity of product x consumed per week	Total utility (TU) (utils per week)	Marginal utility (MU)
0	0	
		30
1	30	
		16
2	46	
		10
3	56	
		4
4	60	
		−5
5	55	
		−10
6	45	

4. Marginal utility

Marginal utility is the additional utility derived from the consumption of one more unit of the product and, as seen in Table 4.1, the marginal utility falls with extra units consumed.

5. The law of diminishing marginal utility

The declining marginal utility can be expressed as the *principle* or *law of diminishing marginal utility* with the first unit of the product yielding 30 utils of satisfaction, the second 16 utils of satisfaction, and so on until the fifth unit is consumed, which actually reduces total utility. The marginal utility derived from the fifth unit is negative and, in fact, the product yields *disutility*. In essence, therefore, the principle of diminishing marginal utility states that the more an individual has of a product, the less the marginal utility will be from each additional unit consumed. This can be seen in Figure 4.1 which has been produced from the data in Table 4.1.

6. The consumer equilibrium

In considering the consumer equilibrium a number of assumptions are made, namely that the individual:

(a) has a limited income;
(b) acts in a rational manner;
(c) aims to maximise his or her total utility subject to the income constraint.

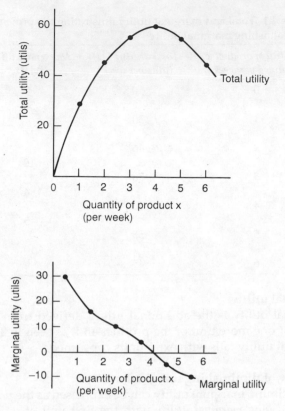

Figure 4.1 *Total and marginal utility.*

The individual is said to be in equilibrium when it is not possible to switch a single penny's worth of expenditure from product x to product y and obtain an increase in total utility, given the individual's income level and the prices that he or she faces. This occurs when:

$$\frac{MUx}{Px} = \frac{MUy}{Py} = \frac{MUn}{Pn}$$

where:

MU	=	marginal activity
P	=	the price
x, y and n	=	the individual products concerned

The above equation states that the consumer equilibrium is where the marginal utility from the last penny spent on product x equals the utility from the last penny spent on product y equals the utility from

Table 4.2 Consumer equilibrium

Product x (price £2.00 each)			Quantity demanded of product x and y	Product y (price £4.00 each)		
Total utility	*Marginal utility*	*MU / P*		*Total utility*	*Marginal utility*	*MU / P*
80	80	40	1	68	68	17
132	52	26	2	100	32	8
152	20	10	3	128	28	7
168	16	8	4	152	24	6
176	8	4	5	172	20	5

the last penny spent on product n, thus taking into account all of the products the individual consumes. When this situation is reached it is not possible for the individual to increase his or her total utility by reallocating expenditure. So the consumer equilibrium is important for it is where the consumer has allocated his or her income in such a way that maximum utility has been achieved.

The consumer equilibrium can be explained by referring to Table 4.2. We assume that there are only two products the individual can consume, product x costing £2.00 each and product y costing £4.00 each, and that the individual has an income per time period of £16.00. Given this situation, it can be seen that the consumer is in equilibrium when he or she consumes four of product x and two of product y. Here MU/P is the same, i.e. 8 for both products, and it is impossible for the consumer with an income of £16.00 to obtain a higher level of total utility. Note that in equilibrium the consumer obtains total utility of 268 utils. If the consumer were not in equilibrium it would be possible for him or her to reallocate income and obtain a greater level of satisfaction.

7. Derivation of the demand curve

It is possible to use marginal utility as a means of deriving a demand curve. If in Table 4.2 the price of product y were to fall to £2.00, then assuming everything else remained constant, there would be a new column for MU/P and a new equilibrium would result. The consumer would reduce consumption of product x by 1 unit and increase consumption of product y by 3 units, hence consuming 3 of product x and 5 of product y. The fall in the price of product y by £2.00 has led to an increase in demand by 3 units (*see* Figure 4.2). You may find it useful at this point to calculate the new MU/P for product y when its price has fallen and prove that the equilibrium is where the individual consumes 3 of product x and 5 of product y given an income of £16.00.

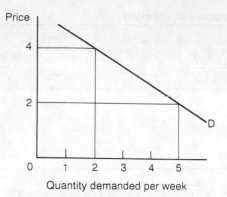

Figure 4.2 *An individual consumer's demand curve for product y.*

Indifference curve analysis (the ordinalist approach)

8.   What is indifference curve analysis?

The marginal utility approach to consumer behaviour has been criticised in that it is not possible to measure utility, which in any case can be viewed as rather abstract and subjective. With this in mind, certain economists including John Hicks in the 1930s developed an *ordinalist approach* to consumer behaviour. The idea was that although the consumer could not measure utility, they could *order* or *rank* their preferences, say preferring bundle of goods A to bundle of goods B and so on. The ordering of preferences meant that the measuring of utility was not required, and the theory became known as *indifference curve analysis*.

9.   Indifference curves

If again we assume two products, x and y, it is possible to produce an indifference schedule (*see* Table 4.3) which shows different combinations of the two products which yield the same level of satisfaction.

Table 4.3 can be represented diagrammatically (*see* Figure 4.3) and

Table 4.3 An indifference schedule

Combination	Units of product x	Units of product y
A	10	30
B	20	16
C	30	9
D	40	5

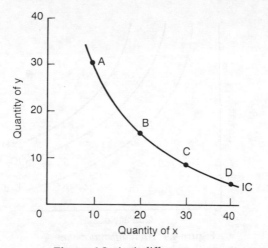

Figure 4.3 *An indifference curve.*

the individual obtains the same level of satisfaction whether at point A, B, C, or D or, in fact, at any points in between. It is possible to define an indifference curve as a line which joins all the combinations of two products at which the consumer obtains the same level of satisfaction.

There are certain points to note with regard to indifference curves:

(a) They are *convex to the origin* (*see* Figure 4.3). The reason for this should be obvious from Table 4.3, for when the individual is at point A he or she has relatively large amounts of product y and is willing to give up 14 units of that product so long as he or she is given 10 units of product x. This will leave the individual at the same level of satisfaction. However, in a move from B to C the individual would be willing to give up only 7 units of product y for 10 of product x, for now product y is becoming relatively scarce. To move from C to D he or she would be willing to give up only 4 units of product y and would require an additional 10 units of product x to remain at the same level of satisfaction. The measure of the amount of one good an individual is prepared to give up in order to acquire additional amounts of the other good, and leave him or her at the same level of satisfaction is called the *marginal rate of substitution* and it can be seen to vary as we move along the indifference curve. To be absolutely accurate, the marginal rate of substitution is the slope of a tangent to the curve at a particular point.

(b) It is possible to produce an *indifference map* (*see* Figure 4.4). There are an infinite number of indifference curves although only 3 are shown in the figure, and a move from IC_1 to IC_2 and so on represents

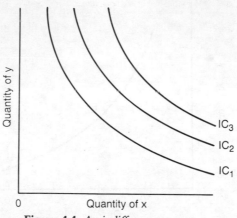

Figure 4.4 *An indifference map.*

an increase in the level of satisfaction. Unlike the cardinalist approach to consumer theory, no attempt is made to quantify the increase in satisfaction.

(c) *Indifference curves cannot cross* for this would suggest irrational consumer behaviour.

10. The budget line

Indifference curves reveal the consumer's preferences for product x and y but they do not tell us which combination of the two products will be chosen. The consumer is constrained by his or her income level and the price of the products. It is necessary, therefore, to introduce what is known as the *budget line* or the *consumption possibility line* which reveals all combinations of the two products that are obtainable, given the individual's income and the prices of the two products.

For example the individual may have £100 to spend on the two products per week. Table 4.4 shows the possible combinations of the two products assuming the individual spends all of the £100 with the price of product x being £2.00 and that of product y £4.00. This can be produced diagrammatically as in Figure 4.5. The individual can be at point A purchasing 10 of product y but unable to buy any of product x, or at point F purchasing 5 of product x but none of product y, or alternatively the consumer could be at a point between A and F on the budget line. Points above and to the right of the budget line are unobtainable and the slope of the budget line depends upon the relative prices of the two products.

Table 4.4 The budget constraint with income equal to £100

	Quantity of product x Price = £20.00	Quantity of product y Price = £10.00
A	0	10
B	1	8
C	2	6
D	3	4
E	4	2
F	5	0

11. The consumer equilibrium

The consumer is in equilibrium, that is at the highest level of satisfaction that his or her income allows, where the budget line is tangential to the indifference curve, and this is the point where the slope of the budget line (as given by the relative prices of the two products) is equal to the slope of the indifference curve (the marginal rate of substitution). This can be seen in Figure 4.6 at point E which is the position of maximum utility for the consumer. As stated, any point on the budget line is feasible but movements to points such as C or D in Figure 4.6 would place the consumer on a lower indifference curve (IC_1) which represents a lower level of satisfaction. Given the consumer's income level and the price of the two goods, indifference curve IC_3 is unattainable.

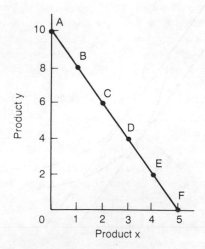

Figure 4.5 *The budget line.*

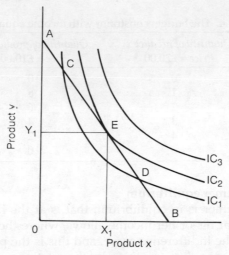

Figure 4.6 *The consumer equilibrium.*

Having outlined the basics of indifference curve analysis it is now possible to analyse how the equilibrium position is affected by changes both in the income level of the consumer and in the price of the two products. These will be analysed in turn.

12. A change in income
An increase in income, assuming the price of the two products

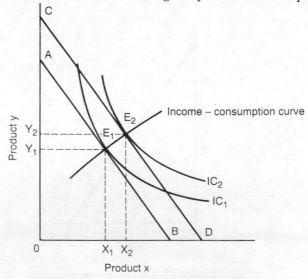

Figure 4.7 *The income–consumption curve.*

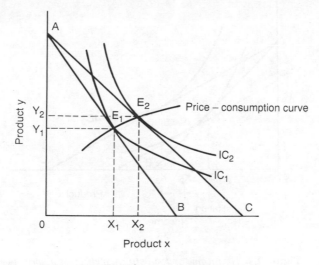

Figure 4.8 *The price–consumption curve.*

remains unchanged, will lead to a parallel shift in the budget line to the right allowing the consumer to buy more of both products.

This can be seen in Figure 4.7 where the budget line shifts from AB to CD, thus allowing the consumer to move onto a higher indifference curve IC_2 with a new equilibrium of E_2. The line through the equilibrium positions is called the *income–consumption curve* and it shows how the consumption of the two products responds to an income change.

If there had been a fall in income the budget line would have shifted to the left.

13. A change in price

If there is a change in price of one of the goods, with income remaining unchanged, the budget line will pivot.

In Figure 4.8 the initial budget line is AB and the consumer is in equilibrium at E_1, where the budget line is tangential to the indifference curve. Following a fall in the price of product x the budget line pivots to AC, thus allowing the consumer to move onto a higher indifference curve (IC_2) resulting in a new equilibrium of E_2. A line that joins all of the points of consumer equilibrium is called the *price–consumption curve* (*see* Figure 4.8).

In Figure 4.8 there has been a fall in the price of product x, but if

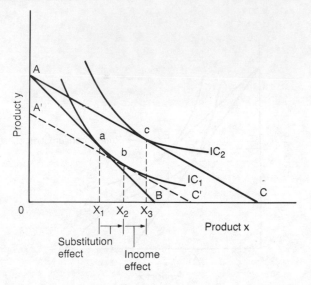

Figure 4.9 *The income and substitution effect for a normal good.*

the price had increased then the budget line would have pivoted again from point A but become steeper. You might like to think about how an increase or decrease in the price of product y would affect the budget line.

Referring back to Figure 4.8, as the price of product x has fallen the quantity demanded has increased from X_1 to X_2. There are two reasons for this which will be analysed in the following section. This is a difficult area of economic theory so care must be taken to make sure you fully understand it.

14. The income and substitution effect

As the price of product x falls it becomes cheaper relative to product y and for this reason the consumer will substitute product x for product y. This is called the *substitution effect* of a price change. It will always be the case that the consumer will substitute towards the product which has become relatively cheaper. As the price of product x falls it also means that the consumer has more money to spend on other products. It can be said that the consumer's real income has increased since it costs less to buy a given quantity of goods. This *may* mean that the consumer buys more of product x and this is called the *income effect* of a price change.

It is possible to distinguish between the income and substitution effect and this is shown graphically in Figure 4.9.

AB is the original budget line with the consumer in equilibrium at point a. If the price of product x falls this will lead to a pivot in the budget line to AC, allowing the consumer to reach a higher indifference curve (IC_2) and a new equilibrium of point c. The result of this is that the consumer has increased the quantity of product x bought from X_1 to X_3. It is possible to distinguish between the income and substitution effect by first eliminating the income effect, which means hypothetically removing the increase in real income until the consumer is back on the original indifference curve. This is achieved by shifting a line back, parallel to the new budget line AC, until it is tangential to the original indifference curve with the consumer obtaining the same level of utility prior to the price change. In Figure 4.9 this is represented by the hypothetical budget line A' C' which is tangential to the original budget line at b. The movement from a to b is the substitution effect, and there is an increase in the quantity consumed from X_1 to X_2.

The movement from point b to point c represents the income effect, allowing the consumer to reach a higher indifference curve IC_2 and consume more of product x, i.e. a move from X_2 to X_3. Figure 4.9 refers to a normal good (*see* 3: **5**) because the income effect is positive, meaning that an increase in income has led to an increase in the

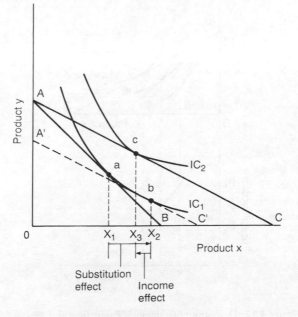

Figure 4.10 *Inferior good.*

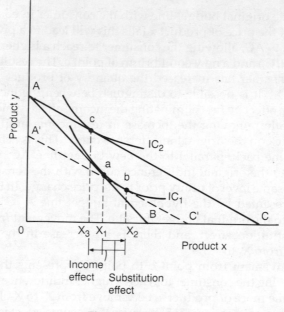

Figure 4.11 *Giffen good.*

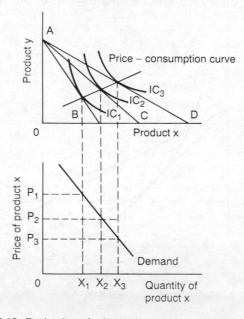

Figure 4.12 *Derivation of a demand curve from indifference curves.*

quantity demanded with the income effect reinforcing the substitution effect. The income effect can, however, be negative as in the case of an inferior good and a Giffen good.

15. Inferior good

In Figure 4.10 we follow the same process as in Figure 4.9 but with one difference. Again the price of product x falls leading to a substitution towards the product, i.e. a movement from a to b, with more being consumed (X_1 to X_2). However, the income effect is negative, unlike the previous example, and this means a movement from b to c with less being consumed, X_2 to X_3.

Although the income effect is negative, in this case it is not sufficient to outweigh the substitution effect, which means that overall there is still more of the product demanded as the consumer has moved from X_1 to X_3. In other words, the demand curve for product x is still downward sloping. It is possible, however, for the negative income effect to be sufficiently large to outweigh the substitution effect.

16. Giffen good

A Giffen good refers to a situation where the substitution effect is outweighed by the negative income effect. This can be seen in Figure 4.11 where the total effect of a price change reveals that the total quantity of the product demanded falls (X_1 to X_3) as the price of the product falls.

In this situation the demand curve is upward sloping from left to right (a positive slope) and this special type of demand curve relates to a type of product which is referred to as a *Giffen good*. The Giffen good (so named after a nineteenth-century economist) is one where demand falls as the price of the product falls and vice versa. For certain very low income groups, potatoes may form an important part of their total expenditure. Therefore, if the price of potatoes falls this group, finding that their real income has increased, may substitute products such as meat for potatoes — thus reducing their demand for potatoes.

17. Derivation of the demand curve

It is possible to use the preceding analysis to derive a consumer's demand curve (*see* Figure 4.12). As the price of product x falls, represented by the budget line pivoting from AB to AC to AD, the quantity of product x demanded increases from X_1 to X_2 to X_3, thus giving a downward sloping demand curve.

Progress test 4

1. Briefly explain what is meant by total and marginal utility. **(3, 4)**

2. Explain the law of diminishing marginal utility. **(5)**

3. Using marginal utility theory, when is a consumer in equilibrium? **(6)**

4. Outline what is meant by an indifference curve. **(9)**

5. Using indifference curve analysis show, with the aid of a diagram, how a consumer maximises satisfaction from a given expenditure on two goods. **(11)**

6. What is the effect on the consumer equilibrium of:
(a) an increase in income; and
(b) an increase in price? **(12, 13)**

7. Distinguish between the income and the substitution effect of a price change **(14, 15, 16)**

5
Production and costs

1. Introduction

Production can be defined as the transformation of inputs, namely land, labour, capital and enterprise, into goods and services in order to satisfy human wants. This chapter deals with the different types of business organisation, how they grow in size and the factors of production they use in the production of goods and services.

The costs of production in the short run and the long run are also covered in this chapter, and it is essential that you understand the relationship between the total, average and marginal cost as these concepts will be used in Chapters 6 and 7.

Types of business enterprise

2. Sole trader

This type of business is also called a *sole proprietor* business and, as the name implies, it is owned by one person. On the whole they tend to be small businesses and are common in retailing and in the provision of personal services such as hairdressing. Since the owner of this type of business is in sole charge, decisions can be taken quickly because no one else has to be consulted. There is also the advantage that they only require a small amount of capital to start up. Also, since the owner is working for him or herself there is an incentive to operate the business as efficiently as possible.

There are, however, a number of disadvantages in this type of business, for example the owner may not be able to specialise in certain functions within the business. Additionally, the owner stands to lose all of his or her personal belongings if the business goes bankrupt — the owner is said to have *unlimited liability*.

3. Partnership

As the name implies a partnership comprises two or more owners. Partnerships are generally allowed to have between 2 and 20 members, although there are exceptions such as banks, accountants and solicitors. All the partners have equal responsibility for the debts of the business, if they occur, since all the partners have unlimited liability. It is, however, possible to have what are known as *sleeping* or *dormant partners* who simply provide capital for the partnership on which they receive a return, but who take no active part in the day-to-day running of the company. These partners have *limited liability*.

Partnerships have the advantage in that the various partners may bring different ideas and extra capital into the business. They may also be able to specialise in a particular area of the partnership's work in which they have expertise. The main disadvantages are that, like a sole trader, the partners have unlimited liability for all the debts of the business, and the actions of one of the partners are legally binding on the other partners.

4.   Joint stock company

Unlike sole traders and partnerships, joint stock companies have *limited liability*. This means that if the company goes bankrupt, the owners'/shareholders' responsibility ends with the money they have invested in the company — they will not be liable to lose all of their personal possessions. The individual will not, therefore, be put off from investing in a limited company by, for instance, fear of losing their home.

There are two types of joint stock company:

(a)   *Private limited company*. These can be identified by 'Ltd' after the name of the company. With this type of enterprise its shares cannot be advertised and offered for sale to members of the general public. They are not, therefore, available for sale on the Stock Exchange. The number of shareholders can start at 2, with no upper limit. Private limited companies are a common form of business and tend to be small family concerns. The advantage of such businesses is that the owners are protected from losing their personal possessions, with the company having limited liability. The company has its own legal identity, unlike a sole trader business or a partnership.

A possible disadvantage for a sole trader or a partnership which has become a private limited company is that they will lose some of their control over how the business is run, for they will be accountable to the shareholders.

(b)   *Public limited company*. These can be identified by the letters PLC (or plc) after the name of the company. As with the private limited company the number of shareholders can range between 2 and no upper limit. However, unlike a private limited company, the shares can be advertised and sold to members of the general public and, once issued, the shares can be traded on the Stock Exchange. The shareholders have certain rights, namely to attend and vote at the annual general meeting (AGM), receive the company annual report and elect the board of directors. PLCs are normally much larger than private limited companies.

The advantages of a PLC are that, like the private limited company, the shareholders have limited liability and, since they are able to sell shares on the open market, PLCs are able to grow and take advantage of internal economies of scale (*see* **21**). One possible disadvantage with a PLC is that their shares are sold on the open market and, therefore, can be bought by a company interested in a takeover bid.

5. Public sector companies

These are enterprises owned by the state on behalf of the general public. There are two types, namely public corporations and nationalised industries. Public corporations are established by a Royal Charter and include the BBC (set up in 1927). Nationalised industries, such as British Rail and British Coal, were established by an Act of Parliament. They have a separate identity from the government, although the government appoints the chairman who, along with the board of directors, is responsible for the day-to-day running of the industry. Unlike PLCs, there are no shareholders in public sector companies as they are owned by the state.

Since 1979 there has been a policy of 'privatisation', i.e. returning state-owned assets to the private sector, and the status of many state-owned companies has changed from being a nationalised industry to being a PLC. The whole issue of privatisation will be dealt with in Part two, 18: **12-14**.

The growth of firms

6. Why do firms wish to grow?

There are a number of reasons why a firm may wish to grow:

(a) in order to reduce their average costs and hence take advantage of economies of scale (*see* **21**).

(b) to diversify, producing a wider range of products in order to ensure their long-term survival. By spreading their risks it can be argued that companies are in a better position to withstand a recession in the economy or a failure of one of their products.

(c) in order to increase its profit and market share and possibly, therefore, its monopoly power.

The next question to ask is, *how* do firms grow?

7.   Internal growth

There are essentially two methods of growth, the first being internal growth. This is where the firm ploughs back its profits into the company and by so doing increases its productive capacity. This is obviously easier if the demand for the company's product/s is increasing.

8.   External growth

External growth has become a common method of growth and involves a *takeover* or a *merger*. A takeover is where one firm purchases another firm from its shareholders, normally with the agreement of the shareholders of the acquired company. It may, however, involve what is known as the 'predatory' company buying up shares in the company it wishes to acquire, over a period of time. By making attractive offers to the shareholders it hopes to persuade them to sell their shares, with the aim of obtaining 51 per cent of the shares in the 'targeted' company.

A merger on the other hand is where both companies agree to combine their resources into a single company. A merger is normally a voluntary agreement.

The amalgamation of two or more companies in the form of a merger can also be called *integration* and this can be classified in the following way:

(a) *Vertical integration*. This occurs when firms amalgamate at different stages of the productive process. Vertical integration can be divided into backward and forward integration:

(i) *Backward vertical integration* refers to a situation where one firm amalgamates with another firm at an *earlier* stage of the productive process. An example of this is a tea producer such as Brooke Bond acquiring a tea plantation. There are certain benefits in that the acquiring firm can directly control the quality and the supply of their raw material requirements. It is also possible to make sure that delivery of the raw material is on time and that other producers (possibly competitors) are denied the raw material supply. It is also the case that the profits which would have been earned by the supplier of the raw material now accrue to the firm at the next stage of production.

(ii) *Forward vertical integration* occurs when a firm acquires another firm at the *next* stage of the productive process. Examples of this include a brewery acquiring a public house or an oil producer acquiring a chain of petrol stations. The reason for this type of integration is that the producer is able to control the quality of the outlet. If a firm, such as a brewing company, has spent substantial amounts of money on advertising its product it will want to make sure that the outlet or the 'point of sale' for its product is satisfactory. Additionally, with a brewing company, the acquisition of a number of public houses also ensures that those outlets are tied to the manufacturer's product.

(b) *Horizontal integration*. This occurs when a firm amalgamates with another firm at the *same stage* of the productive process. An example of this was the acquisition of Rowntree Mackintosh by Nestlé in 1988. There are obvious advantages gained by horizontal integration. Economies of scale can be obtained (*see* 21) and it also allows for rationalisation, with the closure of plant if there is excess capacity. Horizontal integration can also lead to a reduction of competition in the industry and can, therefore, benefit the firm from increased monopoly power.

(c) *Conglomerate integration*. This occurs when firms merge with no obvious link between the goods and services they produce. One of the main advantages of this is the 'spreading of risk' as production is diversified. It is also possible that economies of scale, namely managerial and financial (see 21), can be achieved through conglomerate mergers.

The factors of production

9. What are the factors of production?
There are certain inputs or resources called the factors of production which are the means by which goods and services are produced. These resources can be divided into the four categories of land, labour, capital and enterprise.

10. Land
This can be classed as the natural resource. It is not simply the surface of the earth on which houses and factories can be built but is also the natural resources which can be found on or below the surface. Land, therefore, includes agricultural production, mining such as coal and oil, and the resources obtained from the sea namely fishing. Land can be separated into *renewable* and *non-renewable resources*. For example, fish and forests can be consumed today and also (under careful management) the stocks can be replenished for future use. There is,

however, the current debate on the over-exploitation and destruction of the world's renewable resources. The non-renewable resource refers to raw materials such as coal, iron ore and tin.

11. Labour

If land can be classified as the natural resource, labour can be seen as the human resource. Labour is not simply the physical or manual work undertaken by individuals but also the intellectual and mental skills used in the production of goods and services. The supply of labour is all important and it is determined by the size of the population which in turn depends upon the birth rate, the death rate and the level of migration. Obviously not all of the population will be of working age, i.e. between the ages of 16 and 65, and not all those of working age will be available for work, for example those in full-time higher education.

12. Capital

Unlike land and labour, capital is a man-made resource which can be used in the production of goods and services. It includes plant, machinery and factory buildings. Capital can be divided into *fixed* and *circulating capital*. Fixed capital includes such items as machinery and factories and can be used over a period of time. Circulating capital, which is sometimes called working capital, includes the stock of raw materials, partly finished products and all the finished products in the factory waiting to be sold. An important point to remember when considering capital is that it does not refer to money, for capital consists of real assets.

13. Enterprise

Although land, labour and capital are needed in the productive process they require organising. The enterprise factor, or the entrepreneur, combines the other factors of production in order to produce goods or services, bears the risk and takes decisions as to what is produced.

Production in the short and long run

14. Production in the short run

The production of goods and services requires inputs of the factors of production. The relationship between the two can be summarised in the *production function*, generally given as

$$Qx = f(F1, F2, \ldots Fn)$$

Where:

Qx = the output of product x over a period of time
f = the functional relationship
F1, F2 ... Fn = the factor inputs

So the output of product x is a function of (depends on) the inputs of land, labour, capital and enterprise. The above equation can be simplified to give the following:

$$Qx = f(L, K)$$

where:

L = the quantity of labour
K = the quantity of capital

It is important to distinguish between production in the short run and the long run. In the short run, at least one of the factors of

Table 5.1 Total, average and marginal product illustrating the law of diminishing returns

Number of workers	Total product (TP)	Average product (AP)	Marginal product (MP)
			5
1	5	5	
			19
2	24	12	
			33
3	57	19	
			43
4	100	25	
			50
5	150	30	
			30
6	180	30	
			9
7	189	27	
			–13
8	176	22	
			–23
9	153	17	
			–53
10	100	10	

production is fixed. This is normally taken to be capital because it is not possible to construct a new factory or purchase new machinery overnight. It is, however, possible to employ extra labour and purchase raw materials in the short run, hence they are called the *variable factors*. In the long run, all of the factors of production can be varied.

In the short run, as a firm varies its output it will eventually experience *decreasing returns to the variable factor*. This is known as the *law of diminishing returns* and is illustrated in Table 5.1.

We assume that the quantity of capital and the state of technology are fixed with the only variable factor being labour. Labour is also assumed to be homogeneous (each worker is identical). Table 5.1 shows what happens to production as there is an increase in the number of workers employed. The terms used in the table are defined below.

(a) *Total product (TP)*. This is the total output that the firm produces over a given period of time as the number of workers employed is varied. The total product will increase up to a maximum of 189 units of output, when 7 workers are employed.

(b) *Average product (AP)*. The average product of labour represents the output per worker. It is measured by dividing total product by the number of workers, thus if 5 workers are employed and total output is 150 units then AP is 30:

$$AP = TP/L$$

(c) *Marginal product*. The marginal product is the extra output obtained from the employment of one extra worker. In other words, it is the change in total product as a result of an additional unit of the variable factor, i.e. labour, employed.

$$MP = \Delta TP/\Delta L$$

Where ΔTP is the change in the total product and ΔL is the change in the quantity of labour employed.

The law of diminishing returns, which is sometimes called the law of variable proportions, states that as successive units of the variable factor are combined with the fixed factors (land and capital) both the average and the marginal product will eventually decline. Thus in Table 5.1 diminishing marginal returns occur after the fifth worker is employed and diminishing average returns occur after the sixth worker is employed.

The information from Table 5.1 can be reproduced in a diagram (*see* Figure 5.1). Note that the MP is plotted at the mid-points between

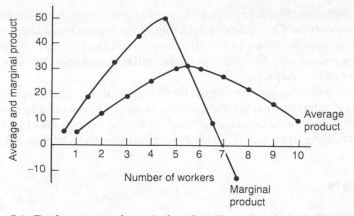

Figure 5.1 *Total, average and marginal product illustrating the law of diminishing returns.*

0 and 1, 1 and 2, etc. and that at some point MP becomes negative, when employing additional units of the variable factor actually reduces the total product of the firm. This occurs after the seventh worker is employed.

15. The average and marginal concept

These are important concepts which you will come across throughout this handbook. Note from Figure 5.1 that the MP cuts the AP at its maximum point. This can be explained by use of the batting average of a cricketer. His latest innings is his marginal score and his average score is the total number of runs he has made so far divided by the number of innings he has batted (the assumption is made that he is out each time). If he has only batted in 4 innings so far and has made scores of 20, 30, 50 and 60 his average is 40. If in the next innings (his 5th) he makes 50, although his marginal score has declined from the previous one of 60 his average, which is now 42, is still increasing because his marginal score was above his average. If in his 6th innings he only scores 42 which is exactly equal to his average score, then his average score does not change. At this point the marginal and the average score are the same. If, however, in the 7th innings the cricketer scores only 28 his average will start to fall, now being only 40. This is because his marginal score is now below his average score.

16. Production in the long run

In the long run it is possible to vary all of the factors of production. A new factory can be built and new machinery can be purchased. It is, therefore, possible to vary the *scale of production*. *Increasing returns to scale* are said to occur if a doubling of the inputs leads to more than a doubling in the output. If this occurs then the firm is experiencing *economies of scale*. Economies of scale will be considered in more detail later in the chapter.

If a doubling of the inputs leads to a doubling of the output then this is referred to as *constant returns to scale*. There could however be *decreasing returns to scale*, where a doubling of inputs leads to less than a doubling in output. This is called *diseconomies of scale* (*see* **23**).

Costs

17. What are costs?

Costs can be viewed as the total amount paid by a firm for the factors of production it uses, such as labour, in the productive process. It is important when considering costs to distinguish between the accountant's and the economist's method of measurement. The accountant measures historical cost which is the price originally paid for the factors of production whereas the economist measures the opportunity cost. Opportunity cost (*see* 1: **4**) is a measure of the best alternative foregone. In certain situations the historical cost and the opportunity cost measurements are the same. For example, when a firm buys raw materials and uses them soon after they are purchased then the historical cost and the opportunity cost are the same because the money spent on the raw materials could have been used to purchase something else. However, the historical cost of the accountant and the opportunity cost of the economist may differ.

Take for example a firm owned by one person (a sole trader) who may obtain a revenue of £140,000 for the sale of his or her product over the year. According to the accountant, subtracting the explicit costs on such things as the purchase of raw materials and the wages of hired labour totalling £100,000 would leave the firm with a profit of £40,000 as shown in Table 5.2

The economist, however, would view this as an over-estimate of the profit earned by the firm. In calculating costs, the economist would also take into account the implicit costs, which refer to the inputs owned and used by the firm when producing goods and services. These costs can be viewed as imputed (or estimated) costs because no actual expenditure has taken place. The imputed costs are based on what the inputs could have earned in their best alternative use and include what the owner of the firm could have earned if he

Table 5.2 Accounting cost and opportunity cost

The accountant (accounting cost) £		The economist (opportunity cost) £	
Sales revenue:	140,000	Sales revenue:	140,000
Less:		Less:	
Explicit costs	100,000	Explicit costs	100,000
		Imputed cost of owner's time	15,000
Accounting profit	40,000	Opportunity cost of finance	5,000
		Opportunity cost of factory and machinery	10,000
		Economic profit	10,000

or she had worked for another company. For example, the owner could earn say £15,000 if he or she was employed by someone else and this is the opportunity cost of the owner's time, which is included in the economist's calculation of costs but not the accountant's.

The economist's opportunity cost is also concerned with the funds the owner has tied up in the business. The opportunity cost is the amount these funds could have earned elsewhere. For example, if the owner has £50,000 in the business this could have been placed in a bank and earned a rate of interest of, say, 10 per cent. The sum of £5,000 interest is the opportunity cost of finance and is also included in the economist's cost calculation.

The sole trader may also own the factory and machinery used in production and it is possible that both could be rented out. The imputed cost is the rent it could have received by letting it out to another business and this could be estimated at £10,000.

As seen in Table 5.2, using the economist's method of calculating cost reduces the profit figure from £40,000 to £10,000. After taking the costs into account as calculated by the economist, the firm is still making a profit. This is called economic profit, pure profit or super normal profit and is a true indicator of how the firm is doing. If the figure had been negative it would have been better for the sole trader to close down the business, place his or her money in the bank, rent out the factory and work for someone else. The concept of supernormal profit will be considered in more detail in Chapter 6.

18. Short-run and long-run costs

When considering costs it is important to distinguish between the short run and the long run. In the short run certain factors are fixed

Table 5.3 Total, average and marginal cost

Units of output Q	TFC (£)	TVC (£)	TC (£)	AFC (£)	AVC (£)	ATC (£)	MC (£)
0	30	0	30				
							30
1	30	30	60	30.0	30.0	60.0	
							11
2	30	41	71	15.0	20.5	35.5	
							8
3	30	49	79	10.0	16.3	26.3	
							9
4	30	58	88	7.5	14.5	22.0	
							12
5	30	70	100	6.0	14.0	20.0	
							15
6	30	85	115	5.0	14.1	19.1	
							20
7	30	105	135	4.2	15.0	19.2	
							25
8	30	130	160	3.75	16.25	20.0	
							30
9	30	160	190	3.33	17.7	21.0	
							41
10	30	201	231	3.0	20.1	23.1	

while others are variable. This means that some costs, namely *fixed costs*, will have to be paid even if there is no output being produced. The fixed costs, which are also called overhead or unavoidable costs, include rent paid on the premises, rates, interest payments on loans and hire purchase repayments. *Variable costs* include raw materials, wages of the operative staff and the cost of fuel. When no output is produced, no variable costs are incurred. As output increases, the firm will incur increasing variable costs and because of this they are also called direct or avoidable costs. In the long run, all the factors of production are variable costs.

19. Total, average and marginal cost

Table 5.3 gives the figures for total, average and marginal cost for a hypothetical firm producing a particular good.

(a) *Total cost (TC)*. Total cost is just that, it is the total cost of producing a particular level of output. Total cost can be divided into total fixed cost (TFC) and total variable cost (TVC), so that:

$$TC = TFC + TVC$$

It can be seen from Table 5.3 and Figure 5.2 (which is based on the data in the table) that total fixed costs do not vary with output and are constant at £30. The total variable costs are zero if no output is produced and then increase as output increases. As illustrated in Figure 5.2, both total variable cost and total cost increase with output, with the vertical distance between the two being equal to the total fixed cost.

(b) *Average cost (AC).* Average cost is the cost per unit and is obtained by dividing total cost by the number of units produced. *Average total cost* (ATC) comprises *average fixed cost* and *average variable cost* so that:

$$ATC = AFC + AVC$$

Average fixed cost is TFC/Q and, as shown in Figure 5.3 (using the data from Table 5.3), AFC declines continuously as output increases. This is because the fixed cost is spread over more units of production and is therefore sometimes called 'spreading the

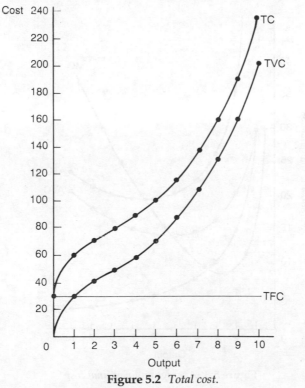

Figure 5.2 *Total cost.*

overheads'. Average variable cost is TVC/Q and is shown in Figure 5.3, again obtained by using the data from Table 5.3.

(c) *Marginal cost (MC).* Marginal cost is the change in the total cost as a result of a change in output of one unit. It can be written as:

$$MC = \frac{\Delta TC}{\Delta Q}$$

The marginal cost cuts the average cost at its minimum point (*see* Figure 5.3).

20. The long-run cost.

In the long run all the factors of production are variable and this means that output can be varied using different capacity.

The long-run average cost (LRAC) curve is the envelope of all the short-run average cost (SRAC) curves and it represents the lowest cost of producing different levels of output. All points above the LRAC curve are attainable levels of cost, whereas the points below the curve

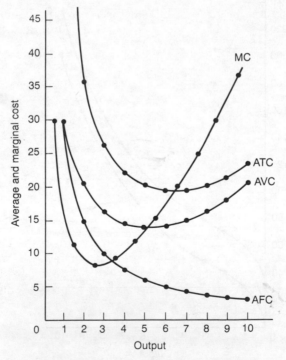

Figure 5.3 *Average and marginal cost.*

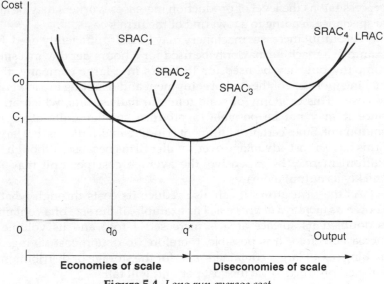

Figure 5.4 *Long run average cost.*

are unattainable levels of cost.

Up to an output level of q^* the LRAC curve is declining, which signifies that the firm is benefiting from economies of scale, there being increasing returns to scale. The minimum point q^* is the minimum efficient scale of production and after q^* the LRAC curve increases, which signifies diseconomies of scale, with the firm experiencing decreasing returns to scale.

An output of q_0 could be produced by using the capacity implicit within the short run average cost curve ($SRAC_1$) at a cost of C_0, but by expanding its capacity to $SRAC_2$, the firm's cost of producing q_0 could be reduced to C_1.

21. Economies of scale

As a firm grows in size it is possible for them to reduce their cost of production. The reduction in costs as a result of increasing production are called economies of scale and in Figure 5.4 they are obtained by the firm up to a level of output q^*, the lowest point on the firm's long run average cost curve.

The sources of economies of scale can be outlined as:

(a) *Technical economies.* As a firm grows in size it may be able to take advantage of increased *specialisation*. If the firm produces only a small output it may not be possible to employ a worker solely on one process but as the level of production increases workers may be able to specialise, leading to a lowering of the firm's costs.

As output increases machinery may be more efficiently used. For example, a machine may only be used for 6 hours per day in a small company but may be used for 18 hours in a large company, thus making more use of the capital equipment and resulting in a lowering of costs. This economy of scale refers to *indivisibility*, which arises since it may not be possible to produce smaller units of capital equipment. Since certain equipment is indivisible, it means that larger firms have a cost advantage over smaller firms because, although the equipment may be expensive, the average cost per unit may fall quickly as output increases.

As the firm grows it can also reduce its costs through what is known as *increased dimensions*. For example, if the size of a container is doubled its surface area is increased 4 fold and its volume is increased 8 fold. It is possible, therefore, to obtain cost savings by making use of larger containers, say, for the storage or distribution of finished products since the cost per unit will fall.

A large firm may also devote proportionately more resources to *research and development* which could lead to an improvement in the quality of the goods and services produced, and possibly to a lowering of the cost per unit.

(b) *Marketing economies.* When a firm buys its raw materials in *bulk* it may obtain preferential terms in the form of a discount, thus reducing the cost of each unit. A large firm may employ specialist buyers whose sole responsibility it is to purchase raw materials at the cheapest price. Administration, advertising, and packaging costs may also be lower for larger companies since they can spread the cost over larger orders. For example, the packaging costs per item for 1 million units is likely to be substantially lower than if 100 items were packaged.

(c) *Financial economies.* Larger firms may be able to obtain finance on favourable terms, obtaining loans from financial institutions at lower rates of interest. Banks will be more willing to loan on preferential terms to a large, well-known company, which can offer more collateral as security for the loan, than it will to a smaller company.

22. Economies of scope

Firms will normally produce more than one product and are, therefore, in a position to take advantage of *economies of scope*. Economies of scope refer to the reduction in average total cost (ATC) made possible by a firm increasing the number of different goods it produces. For example, Cadbury Schweppes could produce a range of confectionery products at a lower ATC than if separate firms were to produce each particular product. The reason for this is that Cadbury Schweppes is able to take advantage of skilled staff and technology which can be shared by the different confectionery goods produced. Economies of scope therefore exist when costs are spread over a range of products, with the result that there are lower costs of production for each good.

23. Diseconomies of scale

As seen in Figure 5.4, at a certain level of output the firm's average costs may increase in the long run with the firm experiencing diseconomies of scale.

The sources of diseconomies are:

(a) As a company grows in size it will possibly have a larger management team and, unlike a sole trader, it will find it difficult to make decisions quickly. This can often be the case where companies have merged and there are two sets of management with different ideas. It may be difficult to coordinate planning, marketing, production and so on, with a resulting increase in the company's cost per unit.

(b) The workforce may feel remote and alienated from the management. They may find their jobs boring and repetitive, particularly if mass production methods are used, and this may result in low morale and poor motivation. There may be a feeling on the part of the workforce that they are not part of the firm and this may lead to a deterioration in the quality of work undertaken. A 'them and us' situation may also develop between the management and the workforce, possibly resulting in an increase in the number of industrial disputes.

Progress test 5

1. Outline the main differences between a sole trader, partnership and a public limited company. **(2, 3, 4)**

2. What are the main reasons for a firm growing in size? **(6)**

3. Distinguish between vertical, horizontal and conglomerate integration. **(8)**

4. Explain the law of diminishing returns. **(14)**

5. Outline the relationship between total, average and marginal product. **(14, 15)**

6. How does the accountant's concept of cost differ from that of the economist? **(17)**

7.	Output	TC	TFC	TVC	ATC	AFC	AVC	MC
	0	15	15	0				0
	1	30						
	2	35						
	3	39						
	4	45						
	5	60						

(a) Complete the above table. **(18, 19)**
(b) Plot the AC and the MC on graph paper. **(18, 19)**
Remember to plot the MC at the mid point, i.e. between 1 and 2, etc.

8. Outline what is meant by economies and diseconomies of scale and how they affect the shape of the long-run average cost curve. **(21, 23)**

9. What is meant by economies of scope? **(22)**

6

Theory of the firm — perfect competition and monopoly

The theory of the firm

1. Introduction

An industry can be defined as a group of firms which produce close substitutes. For example, there are product similarities in the confectionery industry, the car manufacturing industry and the textile industry. Industries, however, are difficult to define accurately since a firm may operate in more than one industry. An industry is made up of a number of firms and it is possible, by summing the output of those individual firms, to obtain the output of the industry as a whole. Industries have different numbers of firms operating within them and this chapter analyses how this may affect the behaviour of firms in their price and output decisions.

The benchmark cases which form the extremes of what is called the *market structure* are *perfect competition* and *monopoly*. In perfect competition there are a large number of firms producing an identical product and there are no barriers to entry into the industry. At the opposite extreme is a monopoly in which the firm is the industry. This situation is maintained through the imposition of barriers to entry of new firms. Perfect competition and monopoly will be dealt with in

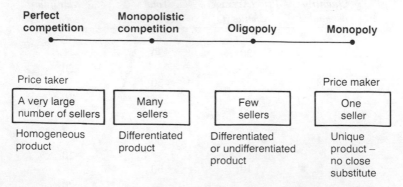

Figure 6.1 *Market structures with the bench-mark cases of perfect competition and monopoly.*

this chapter, while the other types of market structure (*see* Figure 6.1) which lie between these two extremes, namely *monopolistic competition* and *oligopoly* will be discussed in Chapter 7. However, a short explanation may be useful here. In monopolistic competition there are a large number of firms in competition with each other, each producing a similar product. Oligopoly is a market form in which there are a small number of large firms.

2. Cost, revenue and profit maximisation

Central to the theory of the firm is the concept of profit maximisation and in order to analyse the various market structures using profit maximisation a clear understanding of cost and revenue is required. The concept of *cost* was dealt with in Chapter 5 and although *total revenue* was introduced in Chapter 3, a little more detail is required.

3. Revenue

Table 6.1 presents a revenue schedule revealing how the demand for a product changes as the price falls.

(a) *Total revenue* is the price of the product multiplied by the quantity:

$$\text{Total Revenue (TR)} = \text{Price (P)} \times \text{Quantity (q)}$$

As seen in Table 6.1, as the price of the product falls total revenue will initially increase and then decrease. This can be presented graphically (*see* Figure 6.2.).

Table 6.1 Total, average and marginal revenue

Quantity demanded	Price/Average revenue (£)	Total revenue (£)	Marginal revenue (£)
			30
1	30	30	
			20
2	25	50	
			10
3	20	60	
			0
4	15	60	
			−10
5	10	50	
			−20
6	5	30	

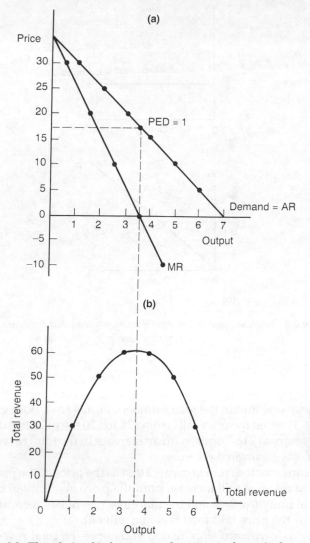

Figure 6.2 *The relationship between total, average and marginal revenue.*

(b) *Average revenue* is total revenue divided by quantity:

$$\text{Average revenue (AR)} = \frac{\text{Total revenue}}{\text{Quantity}}$$

Since average revenue is also $\dfrac{P \times q}{q}$, average revenue is also equivalent to the price.

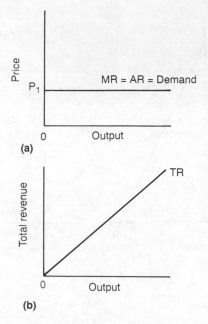

Figure 6.3 *Total, average and marginal revenue given that the demand curve is perfectly elastic.*

(c) *Marginal revenue* is the change in total revenue resulting from a change of one unit in the total number of units sold. For example (*see* Table 6.1) when the price falls from £25 to £20 the quantity demanded increases from 2 to 3 units, with an increase in the total revenue of £10 which is the marginal revenue.

It can be noted from Figure 6.2 that as the price of the product falls the total revenue will increase until the price elasticity of demand is equal to unity (*see* 3: **3**) and the marginal revenue is zero, after which point, as the price falls total revenue will fall.

For a downward sloping demand curve the total revenue curve is as shown in Figure 6.2(b). However, if the demand curve is perfectly elastic as in Figure 6.3(a), then the price charged would also be the average and marginal revenue, and the total revenue curve would be a straight line through the origin as in Figure 6.3(b), with the gradient of the total revenue curve dependent on the price charged.

Using a revenue schedule like Table 6.1 work out why if the price is constant it will also equal both the marginal and the average revenue.

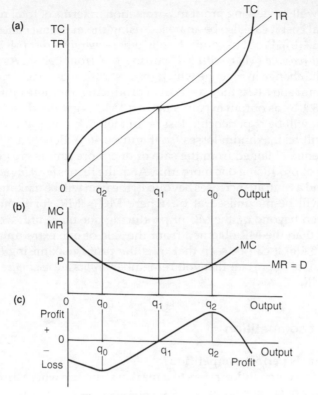

Figure 6.4 *Profit maximisation.*

4. Profit maximisation

Before dealing with the concept of profit maximisation it is important to note a number of points from Figure 6.4.

(a) Figure 6.4 refers to a perfectly competitive firm. This can be seen by the fact that the demand curve in Fig. 6.4(b) is perfectly elastic and the resulting total revenue curve in Fig. 6.4(a) is a straight line through the origin. The demand curve will be referred to later in the chapter.

(b) The figure relates to the short run since in Figure 6.4(a) the total cost curve intersects the vertical axis, which means that there is an element of fixed cost.

Profit (Π) is total revenue (TR) minus total cost (TC):

$$\Pi = TR - TC$$

Profits are maximised when the firm is producing at an output, q_2 in Figure 6.4(a), where the difference between the TR and TC curves is the greatest and positive.

As well as viewing profit maximisation in terms of total revenue and total cost it can also be analysed using the marginal concept (*see* Figure 6.4(b)). Profit maximisation is where *marginal cost (MC) equals marginal revenue (MR)*, with MC cutting MR from below. As stated, MR is the change in revenue which results from an increase in output by one unit and MC is the extra cost of producing one more unit. Using Figure 6.4(b), as output expands up to q_0, MC is greater than MR and the firm will be experiencing losses. In fact, at an output level of q_0 there will be maximum losses (*see* Figure 6.4(c)). Between q_0 and q_2 the revenue obtained from the sale of one more unit is greater than the cost of producing one more unit. At q_1 the firm is *breaking even* (TR = TC) and as output increases beyond q_1 the firm will be making profit. Profit will be maximised at q_2, where MC = MR, for if output is expanded beyond q_2, the MC of producing one more unit would be greater than the MR obtained from the sale of one extra unit. From Figure 6.4(c) it can be seen that q_2 is the profit maximising level of output. It is important that you remember *profits are maximised where MC = MR*.

Perfect competition

5.   What is perfect competition?

Perfect competition refers to a market structure where firms have no power over the market. This means that they accept the price as set by the market and, therefore, they are known as *price takers*. Perfect competition is a theoretical market structure which is unlikely to be found in the real world, although certain markets do tend towards it. Despite the lack of real world examples, the model of perfect competition provides a standard or reference point against which to analyse other market situations. There are a number of simplifying assumptions with respect to perfect competition.

(a) There are many buyers and sellers, none of which is able to influence the market. Each firm is very small in relation to the whole market and is, therefore, unable to affect the price charged. As stated, they are price takers which means that they face a perfectly elastic demand curve at the price set by the market (*see* Figure 6.5).

The industry's demand curve is the normal shape (Figure 6.5(a)) and the demand curve for the firm is such that if they raise their price above P_0 then the demand for their product would fall to zero.

(b) Both the producers and consumers have *perfect knowledge*; they

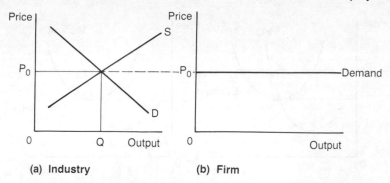

Figure 6.5 *The demand curve for the firm in perfect competition.*

are aware of the ruling market price, P_o. If the producer charges above P_o, consumers, given that in perfect competition there are many small firms, will purchase their products elsewhere.

(c) The product is *homogeneous*, which means that each unit of the product is identical. Thus, following on from the previous assumption, buyers have no preference as to where they purchase the product — they are indifferent — hence the demand curve in Figure 6.5(b).

(d) In a perfectly competitive market there is freedom for firms to enter into and leave the industry. Existing firms cannot prevent the entry of new firms into the market.

6. Short run equilibrium in perfect competition

Figure 6.6 gives three alternative situations for the firm in perfect competition, in the short run.

(a) *In situation (a)* the firm is profit maximising producing an output q_1 where MC = MR. The cost curves incorporate an element of profit called *normal profit*. Normal profit is the return necessary to keep the firm in its present business. The total revenue is OP_1Aq_1 and total cost is $OCBq_1$, hence the firm is making supernormal profit of P_1ABC, represented by the shaded area.

(b) *In situation (b)* the firm is profit maximising, producing an output q_2 and covering its total cost. The firm is breaking even, making normal profit.

(c) *In situation (c)* the firm is profit maximising producing an output of q_3. However, in this situation, the firm is actually *loss minimising* making a loss equal to P_3DEF.

In the long run the firm in this situation will close down, although it may continue to operate in the short run if it can cover its average

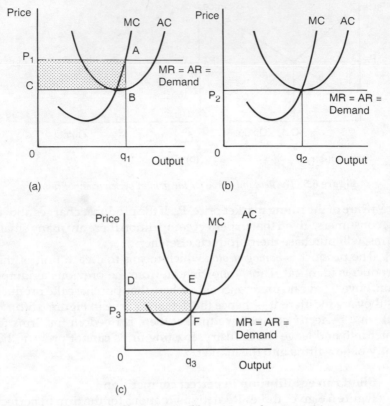

Figure 6.6 *Short run equilibrium in perfect competition.*

variable cost (AVC). The reason for this is that in the short run the firm will have to pay its fixed costs even if it produces nothing, so by producing an output of q (*see* Figure 6.7), the firm can cover its AVC, such as raw materials, wages and fuel costs, and part of its fixed costs.

In Figure 6.7 the firm's total revenue is represented by the area OP_oC_q and therefore the firm can cover all of its total variable costs, represented by area OED_q and some of its fixed costs represented by area EP_oCD. The firm is not, however, able to cover P_oABC of its fixed costs and this represents a loss to the firm. It is, therefore, worth this firm operating in the short run for its total revenue is greater than its total variable cost. If the price line were below point F, then the firm would close down in the short run for it would not even be covering the purchase of such things as raw materials and labour, i.e. the variable costs. At prices above the AVC curve the firm will equate

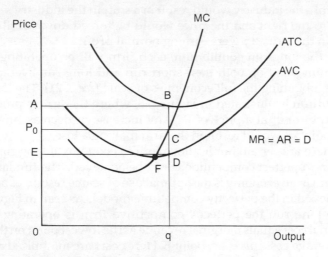

Figure 6.7 *A loss-making firm in perfect competition.*

price (marginal revenue) with marginal cost and, in fact, the marginal cost curve above the AVC curve (i.e. point F) represents the firm's supply curve. The industry supply curve (*see* Figure 6.5(a)) is derived from the horizontal summation of the individual firms' marginal cost curves.

7. Long run equilibrium in perfect competition

In the long run all the firm's costs are variable costs. Thus a firm such as in Figure 6.6(c) would close down, whereas a firm as in Figure 6.6(b) would continue to operate since they are breaking even. The existence of supernormal profit, as with a firm like that in Figure 6.6(a), would attract new firms into the industry for profits act as a 'signal' in a competitive market to enter the industry. The entry of new

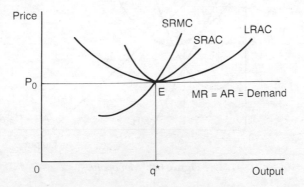

Figure 6.8 *Long run equilibrium for the firm in perfect competition.*

firms into the industry would result in a shift in the industry's supply curve to the right and the price would be forced down until all the firms in the industry were earning normal profit.

In the long run equilibrium, each firm will be operating at the minimum point on both their short run and long run average cost curves, obtaining the full economies of scale (*see* 5: **21**). The long run equilibrium is illustrated in Figure 6.8, where the firm is producing an output of q* at a price of P_o. Any increase or decrease in output from point q* would result in the firm making a loss.

There are certain implications for the economy if long run equilibrium in perfect competition could be achieved. The fundamental problem in an economy is the optimal use of scarce resources and this is achieved in the perfectly competitive model. As seen in Figure 6.8, in the long run the perfectly competitive firm is operating where marginal cost equals marginal revenue at the lowest point on the long run average cost curve, i.e. point E. Here costs are minimised and the firm is making the best use of its resources. If all firms in the economy operated in this way, there would be an optimal or efficient allocation of resources in the economy.

Monopoly

8.   What is monopoly?

Whereas in perfect competition there are many sellers of an

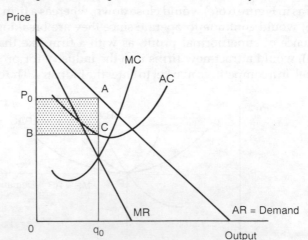

Figure 6.9 *Monopoly.*

identical product, with a 'pure' monopoly there is a single seller of a product for which there is no close substitute. The firm is the industry and, unlike a perfectly competitive firm which is a price taker, a monopolist is a *price maker*. This means that the demand curve is downward sloping from left to right as in Figure 6.9.

Since the demand curve (average revenue curve) is downward sloping, marginal revenue must be less than the average revenue. This was explained earlier in **3**. The monopoly diagram is given in Figure 6.9, with marginal revenue such that it cuts the horizontal axis half-way between the origin and where the average revenue curve cuts the horizontal axis. The monopolist profit maximises where marginal cost equals marginal revenue. The price charged is P_o and an output of q_o is produced, and this results in the supernormal profit of the shaded area. Total revenue is equal to OP_oAq_o and the total cost $OBCq_o$, giving supernormal profit as stated of BP_oAC. As with a perfectly competitive firm, the monopolist must make sure that it is covering its average variable cost in the short run.

In the long run the monopolist can continue to earn supernormal profit and the excess of price over marginal cost is an indication of the firm's monopoly power. For supernormal profit to be earned in the long run it is necessary for there to be *barriers to entry* into the industry.

9. Barriers to entry
There are a number of reasons why monopolists are able to earn supernormal profit in the long run:

(a) The monopolist may have sole ownership of a natural resource. Control over, for example, the supply of a raw material will create an effective barrier to entry.

(b) The monopoly may have been created by the state, making it a legal monopoly.

(c) With either a patent or copyright the firm will have the sole right to produce a particular good or service.

(d) The productive process may be such that a high level of output is required to obtain the full economies of scale. With this being the case, new firms considering entry into the market will face high production costs and will, therefore, find it difficult to compete.

10. Advantages of a monopoly
There are a number of advantages with a monopoly:

(a) Being a large producer of a particular good may mean that the monopolist can benefit from economies of scale which are not possible

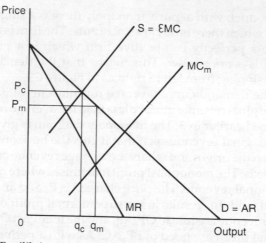

Figure 6.10 *Equilibrium in a perfectly competitive industry and monopoly with different MC curves.*

under perfect competition. In this case the monopolist's marginal cost curve could be lower than the supply curve obtained under perfect competition. This is shown in Figure 6.10 where the monopoly equates MC with MR and produces q_m at a price of P_m.

Under perfect competition the supply curve is the summation of the individual firms' MC curves and the industry will equate supply and demand, producing an output of q_c at a price of P_c. It is, therefore, the case that economies of scale could be so large that the output is higher and the price lower under monopoly than a perfectly competitive industry.

(b) The fact that monopolies earn supernormal profit in the long run means that they can allocate resources to research and development so as to improve the quality of the product, and therefore benefit society.

(c) The existence of long-term supernormal profit under a monopoly situation may mean that they can innovate, not only improving existing products but also introducing new products. ·

11. Disadvantages of a monopoly

There are a number of reasons why a monopoly could be seen as operating against the *public interest*:

(a) There could be an imaginary situation in which a perfectly competitive industry comprising many small firms is taken over by a profit maximising monopolist. This can be analysed by referring to Figure 6.11 in which D is the demand curve for the industry and S_c is

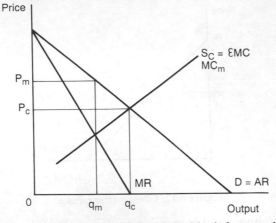

Figure 6.11 *Equilibrium in a perfectly competitive industry and monopoly.*

the supply curve in perfect competition obtained by the summation of individual firms' marginal cost (MC) curves.

In the perfectly competitive situation the quantity produced is q_c and the price charged by each firm is P_c. If the perfectly competitive industry was then taken over by a single firm, i.e. a monopolist with identical cost and demand conditions, then the monopolist would equate MC and MR in order to profit maximise. The perfectly competitive industry's supply curve would then become the monopolist's MC curve (MC_m) and the monopolist would thus reduce its output level to q_m and increase its price to P_m.

(b) Monopolies are able to earn above normal profit in the long run because of the barriers to entry. This represents a redistribution of income from the consumer to the producer which can be criticised on equity grounds.

(c) Since there are barriers to entry, monopolies face no pressure from competition and because of this the quality of the product may decline. This is not the case with perfectly competitive markets where competition forces firms to be efficient, operating at the lowest point on the average cost curve in the long run.

12. Price discrimination

So far we have assumed that the monopolist charges only one price; however, it is possible for a monopolist to charge different prices in separate markets and to obtain some of the consumer surplus which would otherwise go to the buyer of the product. The markets can be separated *geographically*, as with an exporter charging different

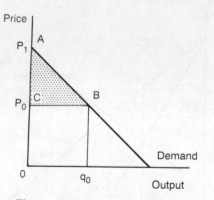

Figure 6.12 *Consumer surplus.*

prices for the home and overseas market, or on the basis of *time*, as with car parking space. Car parking spaces can be charged differently depending on short stay or long stay.

13. Consumer surplus

In terms of Figure 6.12 the market price of the product is P_0 at which q_0 units would be sold. However, certain individuals would have been willing to pay a price for the product in excess of P_0. Some, in fact, would have been willing to pay a price as high as P_1, and the shaded area under the demand curve and above the price is the consumer surplus (area ABC).

14. The operation of price discrimination

Price discrimination is found in a number of industries. British Rail, for example, charges different prices for peak and off-peak users, as does the electricity industry.

There are a number of assumptions necessary for price discrimination to operate:

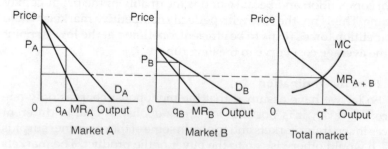

Figure 6.13 *Price discrimination.*

(a) There is a single monopoly supplier of the product.

(b) The market can be divided into two, such as markets A and B in Figure 6.13.

(c) There are different demand and marginal revenue curves in the two markets with different elasticities.

(d) A single price is charged in each market.

(e) It is not possible to resell the product between the two markets. The markets are separated either on the basis of time or geographically.

(f) The cost of providing the product is the same in the two markets.

In Figure 6.13 the demand in the two markets is given by D_A and D_B, and this will result in marginal revenue curves MR_A and MR_B. The marginal revenue curves can be summed horizontally to give the marginal revenue curve for the overall market MR_{A+B}. By equating marginal revenue and marginal cost in the overall market, the monopolist will produce an output q^* and this output can be split between the two markets depending on where MR_A and MR_B equal MC. The result of this is that q_A is sold in market A at a price of P_A and q_B is sold in market B at a price of P_B. Note that $q^*=q_A+q_B$. There is still consumer surplus in the two markets but this is less than was the case prior to price discrimination.

Progress test 6

1. Outline the relationship between total, average and marginal revenue. (3)

2. Outline what is meant by profit maximisation. (4)

3. Why is a firm in a perfectly competitive market said to be a 'price taker'? (5)

4. Distinguish between the short run and long run equilibrium in perfect competition. (6, 7)

5. Why is it possible for a monopolist to earn supernormal profit in the long run? (8, 9)

6. What is meant by consumer surplus? (13)

7. Outline the assumptions necessary for price discrimination to take place. (14)

7
Theory of the firm — monopolistic competition and oligopoly

1. Introduction

Chapter 6 dealt with the theories of perfect competition and monopoly, the perfectly competitive firm being a price taker and the monopolist a price maker. This chapter deals with the theories of monopolistic competition and oligopoly, where firms are able to exercise a degree of control over the price they charge.

In monopolistic competition there are many firms producing slightly different products and, although they are in competition with each other, their product is unique in some way, thus giving them a certain degree of monopoly power. In oligopolistic markets there are a few firms which are *interdependent*, closely monitoring their competitors' actions and responding accordingly.

Monopolistic competition

2. What is monopolistic competition?

The theory of monopolistic competition incorporates features of both perfect competition and monopoly. As with perfect competition there is freedom of entry into and exit from the industry. There are a large number of firms in the market, each producing goods and services which are slightly different from their competitors. The existence of *product differentiation* means that firms have a certain degree of monopoly power, thus if they raise their price they do not lose all of their customers even though they produce products which are close substitutes. The result is a downward sloping demand curve, albeit a relatively elastic demand curve. Thus a monopolistically competitive firm is not a price taker. Product differentiation can be reinforced through advertising which produces an element of *brand loyalty*.

3. Short run equilibrium in monopolistic competition

Assuming the monopolistically competitive firm is a profit max-

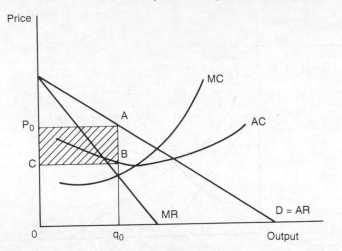

Figure 7.1 *Short run equilibrium for the firm in monopolistic competition.*

imiser, the short run equilibrium is similar to that of a monopoly. The only difference is that the demand curve is relatively more elastic and each firm is producing only a small proportion of the overall market output. As explained (*see* 6: **4**), profit maximisation is where marginal cost equals marginal revenue, and in Figure 7.1 the firm is in equilibrium where it is producing an output of q_0 which it sells at a price of P_0. Supernormal profit is given by the shaded area P_0ABC.

4.   Long run equilibrium in monopolistic competition

Given the assumption of freedom of entry into the industry, the existence of supernormal profit will act as an incentive for new firms to enter the market. This will result in a shift in the firm's demand curve to the left, which will also lead to a shift in the marginal revenue curve.

The supernormal profit will be competed away until, in the long run, the firm will be earning normal profit and producing where price equals average cost, with the firm breaking even (*see* Figure 7.2). At this point there will be no further entry into the industry.

Note that in equilibrium the average cost curve is tangential to the demand curve at point E which is above the minimum point on the average cost curve. Although in the long run firms are making normal profit, this does not mean that the consumer obtains the same benefit from monopolistically competitive firms as they do from perfectly competitive firms. The firm is producing above the minimum point on the average cost curve so the consumer is having to

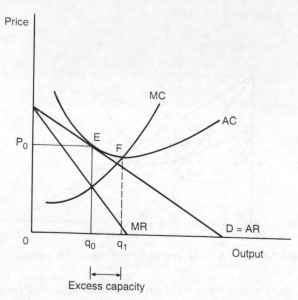

Figure 7.2 *Long run equilibrium for the firm in monopolistic competition.*

pay a higher price than that paid in perfect competition in the long run. Under monopolistic competition, however, the consumer enjoys a greater variety of products and therefore the higher price may, to some extent, reflect the consumer's desire for a wider choice.

In Figure 7.2 the firm is operating on the downward sloping section of its average cost curve at an output of q_0. Average cost is at a minimum denoted by point F, at an output of q_1. Monopolistically competitive firms are not, therefore, operating at the point of *full productive efficiency*, in fact they are operating with spare or excess capacity. In Figure 7.2 the difference between q_0 and q_1 is this *excess capacity*.

Oligopoly

5. What is oligopoly?

Oligopoly refers to a situation where there are a few firms in the market producing a large number of brands. Each firm is of a sufficiently large size that the decision taken by one firm will affect the decisions taken by the other firms in the market. The firms are, therefore, *mutually dependent* and any theory of oligopoly needs to take this into account.

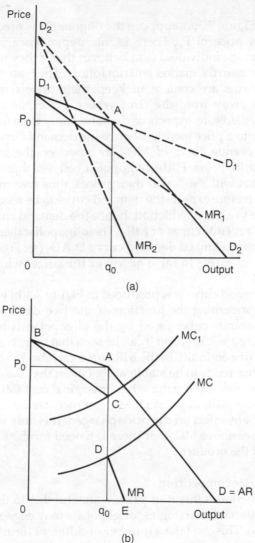

Figure 7.3 *The oligopolist's kinked demand curve.*

6. The kinked demand curve

Figure 7.3 relates to a single firm operating in an oligopolistic market where there are several producers of similar products. The aim of the kinked demand curve, developed by Paul Sweezy in 1939, was to explain price stability and the absence of price wars in oligopolistic markets.

Using Figure 7.3(a), suppose the oligopolist is producing an output q_0 at a price of P_0. There is interdependence in oligopolistic markets and the individual firm believes that if they raise their price the other firms in the market will not follow. The reason for this is that the other firms are content to keep their price fixed and attract consumers away from the firm whose price has increased. The oligopolist, therefore, expects its demand curve to be relatively elastic in response to a price increase, hence the demand curve D_1D_1, with a marginal revenue curve of MR_1. If, however, the individual firm lowers its price below P_0 the oligopolist believes that the other firms in the market will also lower their prices, thus creating a price war. The firm therefore expects the demand curve to be relatively inelastic in response to a price reduction, hence the demand curve D_2D_2, with a marginal revenue curve of MR_2. The oligopolist therefore believes that it is facing a kinked demand curve D_1AD_2 (*see* Figure 7.3(a)) and there is no incentive to raise or lower the price, which is *stable* or *sticky* at P_0.

The demand curve is reproduced in Figure 7.3(b) with the kink at point A representing the junction of the two demand curves. The marginal revenue curve faced by the oligopolist is represented by BCDE (*see* Figure 7.3(b)) and it can be seen that there is a discontinuity of CD. The discontinuity in the MR curve can also be seen as a reason why the price tends to be stable at P_0. Given that the oligopolist is a profit maximiser, producing where marginal cost (MC) equals marginal revenue (MR) at point D, MC can increase up to MC_1 without there being any effect on the price charged. It is only when marginal cost increases above MC_1 that there is a need for the firm to increase the price of the product.

7.   Non-price competition

Since there is a threat of price wars and due to the existence of effective alternative strategies, oligopolists may engage in non-price competition. This can take a number of different forms:

(a) *Product differentiation.* As with monopolistically competitive firms oligopolists can, through advertising, create a brand image for their product. The firm may offer a particular after-sales service or package the product in a particular way.

(b) *Promotional offers.* These can take a number of different forms such as 'buy two and get one free', '20% extra free', or free gifts such as drinking glasses — commonly used by petrol companies.

8. Collusion

Given the level of uncertainty which exists in oligopolistic markets, there is much to be gained from *collusion*. Collusion is a way of dealing with interdependence since coming to an agreement as to what price should be charged or what level of output should be produced makes it possible for oligopolists to act as a monopoly, achieving maximum profits for the industry.

9. Methods of collusion

Collusion can take the following forms:

(a) *Formal collusion.* This can be called *overt* collusion, with agreement being reached between the firms as to what price to charge or what output to produce. This type of formal agreement is known as a *cartel* and is illegal in the UK.

(b) *Tacit collusion.* This is where firms behave in a cooperative way but do not have a formal agreement. Firms in an oligopolistic market may view *covert* collusion as being in their mutual interest. The most common form of tacit collusion is *price leadership* where one firm sets the price and the other firms follow.

(i) *Dominant firm price leadership.* Often the price leader in an oligopolistic market is the dominant firm. In this situation the largest or the most efficient firm takes the lead in setting the price

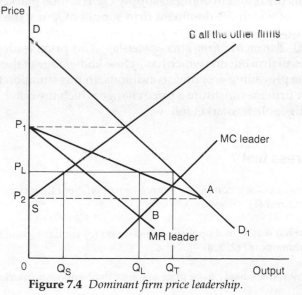

Figure 7.4 *Dominant firm price leadership.*

which the other firms follow, possibly because they fear that not doing so would lead to a price war.

A formal model of the dominant firm price leadership can be explained by the use of Figure 7.4.

The assumption is made that the oligopolistic market consists of one profit maximising dominant firm and many small firms whose behaviour is typical of perfect competition. In Figure 7.4 the total market demand curve is shown as DD_1 and the supply curve of all the small firms in the industry is SS. This is derived from the individual firms' marginal cost curves. Given the market demand curve it is possible for the dominant firm to derive its own demand curve. At a price of P_1 the whole market could be supplied by the small firms, therefore, the demand for the dominant firm's product is zero. At a price of P_2, however, the small firms would supply nothing and the dominant firm would have the market to itself. The demand curve faced by the dominant firm is, therefore, P_1AD_1. Having obtained the dominant firm's demand curve it is possible to construct its MR curve (which is labelled MR leader). If the dominant firm has a MC curve of MC leader then it will profit maximise by producing Q_L at a price of P_L given that MC equals MR at point B. The leader sets the price at P_L and the other small firms in the oligopolistic market follow this price, and in doing so supply Q_S. The total market demand is Q_T of which the dominant firm supplies Q_L and the small firms supply Q_S. The total market output Q_T equals Q_S plus Q_L.

(ii) Barometric firm price leadership. The price leader may be a small firm but one which has a close knowledge of the market and the prevailing economic conditions. In this situation the *barometric* firm may institute a price change which the other firms in the oligopolistic market follow.

Progress test 7

1. Is monopolistic competition more or less efficient than perfect competition? **(4)**

2. In what way is monopolistic competition (a) similar to, and (b) different from, monopoly? **(2, 3, 4)**

3. Why is there likely to be price stability in oligopolistic markets? **(6)**

4. What forms can non-price competition take in monopolistic competition and oligopoly? **(7)**

5. What are the reasons for collusion in oligopolistic markets and what form does the collusion take? **(8, 9)**

6. Outline the different forms of price leadership. **(9)**

8

Wages

1. Introduction

The aim of this chapter is to analyse the reward to the factor of production labour. Labour can be viewed as a *derived demand*, which means that it is not simply demanded for its own sake but for what it can produce.

In a market economy the price of the factor of production is determined by the market demand and supply conditions. Throughout this chapter the *marginal productivity theory* will be used to analyse the demand for labour.

2. The marginal productivity theory

The marginal productivity theory is based on the principle of profit maximisation which was introduced in Chapter 6. Profit maximising firms will employ additional workers up to the point where the extra cost of the additional unit of labour employed is equal to the extra revenue obtained.

In outlining the theory we will initially assume a perfectly competitive product and labour market.

3. Perfectly competitive product and labour market

Assuming a perfectly competitive product market means that a firm can sell each unit of output at the same price, assumed to be £10 in the hypothetical data given in Table 8.1. This means that the firm is a price taker and thus faces a perfectly elastic demand curve for its product.

Perfect competition in the labour market means that the firm can employ extra workers at the same wage rate, assumed to be £200 per worker per week in Table 8.1. We also make the assumption that labour is the only variable factor.

The data given in Table 8.1 can be plotted as in Figure 8.1.

The marginal revenue product of labour is the output each extra worker produces, i.e. the marginal physical product (MPP) multiplied by the price (P) the extra output can be sold at. Hence:

$$MRP = MPP \times P$$

Table 8.1 The marginal revenue product

Number of workers	Marginal physical product (MPP)	Price of the product (P) (£)	Marginal revenue product (MRP) (£)	Wage rate (W) (£)	Additional profit (MRP - W) (£)
1	5	10	50	200	−150
2	19	10	190	200	−10
3	33	10	330	200	+130
4	43	10	430	200	+230
5	50	10	500	200	+300
6	30	10	300	200	+100
7	9	10	90	200	−110

The average revenue product of labour (ARP) is derived by multiplying the average physical product by the price of the product. Both the ARP and the MRP rise and then decline since labour is subject to the law of diminishing returns (*see* 5: **14**). The wage rate (W) is constant at £200 and this represents the marginal cost (MC_L) and the average cost (AC_L) of labour, and also the supply curve of labour. The profit maximising position for the firm is where:

$$MRP = MC_L$$

In Figure 8.1 this is where 6 workers are employed. The firm

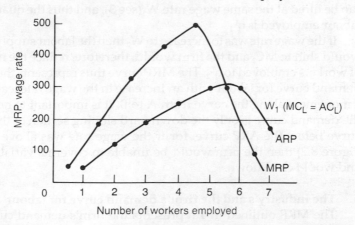

Figure 8.1 *The wage rate and employment in a perfectly competitive market.*

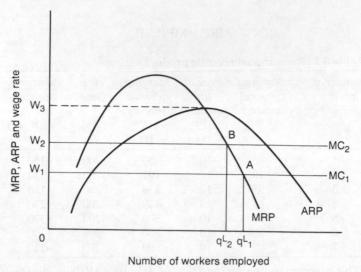

Figure 8.2 *The firm's demand curve for labour.*

would not employ the 7th worker since he or she would only add £90 to revenue but would cost the firm £200 — hence a reduction in profit of £110 (*see* Table 8.1).

4. The firm's demand curve for labour

The profit maximising firm in Figure 8.2 faces a perfectly elastic supply curve for labour (MC_1) which means that additional labour can be hired at the same wage rate W_1(see **3**), and thus the quantity of labour employed is q^L_1.

If the wage rate was to increase to W_2 then the labour supply curve would shift to MC_2 and the firm would, therefore, reduce the number of workers employed to q^L_2. The MRP curve thus represents the firm's demand curve for labour with an increase in the wage rate leading to a movement along the curve from A to B. It is important to note that the demand curve is only the downward sloping section of the MRP curve below the ARP curve, for if the wage rate was above W_3 (in Figure 8.2) then the firm would be unable to cover its variable cost and would close down.

5. The industry's and the firm's demand curve for labour

The MRP outlined in **4** represents the firm's demand curve for labour, thus when the wage rate decreases the firm takes on additional labour and output subsequently expands. This is based on the

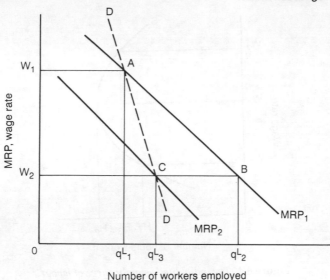

Figure 8.3 *The firm's demand curve for labour, taking into account a change in the price of the product.*

assumption that the other firms in the industry hold their output constant, which is an assumption we can now relax.

With reference to Figure 8.3, as the wage rate falls from W_1 to W_2 the firm will initially employ additional workers, increasing the numbers employed from q^L_1 to q^L_2. This represents a movement along the MRP, MRP_1 curve from A to B. If all the other firms in the industry also increase the numbers they employ, there will be a significant increase in output, with the supply curve for the product shifting to the right. Assuming a downward sloping demand curve for the product, price will fall and this will lead to a shift in the MRP curve to the left, i.e. to MRP_2 in Figure 8.3. (Remember that the MRP equals the MPP $\times$ P, so if the price falls the MRP will shift to the left.) This being so, the firm will now reduce the numbers employed to q^L_3 at the wage rate W_2, represented by point C in Figure 8.3. Joining A and C gives the firm's demand curve for labour. This is steeper than the initial MRP curve and is represented by the dotted line DD in Figure 8.3.

In order to obtain the industry's demand curve for labour, the individual firms' demand curves are summed horizontally in much the same way the market demand curve for goods and services was obtained in 2: 5.

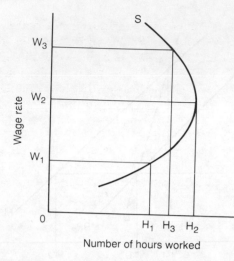

Figure 8.4 *The individual's supply curve of labour.*

6.   The supply of labour

The total supply of labour to a market depends on the price of labour (i.e. the wage rate), the size of the population, the age composition of the population, the labour force participation rate, the occupational and geographical distribution of the labour force and the tastes of the labour force in terms of their trade-off between work and leisure. The wage rate is all important in determining the supply of labour and this section begins by deriving the supply curve of labour for an individual. The market supply curve is simply the summation of the individual supply curves.

(a) *The individual's supply curve.* The supply curve of labour may be backward bending (*see* Figure 8.4). This means that after a certain wage rate, higher wages will result in fewer hours being worked per day, with individuals demanding more leisure time. In Figure 8.4, as the wage rate increases from W_1 to W_2 the individual is prepared to increase the number of hours worked from H_1 to H_2. At a wage rate above W_2, however, the supply curve is backward bending or negatively sloped, with the individual supplying less hours of labour and preferring to use his or her income on leisure activities. So as the wage rate increases from W_2 to W_3, the number of hours worked is reduced from H_2 to H_3.

The backward bending supply curve can be analysed using indifference curve analysis and, in particular, the income and substitution effect (*see* 4: **14**). As the wage rate increases, assuming leisure is a normal good, individuals will substitute extra hours of work for leisure, hence the *substitution effect*. An increase in the wage rate will increase the individual's income and as this takes place there will be an increase in the demand for normal goods, including leisure time. The *income effect* operates in such a way that fewer hours of work are supplied as income increases. When the income effect outweighs the substitution effect, higher wages can lead to less hours worked and a backward bending supply curve.

(b) *The industry's supply curve of labour.* This is obtained by the horizontal summation of the supply curves of individuals and it will normally be positively sloped. As the wage rate increases in a particular industry, workers will be encouraged to transfer from other industries.

7.   The labour market equilibrium

Having derived the market demand and supply curves for labour in a particular industry it is possible to determine the labour market equilibrium.

Figure 8.5 gives the market demand (D_{L1}) and the market supply (S_L) for labour in a particular industry, with an equilibrium wage of W_1 and employment of L_1.

If we take the example of the construction industry, an increase in the demand for buildings will lead to an increase in their price, assuming *ceteris paribus*. With labour being a derived demand, the

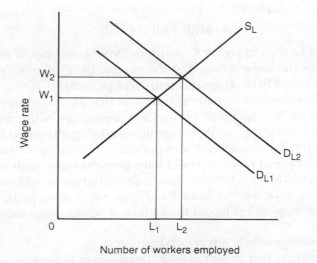

Figure 8.5 *Labour market equilibrium.*

increase in the demand for the products of the construction industry will increase the demand for construction workers. The demand curve for labour will, therefore, shift to the right (D_{L2} in Figure 8.5) and there will be new equilibrium wage and employment (W_2 and L_2 respectively).

8.   Imperfect labour market

The previous sections have assumed that all markets are perfectly competitive, however, labour markets are likely to contain imperfections. These can be on the *demand side*, in terms of the employer, who may be a producer monopoly or a (monopsonist i.e. a monopoly buyer of labour), or on the *supply side* in terms of the employee, who may belong to a trade union.

9.   A product monopolist

A product monopolist will face a downward sloping demand curve for its product. This means that the monopolist must lower the price charged for the product if it wishes to sell more. We can, therefore, distinguish between the *value of the marginal product* (VMP) which is the marginal physical product (MPP) multiplied by the price of the product (P):

$$VMP = MPP \times P$$

and the *marginal revenue product* (MRP) which is the marginal physical product (MPP) multiplied by the marginal revenue (MR):

$$MRP = MPP \times MR$$

This can be seen in Figure 8.6, with the MRP curve below the VMP curve, for the same reason that the monopolist's marginal revenue curve is below the average revenue curve (*see* 6: **3**).

The assumption is made in Figure 8.6 that the wage rate remains constant at W. The profit maximising monopolist will employ L_1 workers at the wage rate W, the equilibrium being illustrated by point A. If the product market had been perfectly competitive then the price and the marginal revenue would have been the same, with the MRP equal to the VMP and L_2 rather than L_1 units of labour would have been employed, illustrated by point B in Figure 8.6. A monopolist would, therefore, employ less labour than a firm in perfect competition.

10.   A monopsonistic buyer of labour

There may be a single buyer of labour — a monopsonist — which could be an employers' association acting as a single decision making

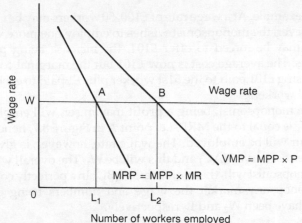

Figure 8.6 *Demand for labour with an imperfect product market.*

body, selling a product in a perfectly competitive market. If this is the case then it means that in order to recruit additional workers it has to offer a higher wage rate. This is illustrated in Figure 8.7 with the marginal cost curve for labour (MC_L) being above the average cost curve for labour. The reason for this can be explained by the use of a

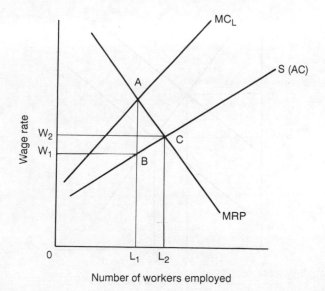

Figure 8.7 *The wage rate and the demand for labour in an imperfect labour market.*

simple example. At a wage rate of £100, 50 workers may be employed. If, however, the monopsonist wishes to employ one more worker he or she may be forced to offer £101, the increase being paid to all workers. The average cost is now £101 but the marginal cost is £151, comprising £101 paid to the 51st worker plus £1 paid to each of the 50 original workers.

The monopsonist, being a profit maximiser, will employ where the MC_L is equal to the MRP, i.e. point A in Figure 8.7, hence L_1 units of labour will be employed. The wage rate, however, is given by the average cost curve S(AC) and this will be W_1. The overall wage bill to the monopsonist will, therefore, be OW_1BL_1. In a perfectly competitive non-monopsony market the wage and numbers being employed would have been W_2 and L_2 respectively.

11. Trade unions

Trade unions are made up of groups of workers who have a common interest. This could be a common skill, a similar job or working in the same industry.

The aims of a trade union can range from improving the working environment to taking up the case of those members the union see as being unfairly dismissed. An important function is to increase the wage rate of its members and this section will concentrate on the way

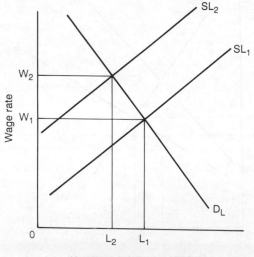

Figure 8.8 *Restricting the supply of labour.*

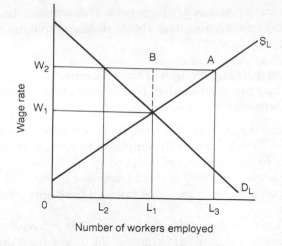

Figure 8.9 *Collective bargaining and the wage rate.*

in which trade unions seek to achieve that objective.

(a) *Restrict the supply of labour.* Restricting the supply of labour could be achieved through the use of a closed shop or by lengthening the time it takes to complete an apprenticeship.

Over a period of time the trade union could reduce the supply of labour to an industry, shifting the supply curve from SL_1 to SL_2 (*see* Figure 8.8). The result would be an increase in the wage rate from W_1 to W_2, but with a reduced number employed, i.e. L_2 instead of L_1.

(b) *Collective bargaining.* Collective bargaining involves the direct negotiation between a trade union, bargaining collectively on behalf of its members, and the employer/s. Successful collective bargaining could raise the wage rate from OW_1 to OW_2, as illustrated in Figure 8.9.

The trade union may be unwilling to supply labour below the wage rate of W_2, therefore, the supply curve becomes $W_2 AS_L$, being perfectly elastic over the section W_2A. At the equilibrium wage of W_1, with no trade union involvement L_1 workers would be employed. However, with a wage of W_2, only L_2 are demanded and therefore $L_3 - L_2$ are unable to find employment. There may be individuals who are willing to work for a wage below OW_2 but they would be prevented from doing so by the union agreement.

Through collective bargaining a wage rate of W_2 has been agreed, with L_2 being employed. The union, however, could attempt to maintain employment at the equilibrium level of L_1 while obtaining a wage W_2. This would involve forcing the employer off the demand curve, thus obtaining position B in Figure 8.9. This will only be successful if the firm is profitable and, thus, able to sustain employment at L_1 while paying a wage rate of W_2.

12. The bargaining strength of trade unions

The bargaining strength of trade unions when dealing with employers depends on a number of factors:

(a) *The demand for the product being relatively inelastic.* If this is the case then it is relatively easy for the employer to pass on an increase in the wage rate to the consumer of the product.

(b) *The labour cost being a small proportion of the total cost.* In this situation an increase in the wage rate will have only a small effect on total cost.

(c) *The level of profit earned by the industry.* This will have an important bearing on the bargaining strength of the union, for if the industry is earning substantial profit there is more chance of the trade union obtaining a wage increase for its members.

(d) *The ease of substituting the factors of production.* It may be easy for an industry to substitute capital for labour. If this is the case, it will weaken the bargaining strength of the trade union.

(e) *The strength of the trade union itself.* If the majority of the workers in a particular industry belong to the union or the union has sufficient funds to withstand a prolonged period of industrial action, it will have added strength when bargaining with the employer.

(f) *The economic and political climate.* In a period of high unemployment, with a government determined to resist wage increases, the power of a trade union will be severely restricted.

Progress test 8

1. Number of workers employed	1	2	3	4	5	6
Total product (output per week)	10	22	36	44	50	50

If the price of the product is £20 per unit, given the information in the table, calculate the marginal physical product of labour and the marginal revenue product of labour. Assuming the producer is a profit maximiser, how many workers would be employed if the wage rate was £160 per week? How many would be employed if the wage rate fell to £120? **(3, 4)**

2. How will the firm's demand for labour be affected by a decrease in the wage rate, assuming:

(a) all other firms hold their output constant? **(5)**
(b) all other firms expand their output? **(5)**

3. Why may the individual's supply curve of labour be backward bending? **(6)**

4. Explain how the equilibrium wage rate is determined in a monopsony market for labour. **(10)**

5. Outline the influence a trade union may have on the perfectly competitive equilibrium wage rate and employment. **(11)**

6. Outline the factors which influence a trade union's ability to increase the wage rate. **(12)**

9

Interest, rent and profit

1. Introduction

In the previous chapter the reward to labour, i.e. wages, was outlined. This chapter concentrates on the rewards to the other factors of production, namely interest being the reward to capital, rent being the reward to land and profit being the reward to the entrepreneur. In practice, however, it is often difficult to separate them totally.

Interest

2. What is interest?

The rate of interest has two roles. *To a borrower* the rate of interest is the payment which has to be made in order to obtain liquid assets, namely cash. *To the lender* it is the reward received for parting with liquid assets. When the term 'the rate of interest' is used it appears to imply a single rate of interest. There are, however, many rates of interest on such things as mortgages, bank loans and government securities, with the rate depending on such factors as how credit-worthy the borrower is and the length of time the loan is required for. The level of inflation present in the economy will also affect the rate of interest. If inflation is increasing then one would expect lenders to seek a higher rate of interest to compensate for the loss in the real value of the capital.

It is important to distinguish between nominal and real rates of interest. The *nominal* or *money rate of interest* is the annual amount paid on funds which are borrowed, whereas the *real rate of interest* takes account of inflation, therefore:

Real rate of interest = Nominal rate of interest − Inflation rate

3. The theory of interest rates

There are two main approaches to the theory of interest rates, the loanable funds theory and the monetary theory.

4. The loanable funds theory

The loanable funds theory is an early attempt to explain how

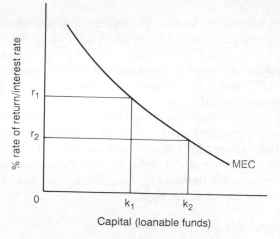

Figure 9.1 *A firm's demand for capital.*

interest rates are determined and is based on the total demand for and the supply of funds.

5. The demand for funds

The loanable funds theory assumes that the demand for funds is not demand for money for its own sake but for the capital goods which it can obtain. Capital goods, such as machinery and equipment, are used to make consumer goods and firms will invest in capital goods if they believe they will eventually obtain a positive net return. The marginal product of capital is the increase in total output obtained by employing one extra unit of capital, assuming other things remain constant. Marginal product is measured in physical terms but the value of the marginal product can be obtained by establishing its market price and multiplying this by the increase in total output, thus obtaining what is known as the *marginal efficiency of capital (MEC)*. The marginal efficiency of capital can be seen in Figure 9.1. It is downward sloping since capital, like labour, is assumed to be subject to the law of diminishing returns. For an explanation of the law of diminishing returns, *see* 5: **14**.

In Figure 9.1 the firm's capital stock is measured along the horizontal axis and the percentage rate of return on the vertical axis. A firm is likely to undertake the most profitable capital projects first and so, as further investment in capital equipment occurs, the rate of return on successive units of investment will be lower, i.e. marginal productivity will fall. The firm will invest up to the point at which the rate of return is equal to the market interest rate. So with an interest rate r_1 the firm will invest in capital projects up to k_1. If the market rate of interest was then to fall to r_2, further capital projects would prove profitable and the firm would invest up to k_2. The marginal efficiency of capital (MEC) curve (*see* Figure 9.1) can be seen as the firm's demand curve for capital.

Once all the firms' demand curves for capital have been obtained it is possible to aggregate them in order to produce the total demand for funds at different market rates of interest. A rise in the demand for capital, which could be brought about by an improvement in technology, would increase the demand for loanable funds, thus shifting the MEC curve in Figure 9.1 to the right.

6. The supply of funds

According to the loanable funds theory an increase in the interest rate will induce individuals to sacrifice current consumption, i.e. save, in order to obtain higher levels of consumption in the future. This being the case the supply of funds will be directly related to the interest rate (*see* Figure 9.2).

If the interest rate rises from r_1 to r_2, the supply of loanable funds will increase from S_1 to S_2, the supply curve (S) thus representing the total supply of savings.

7. The interest rate determined

The equilibrium rate of interest is determined by the interaction of the total demand for and the supply of funds, as shown in Figure 9.3.

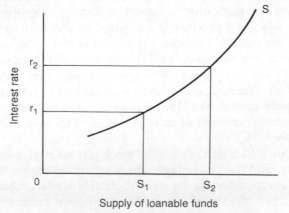

Figure 9.2 *The supply of loanable funds.*

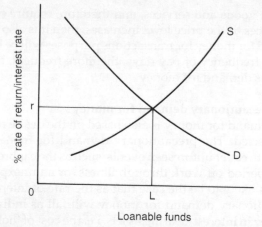

Figure 9.3 *The determination of the interest rate.*

The loanable funds theory (or what is sometimes called the *neo-classical theory*) of the rate of interest is based on the demand and supply of loanable funds, whereas the Keynesian or monetary theory of interest rates is determined by the interaction of the demand for money and the supply of money. The following sections (8–13) will outline the Keynesian theory of interest rates which is also called the *liquidity preference theory*.

8. The liquidity preference theory

In the Keynesian analysis of the rate of interest, unlike the loanable funds theory, the demand for money is not based purely on the demand for new capital goods. In fact, Keynes argued that there are three motives for preferring to hold wealth in the form of money:

(a) the transactions demand for money;
(b) the precautionary demand for money;
(c) the speculative demand for money.

9. The transactions demand for money

Individuals need to hold money in order to meet daily transactions such as buying petrol, paying for groceries or purchasing a newspaper. Everyone will hold a certain amount of money since they are normally paid weekly or monthly whereas their expenditure is spread over the whole period. The average amount held for transactions purposes depends upon the level of money income, the price level and the frequency of pay days. In terms of money income, the higher the money income, the more likely the individual is to purchase more goods and services, and therefore require extra transactions balances. If the price level increases, then it is also the case that the demand for money for transactions purposes will be higher. In the case of the frequency of pay days, the more frequent, the lower the transactions demand for money.

10. The precautionary demand for money

The demand for money is also based on the desire to provide for the unexpected. The precautionary demand for money allows the individual to cover unforeseen events, such as the car breaking down, a lengthy period off work through illness, or an unexpected redundancy. It is likely to be the case that as the rate of interest increases, the precautionary demand for money will fall as individuals place their money in interest-bearing assets, i.e. the cost of 'holding' money has increased. In terms of the following analysis, however, we will assume, as with the transactions demand for money, that the precautionary demand for money does not vary with the rate of interest, i.e. it is *interest inelastic*.

11. The speculative demand for money

The third motive for holding money differs from the other two. The transactions and precautionary motives relate to the function of money as a medium of exchange, whereas the speculative demand for money is based on the expectation of making a speculative gain or avoiding a loss. Keynes outlined the speculative demand for money in terms of the desire to hold money or fixed income bonds, and in order to explain the speculative demand for money it is necessary to outline the relationship between the price of bonds and the rate of interest.

It is important to note that the price of bonds and the rate of interest are inversely related. For example, consider a fixed income bond which yields a return of £10 per year. If the price of the bond is £100 then the rate of interest will be 10 per cent, since the £100 invested in the bond by savers must equal what savers could earn in any other income earning asset. If the market rate of interest were to rise to 20 per cent, then the price of the bond would fall to £50, since £50 invested in an income earning asset would yield £10. If, on the other hand, the market rate of interest were to fall to 5 per cent, then the price of the bond would rise to £200, since £200 invested in an income earning asset would yield £10. It can thus be seen that there is an inverse relationship between the price of a fixed return bond and the market rate of interest. If the rate of interest falls it increases the price

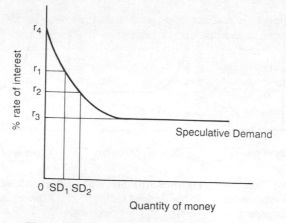

Figure 9.4 *The speculative demand for money.*

of bonds and thus makes them a more attractive proposition for an investor and vice versa.

The speculative demand for money is influenced by what individuals expect to happen to the rate of interest, bearing in mind that investors will have different expectations of how the rate of interest, and hence bond prices, will move. Some investors will expect the rate of interest to rise while others will expect it to fall. When the rate of interest is perceived to be unduly high by individuals they will assume that the next move is in a downward direction. As stated, when the rate of interest falls the price of bonds increases and so there are capital gains to be made. This being so, when the rate of interest is high there will be a substantial demand for bonds and hence a low speculative demand to hold money. If, however, the rate of interest is perceived to be unduly low then individuals will assume that the next move is upwards, resulting in a fall in bond prices and, therefore, a capital loss for those who own bonds. If this is the case the demand for bonds is likely to be low and those owning bonds will be looking to sell them before the price falls. In this situation the speculative demand for money to hold will be high.

The speculative demand for money can be observed by studying Figure 9.4. At a rate of interest r_1 the speculative demand for money is SD_1, whereas at a rate of interest r_2 the speculative demand is SD_2. At a rate of interest r_3 the price of bonds is perceived to be so high that it is expected that the only way they can move is in a downward direction, hence the speculative demand for money is perfectly elastic. On the other hand the rate of interest can be viewed as being so high,

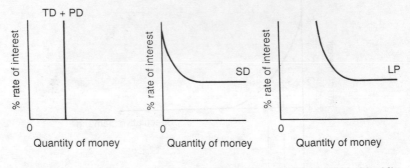

Figure 9.5(a) *Transactions and precautionary demand for money (TD + PD).*

Figure 9.5(b) *Speculative demand (SD).*

Figure 9.5(c) *Liquidity preference (LP).*

such as r_4, that the speculative demand for money is zero since everyone expects the rate of interest to fall, thus leading to an increase in the price of bonds and, therefore, to a capital gain.

12. Total demand for money

The total demand for money comprises the transactions, precautionary and speculative demand. It was stated (*see* **10**) that the transactions and precautionary demand for money is interest rate inelastic, thus they can be represented as a vertical line (*see* Figure 9.5(a)).

By adding the transactions and precautionary demand for money, as in Figure 9.5(a), to the speculative demand, as in Figure 9.5(b), it is possible to obtain the total demand for money referred to as the liquidity preference (LP), given in Figure 9.5(c).

13. The determination of the rate of interest

It is assumed that the money supply is determined by the monetary authorities and is taken to be fixed for the purposes of analysing the determination of the rate of interest. This being so, the interaction of the demand for money and the supply of money will give the equilibrium rate of interest. This can be seen in Figure 9.6, where the liquidity preference (LP) and the money supply MS_1 give the equilibrium rate of interest r_1. If the money supply were to increase to MS_2 then the equilibrium rate of interest would fall to r_2. The reason for this is that if the money supply were to increase at the initial equilibrium rate of interest r_1 from MS_1 to MS_2, there would be an excess

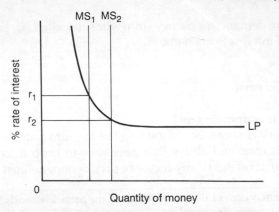

Figure 9.6 *The determination of the rate of interest.*

supply of money. Individuals would respond by demanding more bonds, which would bid up their price. As stated (in **11**), a rise in the price of bonds has the effect of bringing down the rate of interest, and as this occurs the speculative demand for money would increase until the new equilibrium rate of interest r_2 is reached.

14. The liquidity trap

The liquidity trap occurs when an increase in the money supply — such as that shown in Figure 9.7 by a movement from MS_1 to MS_2 — has no effect on the rate of interest. The reason for this is that at a very low rate of interest, such as r, everyone expects the rate to rise and, therefore, the bond price to fall causing a capital loss. In this situation an increase in the money supply is simply absorbed into

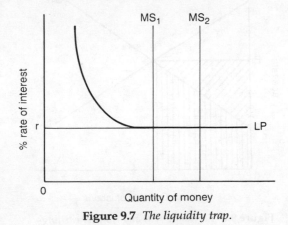

Figure 9.7 *The liquidity trap.*

speculative demand for money (into what are called *idle balances*) and the rate of interest is unchanged.

Economic rent

15. What is economic rent?

Economic rent can be defined as the amount paid to a factor of production over and above that necessary to keep it in its present occupation. It relates to any factor of production, not just land.

Example
A footballer may earn £1,000 per week given the particular skills he possesses. His next best occupation may be a salesman for which he could earn only £400 per week, the £600 difference between the two is called *economic rent* or *rent of ability*.

16. Transfer earnings

If the earnings of a factor of production decline, there will come a point when the factor will transfer to another use. The minimum payment necessary to keep the factor of production in its present

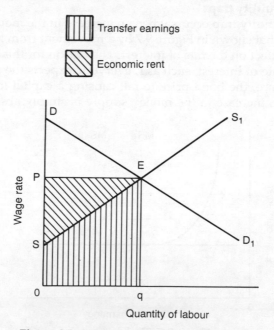

Figure 9.8 *Economic rent and transfer earnings.*

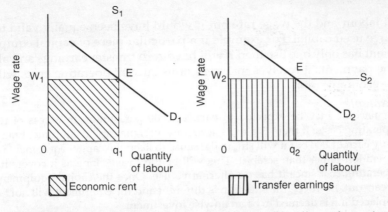

Figure 9.9(a) *All economic rent.*   **Figure 9.9(b)** *All transfer earnings.*

occupation is called its *transfer earnings*. The excess of earnings above the transfer earnings is called the *economic rent*.

These two concepts can be illustrated by reference to Figure 9.8. Although the figure relates to the labour market it could equally be the market for any other factor of production. The equilibrium wage rate in this particular labour market is OP and the numbers employed Oq. Thus total earnings are OPEq. The shaded area SEP represents economic rent and is the amount above the minimum payment necessary to keep labour in the particular industry concerned. The last worker employed may only be willing to work for OP, thus he or she obtains zero economic rent. All previous workers would receive economic rent and their transfer earnings are represented by the area OSEq. SE in Figure 9.8 is the 'necessary supply price', i.e. the minimum payment necessary to keep the factor in its present occupation.

Two extreme situations are represented in Figures 9.9(a) and (b). In Figure 9.9(a) the supply curve for labour is perfectly inelastic (S_1). If this is the case then with a demand curve (D_1) the earnings are OW_1Eq_1 and this is all economic rent since Oq_1 units of labour would have been willing to work for nothing. The situation in Figure 9.9(b) is somewhat different in that the supply curve (S_2) is perfectly elastic at a wage rate W_2, and total earnings are represented by area OW_2Eq_2 and this represents all transfer earnings. The reason for this is quite simple in that if the employer reduced the wage rate below W_2, labour would be unwilling to supply its services. It should be clear from Figures 9.9(a) and (b), therefore, that the more inelastic the supply curve, the greater the economic rent.

We have analysed economic rent and transfer earnings in terms of labour and the wage rate but it would have been equally valid to have used capital. For example if a particular piece of capital equipment has only one use then it will have zero transfer earnings and all the payments it receives in excess of its current operating costs will be economic rent.

Example

A machine may be expected to earn £10,000 per annum in excess of its operating costs. If there is a recession, however, the capital equipment may only earn £1,000 but it will still make sense to keep the capital equipment in operation rather than scrap it. This will be the case as long as it covers its operating cost since it has no alternative use. Once the capital equipment wears out, however, the situation is different and the equipment will not be replaced if it is deemed to be an unwise investment.

Profit

17. What is profit?

The concept of profit was introduced in 5: **17**. Profit can be seen as the reward for risk-taking and it differs from the reward to the other factors of production in several ways:

(a) *Uncertainty surrounds profit* since it is a residual paid to the entrepreneur after all the other factors of production have been rewarded. So, whereas labour receives a reward in the form of either a wage or a salary, it is not certain that the shareholders will receive a dividend. Uncertainty is fundamental to the activities of the entrepreneur and it will generally be the case that the greater the uncertainty, the greater the risk and the potential rewards.

(b) *Profit can be negative* in which case the firm is making a loss. This is unlike the returns to the other factors of production which are positive since they are contracted prior to the commencement of production. For example, labour is paid an agreed contractual amount.

(c) *Profit can fluctuate much more than the other factor rewards*. With regard to wages, for example, the rates are normally fixed by the employer for a particular period of time, so too is rent, but profit depends on the cost of production and the demand for the product — which may change dramatically.

18. Profit as a cost of production

If the profit of a particular company falls below a particular level the entrepreneur will switch into another form of economic activity.

It is, therefore, the case that the entrepreneur must earn normal profit to prevent him or her transferring to another type of economic activity in the long run. *Normal profit* is the minimum return necessary to keep the entrepreneur in a particular line of business and it can, therefore, be seen as a cost of production. Profit above normal profit is referred to as supernormal profit.

19. The function of profit

In the free market economy (*see* 1: 8) the profit motive is all important as a key motivator in allocating resources in line with consumer demand. Consumers indicate their preferences by being willing to pay a higher price for a certain quantity of a particular good or service. If this is the case it will encourage the entrepreneur to increase the supply of that good or service since the higher price, assuming other things remain constant, will increase the sales revenue and, therefore, the total profit received. Demand for other products may have fallen, leading to a reduction in price, and thus a fall in sales revenue and total profit. The result of this will be a reduction in the supply of these products since there is less profit to be earned and resources will reallocate to more profitable areas of production.

Profit acts as an incentive to reallocate resources, for it is the prospect of profit that encourages firms to enter a market and add to the productive capacity of that particular industry. There are, however, certain sectors of the economy where it is not feasible to operate on the basis of the profit motive as a means of allocating resources. This is frequently the case with public services which are state controlled and run as public corporations.

20. Determination of profit

The profits earned by a particular company depend upon:

(a) How successful the entrepreneur is in anticipating changes in the market demand for particular products.

(b) The successful installation of new productive techniques, the result of which could be a lowering of the firm's costs, leading to an increase in the company's profit.

(c) The company may be able to take advantage not only of internal but also external economies of scale (*see* 5: 21).

(d) The company could be a monopolist and, as such, able to restrict the entry of new firms into the market. This will certainly affect profits in the long run.

Progress test 9

1. Outline the loanable funds theory of interest rate determination. **(4–7)**

2. Explain what determines the transactions demand for money. **(9)**

3. What is meant by liquidity preference? **(8–13)**

4. Outline the liquidity preference theory of interest rate determination. **(12, 13)**

5. What is meant by the liquidity trap? **(14)**

6. Distinguish between economic rent and transfer earnings. **(15, 16)**

7. How does the elasticity of supply affect economic rent? **(16)**

8. How does profit differ from the other factor rewards? **(17)**

9. What role does profit play in the allocation of resources? **(19)**

Part two

Macroeconomics

10

National income accounting

1. Introduction

In the preceding chapters we have concerned ourselves with microeconomics, dealing with specific aspects of the economy. This has included how individual consumers and firms behave, how the price of a product is determined and how certain markets, such as the labour market, operate.

The following chapters concentrate on macroeconomics, which deals with the economy as a whole. It will cover topics such as consumption and saving, unemployment, the price level and changes in government policy which affect the whole economy.

2. What is national income?

Central to the study of macroeconomics is the notion of *national income*. This is a measure of the total level of economic activity in an economy over a period of time, normally taken to be one year. It represents the total value, in monetary terms, of all the goods and services produced over that year.

This chapter will deal with how national income is measured, the possible problems encountered in its measurement and what purpose national income statistics serve.

3. The circular flow of income

National income *accounting* is the process by which the millions of transactions which occur in an economy over the course of a year are collated. In the production of those goods and services the factors of production (*see* 5: **9–13**) will receive rewards of wages, rent, interest and profit. These rewards will be used to purchase those goods and services produced by firms. The relationship between production, rewards and expenditure can be seen in Figure 10.1.

The economy (*see* Figure 10.1) comprises households who are the consumers and firms who are the producers. There are two flows taking place between them, namely 'real' flows and 'monetary' flows. The real flow (the unbroken line) refers to the flow of factor services from the household to the firm and the flow of output from the firm

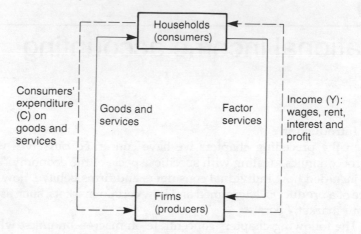

Figure 10.1 *The circular flow of income.*

to the household. In other words, the household works *for* the firm and will obtain the goods and services they need *from* the firm. The monetary side of the circular flow of income (the dotted line) refers to the monetary flow, i.e. the flow of income from the firm to the household for their services in the form of wages, rent, interest and profit, which the household in turn spends on the goods and services they require.

In this simple economy all output is sold and all income is spent. There is no saving, no investment, no government expenditure and taxation, and no foreign trade with exports and imports. These additional flows, which will be dealt with in more detail in Chapter 11, can be incorporated into the circular flow of income (*see* Figure 10.2). It can be noted that savings, taxation and imports are called *leakages* (or withdrawals) from the circular flow of income and investment, government expenditure and exports are called *injections* into the circular flow of income.

4. The circular flow of income and national income accounting methods

The simple circular flow of income clearly shows the three national income accounting methods of measuring the level of economic activity (*see* Figure 10.1). The three methods are the income approach, the output (or product) approach and the expenditure approach. They are identical in the sense that whichever measure is used they should give exactly the same result:

National income ≡ National output ≡ National expenditure

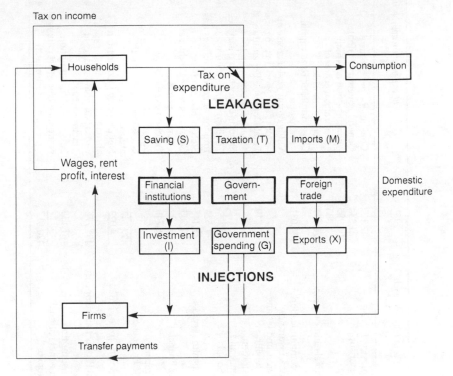

Figure 10.2 *The circular flow of income including the government and foreign trade.*

5. The UK National Income and Expenditure Accounts

In Figure 10.1 the income received by households equals the expenditure by households (consumers) on goods and services which are the output of firms. Each year the Central Statistical Office (CSO) publishes the *UK National Income and Expenditure Accounts* (called the Blue Book) which gives detailed figures of the three approaches. The figures for 1990 are to be found in Table 10.1.

Before dealing with the three methods of measuring national income it is important to explain a number of the terms that are used in Table 10.1.

Terms and concepts involved in national income accounting

6. Statistical discrepancy

The data from which national income is calculated are taken from

Table 10.1 United Kingdom National Income Accounts in 1990 (£m)

The income approach (£m)

Item	£m
Income from employment	316,408
Income from self-employment	57,661
Gross trading profits of companies	62,916
Gross trading surplus of public corporations	4,265
Gross trading surpluses of general government enterprises	17
Rent	38,433
Imputed charge for consumption of non-trading capital	4,278
Total Domestic Income	483,978
Less stock appreciation	−6,391
Statistical discrepancy	160
Gross Domestic Product at factor cost	477,747
Net property income from abroad	4,029
Gross National Product at factor cost	481,776
Less capital consumption	−61,159
National Income (net national product at factor cost)	420,617

The output approach (£m)

Item	£m
Agriculture, forestry, fishing	7,102
Energy and water supply	24,334
Manufacturing	106,995
Construction	36,085
Distribution, hotels and catering repairs	70,151
Transport and communication	34,031
Banking, finance, insurance, business services and leasing	87,260
Ownership of dwellings	30,719
Public administration, national defence and compulsory Social Security	31,524
Education and health services	45,143
Other services	30,983
Adjustment for financial services −	−26,740
Statistical discrepancy	
Gross Domestic Product at factor cost	477,747
Net property income from abroad	4,029
Gross National Product at factor cost	481,776
Less capital consumption	−61,159
National Income (net national product at factor cost)	420,617

The expenditure approach (£m)

Item	£m
Consumers' expenditure	349,421
General government final consumption of which:	
Central government	66,858
Local authorities	42,637
Gross domestic fixed capital formation	105,195
Value of physical increase in stocks and work in progress	−718
Total Domestic Expenditure at market prices	563,393
Exports of goods and services	134,108
Total final expenditure	697,501
Imports of goods and services	−147,582
Statistical discrepancy	678
Gross Domestic Product at market prices	550,597
Taxes on expenditure	−79,067
Subsidies	6,217
Gross domestic product at factor cost	477,747
Net property income from abroad	4,029
Gross National Product at factor cost	481,776
Less capital consumption	−61,159
National income (net national product at factor cost)	420,617

Source: United Kingdom National Accounts (Central Statistical Office), HMSO, 1991.

a number of sources, for example the income approach relies on income tax returns. It is likely that for all three methods the calculations are not entirely accurate for there will be errors and omissions from the statistics. The 'black economy' is one such area. The black economy describes a situation in which work is undertaken for payment, but not reported to the Inland Revenue for income tax purposes. In this case the payment will go unrecorded and, therefore, understate the country's national income. As stated, the income, output and expenditure approaches should yield exactly the same result, therefore any discrepancies can be overcome by including the *statistical discrepancy.*

7. Net property income from abroad

British citizens and companies are likely to earn income from investments abroad in the form of interest from bank accounts, dividends on shares owned in foreign companies, and rent on property and land owned in foreign countries. These payments will lead to an inflow of income into the UK from abroad. In the same way foreign citizens and companies will receive similar payments from the UK, leading to an outflow of income from the UK. The inflow and the outflow of these incomes taken together will give the figure called the net property income from abroad. Taking this figure into account when calculating national income will result in the figure being changed from *Gross Domestic Product* (GDP) to *Gross National Product* (GNP).

GDP + Net property income from abroad = GNP

The figure for net property income from abroad can either be positive or negative depending on the relative sizes of the inflow and outflow of income.

8. Capital consumption

This can also be called *depreciation* and, although it is difficult to calculate accurately, it describes the amount of capital which wears out or becomes obsolete. In calculating national income the *gross* figure minus capital consumption gives a *net* figure, as can be seen in Table 10.1.

GNP – Capital consumption = NNP

As there is difficulty in accurately calculating capital consumption, economists tend to favour the use of the gross product figure rather than the net product figure.

9. Factor cost

In order to obtain an accurate figure for national income, i.e. economic activity, it can be expressed at *factor cost*, which means that it is calculated in terms of payments made to the factors of production for their services. In the expenditure approach, however, the figure is at *market prices*, which means it contains an element of indirect tax (*see* 15: **7**) and subsidy. It is important when calculating national income using the expenditure approach that indirect taxes are subtracted and subsidies are added in order to give the figure at factor cost:

> Market prices – indirect taxes + subsidies = Factor cost

Measuring the national income

10. The income approach

The three methods of calculating national income can be seen in Table 10.1, the first being the income approach. This approach to calculating national income involves adding together the income of the factors of production for their services rendered in the production of the national output. The figures included in this method are gross figures, which means that they state income before taxation has been accounted for. So income from employment and self-employment, which form the largest share of the national income, is included before income tax and national insurance have been deducted. The income approach also excludes transfer payments such as pensions, sickness benefit and child benefit. A fuller explanation of these items will be given later in the chapter.

The gross trading profit of private and public companies can be seen as income to the firm. The actual figures in 1990 were, respectively, £62,916m and £4,265m for private and public corporations.

A figure for rent is also included as part of income. Those who own property will be able to rent it out and receive an income, which was estimated at £38,433m in 1990.

Stock appreciation has to be subtracted from the figures. The monetary value of stocks of raw materials and components at the beginning and the end of the year will differ if there has been a change in the level of prices. This change in prices will have been reflected in the company profit figure and, therefore, needs to be deducted since inflation is not a reward to the factor of production.

As stated earlier (*see* 6) the statistical discrepancy also has to be taken into account because, although by definition national income equals national output and national expenditure, problems in the collection of data mean that the three methods do not give exactly the same result. The statistical discrepancy 'corrects' the differences. Once this has been taken into account, we have gross domestic product at factor cost which is the income received by the factors of production within the UK. However, income is also earned abroad just as foreigners earn income from the UK and by taking net property income from abroad into account the figure for GNP at factor cost is obtained. There then remains the task of subtracting capital consumption (depreciation) from GNP to obtain net national product at factor cost or national income, which totalled £420,617m in 1990 (*see* Table 10.1).

11. The output approach

This approach involves adding together the money value of the output from the various sectors of the economy, namely agriculture, manufacturing, construction, transport and so on. Great care must be taken when aggregating the values of each sector because of the danger of double counting (*see* 13). This can be overcome by summing either the value added at each stage of production or the final value of output of the various sectors of the economy. The figures for national output in 1990 are given in Table 10.1 and, as previously with the income method, certain adjustments have to be made in order to calculate the figure for national income. To proceed from GDP at factor cost to NNP at factor cost both net property income from abroad and capital consumption have to be taken into account.

12. The expenditure approach

This method of calculating national income involves totalling the expenditure of the various agents in the economy on final output. It is important to note that it is expenditure on *final output* which is involved here otherwise, like in the output approach, we could be guilty of double counting. This means that intermediate expenditure, say, on raw materials are excluded as are the purchases of second-hand products because they have already been included once in national income when they were sold new. However, although expenditure on, say, a second-hand car would be excluded from the calculations, the commission received by the dealer would be included since it represents current economic activity.

Expenditure can be classified as:

(a) *Consumers' expenditure (C)*. This is the expenditure by individuals on consumer goods and services over the year. This was the largest element of expenditure in 1990 accounting for 62 per cent of the total domestic expenditure (*see* Table 10.1).

(b) *Government expenditure (G)*. Both central and local government spend on goods and services and this has to be included in the expenditure method of calculating national income. As stated earlier, care must be taken, however, to exclude transfer payments because they are not part of current output.

(c) *Investment (I)*. This is the value of capital goods produced in the economy during the year. It refers to fixed capital which covers items such as plant and machinery, and the figure is gross, i.e. before capital consumption (depreciation) has been accounted for. The figure is called *gross domestic fixed capital formation*.

Also, at the end of the year there will be a certain amount of work in progress, where the product has still to be completed. There will also be stocks of finished products waiting to go out of the factory. To not include these items would underestimate the figure for total expenditure and, therefore, they are included as the 'value of physical increase in stocks and work in progress' and are classed as investment. Totalling consumption (C), government expenditure (G), and investment (I) gives the figure for *total domestic expenditure at market prices*. If the figure were left at this it would represent a *closed economy*, i.e. an economy with no foreign trade. We are, however, an open economy for there is expenditure on foreign goods and services by UK residents called *imports* (M) and also expenditure by foreigners on UK goods and services called *exports* (X). It is important, therefore, to add exports and subtract imports in order to obtain *gross domestic product at market prices*. Unlike the other two methods of calculating national income, the expenditure approach is at market prices and so to obtain an accurate measure of national income the figure must be at factor cost. For this reason taxes on expenditure (indirect taxes, *see* 15: 7) need to be deducted and subsidies added:

> Gross domestic product at market prices − indirect taxes + subsidies = Gross domestic product at factor cost.

The procedure is then identical to the other two methods. Accounting for net property income from abroad and capital consumption gives net national product at factor cost or national income.

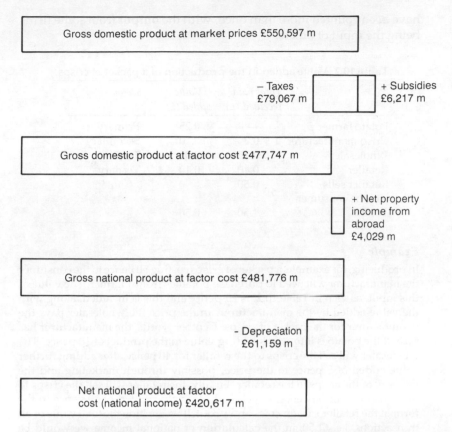

Figure 10.3 *The various stages in calculating national income ,1990.*

In order to make sure that the various steps in calculating national income are fully understood, Figure 10.3 summarises the important stages using the 1990 national income statistics.

Problems with measuring the national income

13. Double counting

There are certain problems encountered when measuring national income, the first being *double counting*. If, in calculating national income, the total output of all firms in the economy were included the figure obtained would be substantially greater than the actual value of domestic product. The reason for this is that certain items would have been counted more than once, with the output from some firms being the input of others.

Table 10.2 Value added in the production of a packet of crisps

	Total paid/ received (£)	Value added (£)	Sector
Potato farmer	—	0.25	Primary
Crisp manufacturer	0.25	0.10	Secondary
Wholesaler	0.35	0.05	Tertiary
Retailer	0.40	0.10	Tertiary
Retailer sells to the consumer	0.50		
Total	1.50	0.50	

Example

In producing, for example, a packet of crisps costing 50 pence to the consumer the manufacturer will need to purchase potatoes from a farmer. The value of this input, as seen in Table 10.2, is 25 pence and this is included, along with the value added by the manufacturer, in the price the wholesaler pays the manufacturer for the packet of crisps. In other words, the manufacturer has turned the potatoes into crisps adding value to the product of 10 pence. The wholesaler will sell the crisps to the retailer for 40 pence after adding further value added of 5 pence to the price, possibly through marketing and the delivery of the crisps to the retailer. Finally, the retailer will sell the crisps to the consumer for 50 pence, which includes value added of 10 pence in the form of the retailer's factor costs and profit. If we include the total value of all transactions, i.e. £1.50, in the calculation of national income we would be guilty of double counting.

This problem can be overcome by either totalling the value added at each stage of production, giving us a figure of 50 pence in the example above or taking the value of the final good, i.e. the price of the packet of crisps, which is in fact the only product which has been produced. All the other transactions involve the sale or purchase of intermediate goods or services.

14. Self provided products

There is a substantial amount of economic activity which is not taken into account when calculating national income. For example DIY, making your own clothes, growing your own vegetables and washing your own car are all productive activities but there is no market value given to these items. There would be a problem in accurately estimating their monetary value for inclusion in national income and for this reason they are excluded.

On the other hand, houses are considered to provide a service to owner-occupiers and an estimate of the benefit they provide is included in national income. Imputed rents are estimates based on what the house owner would receive had the house been rented out.

15. Non-marketed output

When a product is sold in the market, such as the packet of crisps in the example above, it can be valued at its market price. There is, however, a problem when the item produced is non-marketed — such as defence, law and order, and state education. Where there is no market price, the items are valued 'at cost' which means the cost to the government of providing the service.

16. Transfer payments

National income is a measure of the total level of economic activity in an economy over a period of time (*see* 2). Transfer payments such as pensions, unemployment benefit and child benefit are, therefore, excluded from national income calculations because they are not payments for services rendered. In fact, transfer payments are simply a *redistribution* of income from the taxpayer to the recipient.

Using national income statistics

17. Why calculate national income?

Two of the main reasons for calculating national income are:

(a) As a means of expressing changes in the nation's standard of living over time; and
(b) as a means of comparing the standard of living in different countries.

18. Comparing national living standards over time

Great care has to be taken when using national income figures as an indication of living standards. In the UK in 1980 national income was £172,883m but by 1990 it had risen to £420,617m. However, this does not mean that we are 2.5 times better off. The reasons for this are:

(a) There has been *inflation* over the ten year period which needs to be taken into account. We are not interested in money national income, as given by the above figures, but real national income so that the effect of price changes can be eliminated and comparisons between 1980 and 1990 can be made. 1990 prices need to be expressed as 1980 prices, which is achieved by using index numbers. A simple example can clearly explain this point.

Table 10.3 Money and real national income

	Year 1	Year 2
National income	£18m	£24m
Price index	100	110
Real national income [Year 2 national income expressed at Year 1 prices]	£18m	£21.8m $\left[24 \times \dfrac{100}{110}\right]$

Example

If the national income figures are taken at face value they would seem to suggest an increase in national income between Year 1 and Year 2 of 33 per cent (£18m to £24m). Over that period however, inflation has been at 10 per cent so part of the 33 per cent increase in national income has been due to an increase in prices rather that an increase in output. By dividing the Year 2 national income by the price index and multiplying by 100 the real national income can be obtained. The result is that instead of an increase in national income of 33 per cent, the increase is only 21 per cent.

Allowing for inflation when calculating national income gives what is known as *constant price national income*.

(b) Although real national income may have increased, there may have been an increase in population over the period in question. If this is the case the real national income would have to be shared out among more people. It is important, therefore, that changes in the population are taken into account. It is possible to obtain *real per capita income* (or real income per head) by dividing real national income by the population. This will give an average figure for how much national income there is for each member of the economy.

(c) Obtaining a figure for real income per head may still not give a true picture of the nation's living standards. Real income per head could have increased as a result of a longer working week. With less leisure time there may, in fact, be a reduction in the well-being of society not an increase. Furthermore, real income per head is as stated 'an average'; it does not, therefore, indicate how the real national income is distributed in the economy. There may be a skewed distri-

bution with a few very rich members, and a large percentage of the population poor and not sharing in any increase in living standards.
(d) Figures for real income per head do not reveal how government spending is allocated. If the government were to spend £1bn on defence, it would make the same addition to national income as £1bn spent on the health service, but in terms of living standards the two would have different outcomes.
(e) The figure for per capita income cannot take account of quality. A car purchased in 1992 will give a better performance and be more reliable — and, therefore, arguably confer a larger increase in welfare — than a car purchased in 1952.
(f) A major limitation of per capita income is its failure to take account of environmental issues. An increase in pollution and transport congestion will influence living standards negatively but this effect is not yet measured in the national income statistics.

19. Comparing living standards of different nations
National income statistics are used to compare the living standards of different countries. Apart from the problem of exchange rate fluctuations over time between the countries being compared, there are a number of other difficulties when making international comparisons.

(a) There may be differences not only in the way national income is calculated but also in the reliability of the collected data.
(b) The two countries in question may have different climates. So, for example, when comparing Sweden and Greece, Sweden may spend a higher proportion of its national income on heating and clothing. Countries will, therefore, have different needs and tastes which cannot be readily taken into account when making international comparisons.
(c) The two countries may have a different length of working week, with standard of living implications.
(d) The countries may devote different proportions of their national income to defence, which will influence their living standards even if the two countries have similar per capita incomes.

Progress test 10

1. What is meant by the circular flow of income? **(3, 4)**

2. Define net property income from abroad. **(7)**

3. Outline the three methods of calculating national income. **(10, 11, 12)**

4. How do you get from gross domestic product at market prices to net national product at factor cost? **(12)**

5. What are the difficulties encountered in calculating national income? **(13–16)**

6. Explain what is meant by double counting and how the problem is overcome. **(13)**

7. How useful are national income statistics as an indicator of a country's standard of living? **(18, 19)**

11
National income determination

1. Introduction

Chapter 10 dealt with how national income is measured, the problems encountered in its measurement and the use to which national income statistics can be put. This chapter is concerned with what *determines the size* of the national income, the size being an important influence on our living standards and the level of employment.

The Keynesian theory of national income determination, developed by John Maynard Keynes and published in a book called *The General Theory of Employment, Interest and Money* in 1936, will be outlined. The basic idea central to the Keynesian theory of national income determination is that the level of real national income and, thus, employment is determined by the level of aggregate demand (AD) in the economy.

Aggregate Demand is the total planned expenditure on goods and services in an economy and consists of consumer spending (C), investment expenditure by firms demanding investment goods (I), government demand for goods and services (G), exports (X) relating to foreigners demanding an economy's goods and services minus imports (M) which represent the demand for goods and services from abroad. Thus:

$$AD = C + I + G + X - M$$

There is only one level of national income where AD equals the total value of goods and services produced and this is called the *equilibrium level of national income*. This may not, however, be the full employment level of national income, thus the idea underlying Keynesian theory that the factors which determine AD could be manipulated in order to achieve full employment. Throughout this chapter the assumption will be made that prices are constant and the interest rate is fixed.

2. The circular flow of income

In Chapter 10 the circular flow of income was introduced and a

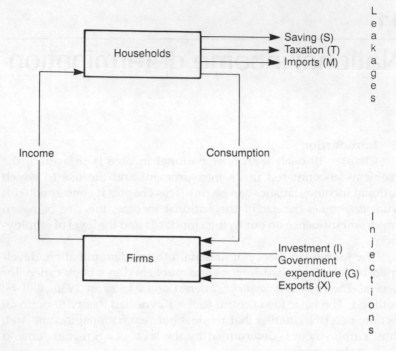

Figure 11.1 *The circular flow of income.*

simple model of the whole economy is reproduced here in Figure 11.1.

Figure 11.1 illustrates that there are certain *injections* into and *leakages* out of the circular flow of income.

Injections and leakages

3. Injections

An injection represents an autonomous addition to spending and there are 3 injections into the circular flow of income:

(a) Investment (I)
(b) Government expenditure (G)
(c) Exports (X)

(a) *Investment (I)*. Investment is referred to as an addition to the *real capital stock* of the economy and it comprises such things as the purchase of new capital equipment, the construction of buildings and the addition to the stock of raw materials, semi-finished and finished goods.

In the analysis which follows, investment will be taken to be *autonomous* which means that it does not vary with national income. In other words, investment is assumed constant at all levels of national income. The factors which influence investment will be dealt with in more detail later in the chapter.

(b) *Government expenditure (G).* In 1990 central and local government expenditure comprised 19 per cent of total domestic expenditure at market prices (*see* Table 10.1). The government purchase of goods and services adds to national income and is, therefore, classed as an injection into the circular flow.

(c) *Exports (X).* When foreigners purchase goods and services produced in the UK they are adding to the income of UK households and firms. Exports net of import content thus provide an injection into the economy's circular flow. As with investment, government expenditure and exports are assumed to be autonomous.

$$\text{Total injections equal } I + G + X$$

4. Leakages

Leakages can be classified as a *withdrawal* from the circular flow. A leakage is any part of the income that is not passed on as part of the circular flow but is withdrawn, which means it is not used to purchase other domestic goods and services. There are 3 leakages from the circular flow of income:

(a) Savings (S)
(b) Taxation (T)
(c) Imports (M)

(a) *Savings (S).* Savings are that part of income which is not spent and savings can be seen as income (Y) minus consumption (C):

$$S = Y - C$$

(b) *Taxation (T).* The government can influence the circular flow of income through its expenditure and also through its levying of taxation, which represents a leakage. *Direct taxes,* such as income tax, reduce disposable income whereas *indirect taxes,* such as VAT and Excise Duty, reduce the producers' receipts relative to total expenditure. The whole area of taxation will be dealt with in more detail in Chapter 15.

(c) *Imports (M).* Imports can be classed as a leakage since the amount spent on foreign goods and services represents money flowing out of the economy. It leaks out of the circular flow and forms part of the demand for output from foreign countries.

$$\text{Total leakages} = S + T + M$$

The consumption function

5.   What is meant by the consumption function?

Consumption is an important component of national income and, as seen in Table 10.1, it comprised 62 per cent of total domestic expenditure at market prices in 1990.

As national income increases so does consumption, simply because as incomes rise, individuals can afford to increase their spending. The relationship between consumption and income is referred to as the *consumption function* and can be expressed as:

$$C = f(Y)$$

Consumption is a function of income.

Table 11.1 presents hypothetical data to illustrate the relationship between consumption and income. It can be noted in column 3 that what is not consumed is saved.

Table 11.1 The relationship between income, consumption and saving

(1) National income (£bn)	(2) Con- sumption (£bn)	(3) Saving (£bn)	(4) APC (C/Y)	(5) MPC (ΔC/ΔY)	(6) APS (S/Y)	(7) MPS (ΔS/ΔY)
0	120	−120				
				0.6		0.4
100	180	−80	1.8		−0.8	
				0.6		0.4
200	240	−40	1.2		−0.2	
				0.6		0.4
300	300	0	1.0		0	
				0.6		0.4
400	360	40	0.9		0.1	
				0.6		0.4
500	420	80	0.84		0.16	
				0.6		0.4
600	480	120	0.8		0.2	

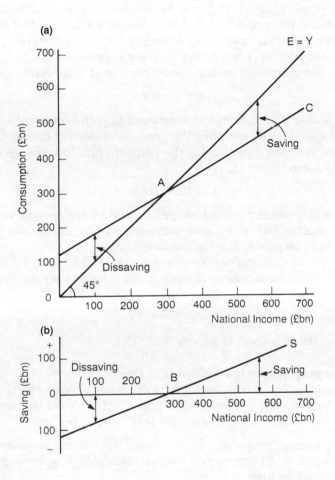

Figure 11.2 *The consumption function and savings function.*

The information given in Table 11.1 is presented graphically in Figure 11.2

The 45° line in Figure 11.2(a) illustrates the points where expenditure, namely consumption, is equal to income. When income is at £300bn all income is consumed and this is indicated by point A. At this point saving is zero which can be illustrated by point B in Figure 11.2(b). Figure 11.2(b) represents the savings function. To the left of points A and B saving is negative and this is commonly called *dissaving* or borrowing, i.e. using past saving to finance current consumption. To the right of points A and B saving is positive.

The consumption function can be presented in the form:

$$C = a + bY$$

where a and b are constants; a representing the intercept on the vertical axis and b representing the gradient or slope of the consumption function. The equation for the consumption function given in Table 11.1 and Figure 11.2(a) is:

$$C = 120 + 0.6Y$$

This means that the consumption function intercepts the vertical axis at £120bn and as income increases, say by £1, consumption increases by 60 pence, thus the gradient is 0.6.

Given the consumption function, Figure 11.2(b) shows the relationship between income and saving, the equation for the savings function being

$$S = -120 + 0.4Y$$

based on the hypothetical data in Table 11.1.

6.   The propensities to consume and save

In relation to the consumption function and savings function the *average propensity to consume* (APC) and *save* (APS) and the *marginal propensity to consume* (MPC) and *save* (MPS) are important.

(a) The average propensity to consume (APC) is the proportion of total income that is consumed and is calculated by dividing total consumption by total income:

$$APC = C/Y$$

It can be seen from Table 11.1, column 4, that the APC declines as income increases.

(b) The average propensity to save (APS) is the proportion of total income which is saved and it is calculated by dividing total saving by total income:

$$APS = S/Y$$

The APS is given in Table 11.1, column 6.
It should be noted that:

$$APC + APS = 1$$

(c) The marginal propensity to consume (MPC) relates to the change in consumption as income changes and is measured by dividing the change in consumption by the change in income:

$$MPC = \Delta C/\Delta Y$$

The MPC is given in Table 11.1, column 5. It is calculated from the hypothetical data and is constant at 0.6. This is in fact the slope of the consumption function in Figure 11.2(a) and represents b in the linear equation, $C = a + bY$.
(d) The marginal propensity to save (MPS) relates to the change in saving as income changes and is measured by dividing the change in saving by the change in income:

$$MPS = \Delta S/\Delta Y$$

In the example used, the MPS is 0.4 and this represents the gradient of the savings function in Figure 11.2(b).
It should be noted that:

$$MPC + MPS = 1$$

National income equilibrium

7. Equilibrium in a 2 sector economy

Initially we assume an economy in which there is no government and no foreign trade, thus the only injection is investment and the only leakage is saving. This is the simplest model of the economy and is referred to as a *closed economy with no government intervention*. The 2 sector economy thus comprises households and firms.

Equilibrium refers to a situation where there is no tendency for change, thus national income equilibrium can only exist when national income is neither increasing nor decreasing. A situation where it is not in equilibrium is called *disequilibrium*. National income equilibrium can be expressed in two ways: the income–expenditure approach and the leakages–injections approach.

Table 11.2 National income equilibrium

National income	Planned con-sumption	Planned saving	Planned invest-ment	Planned expenditure	Tendency of national income to:
(Y) (£bn)	(C) (£bn)	(S) (£bn)	(I) (£bn)	(E = C+I) (£bn)	
0	120	−120	40	160	Increase
100	180	−80	40	220	Increase
200	240	−40	40	280	Increase
300	300	0	40	340	Increase
400	360	40	40	400	No change
500	420	80	40	460	Decrease
600	480	120	40	520	Decrease
700	540	160	40	580	Decrease
800	600	200	40	640	Decrease

(a) *The income–expenditure approach.* Table 11.2 represents data for a hypothetical 2 sector economy. The data for income, consumption and saving is the same as that used in Table 11.1.

If we assume that the economy is in a situation where firms are producing an output of £300bn, then with household income of £300bn, planned expenditure by households and firms (i.e. C + I) totals £340bn at that income level. In this situation either households or firms will be unable to spend the extra £40bn they want to since there may be shortages of goods and services. Alternatively, stocks of goods already produced may be run down by the £40bn households and firms plan to spend, but this can only carry on as long as stocks last. In both situations, firms are likely to expand their output and thus national income will increase. If planned expenditure, which is C + I in a 2 sector economy, exceeds total output then national income will increase.

Again referring to Table 11.2, if national income were £600bn then households' and firms' planned expenditure would only be £520bn. If a level of output totalling £600bn continues to be produced then firms will find they have unsold stocks and it will not be long before they reduce their output. When this occurs national income will decrease.

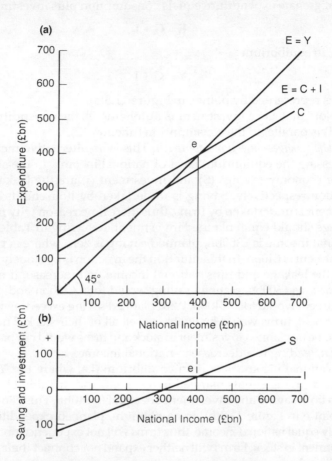

Figure 11.3 *The equilibrium level of national income.*

If national income were £400bn in Table 11.2, planned expenditure by households and firms would equal national income. Firms would not change the level of output they produce and stocks would remain unchanged. National income would thus be in equilibrium, where planned expenditure (C + I) equals planned output.

The data in Table 11.2 are produced graphically in Figure 11.3.

The 45° line represents all points where expenditure equals income:

$$E = Y$$

and aggregate expenditure equals consumption plus investment:

$$E = C + I$$

Thus, in equilibrium

$$Y = C + I$$

This is represented by point e in Figure 11.3(a).

Note that since investment is autonomous, the expenditure line (C + I) is parallel to the consumption function (C).

(b) *The leakages–injections approach.* This is an alternative method of expressing the equilibrium level of national income. In the simple 2 sector economy savings (S) and investment (I) are the leakage and injection respectively. Saving is undertaken by households and investment is undertaken by firms, thus there is no reason why planned savings should equal planned investment. Referring to Table 11.2, if national income is £300bn, planned saving is zero whereas planned investment is £40bn. In this situation the injection is obviously greater than the leakage and thus national income will increase. If national income was £600bn, planned saving would total £120bn and planned investment would total £40bn. With planned saving exceeding planned investment, firms would be unable to sell all of their stock. Thus there would be unplanned investment in stock and firms would cut back their output, leading to a decrease in national income.

National income is only in equilibrium (i.e. where E = Y) when planned saving equals planned investment, and in Table 11.2 this is when both saving and investment are equal to £40bn. This can be seen as point e in Figure 11.3(b). In equilibrium, planned expenditure will exactly equal national income, thus firms will not experience unplanned investment in stock. Firms will neither expand nor contract their output.

Since households' income is either consumed or saved:

$$Y = C + S$$

In the previous section it was stated that in equilibrium:

$$Y = C + I$$

It is thus the case that:

$$C + I = C + S$$

This means that:

$$S = I$$

which is the equilibrium in the leakages–injections approach.

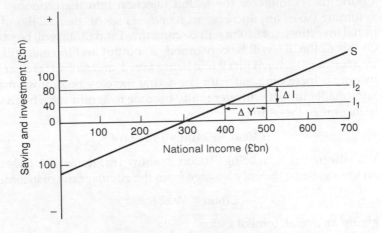

Figure 11.4 *The multiplier effect.*

8. The investment multiplier

The multiplier is all important in Keynesian analysis for it shows how a change in injections (I in the 2 sector economy) or leakages (S in the 2 sector economy) will influence national income.

In the previous section the equilibrium level of national income was £400bn. Suppose there is now an increase in investment from £40bn to £80bn, then the equilibrium level of national income will rise from £400bn to £500bn as seen in Figure 11.4. This example reveals the *multiplier effect*, since a change in investment of £40bn has led to an increase in national income of £100bn. The multiplier is thus 2.5. Referring to Figure 11.4, the multiplier (K) can be given as:

$$K = \frac{\Delta Y}{\Delta I} = \frac{100}{40} = 2.5$$

The size of the multiplier is determined by the MPC, for the value of K can be obtained by:

$$K = \frac{1}{1 - MPC} \quad \text{or} \quad \frac{1}{MPS}$$

So from the hypothetical data given in Table 11.1, an MPC of 0.6 will give a multiplier of 2.5:

$$K = \frac{1}{1 - 0.6} \quad \text{or} \quad \frac{1}{0.4} = 2.5$$

Taking the example of the £40bn injection into the economy and assuming 0.6 of any increase in income is spent, then £24bn of the initial investment of £40bn will be consumed and £16bn will be saved. Of this £24bn, 0.6 will be consumed, so output and income will rise by a further £14.4bn with £9.6bn being saved, and so on. It is clear that income is increasing but with the actual increase becoming smaller and smaller until it will eventually become insignificant. The change in income is, therefore:

$$£40bn + £24bn + £14.4bn + \dots$$

With the overall total being £100bn, as shown in Figure 11.4. The effect on saving, being the only leakage from the circular flow of income, is:

$$£16bn + £9.6bn + \dots$$

giving an overall total of £40bn.

In an extreme situation the MPC could be zero, in which case the multiplier would be 1 and national income would only increase by as much as the initial increase in investment. Thus the bigger the MPC, the larger the multiplier.

9.   Equilibrium in the 4 sector economy

Having developed the equilibrium in the simple closed economy with no government it is now possible to expand the model to include the government and foreign trade.

10.   The government sector

Government expenditure (G) adds to aggregate demand in the economy while government taxation takes money out of the economy. Government expenditure is an injection into the circular flow of income while taxation is a leakage (*see* Figure 11.1). Government expenditure is determined by government policy and it is assumed to be autonomous. Taxation is a function of national income:

$$T = f(Y)$$

Relating to the equations introduced in 7:

$$E = Y$$

and since we now have the government sector:

$$E = C + I + G$$

Thus the equilibrium will be:

$$Y = C + I + G$$

This represents the equilibrium in a closed economy, using the income–expenditure approach.

With the leakages–injections approach, injections will be $I + G$ and leakages will be $S + T$, thus the equilibrium is:

$$S + T = I + G$$

11. Foreign trade

Introducing foreign trade means that exports and imports will be incorporated into the model which is now an open economy. Exports (X) represent an inflow into the circular flow of income and can therefore be seen as an injection, while imports (M) represent spending on foreign goods and services and are classed as a leakage. Exports like investment and government expenditure are assumed to be autonomous whereas imports are determined by income. A rise in national income will thus lead to an increase in the demand for imports thus:

$$M = f(Y)$$

Incorporating foreign trade into the model means that we now have an open economy and using the income–expenditure approach:

$$Y = C + I + G + X - M$$

$C + I + G + X - M$ represents the total expenditure on goods and services in the economy minus the expenditure on imports. Total expenditure can be referred to as *aggregate demand* or *aggregate expenditure*.

12. Equilibrium

Using the leakages–injections approach the equilibrium is where:

$$S + T + M = I + G + X$$

Injections (J) = Leakages (L) or Withdrawals (W)

The 4 sector model can be presented graphically as in Figure 11.5. The J line in Figure 11.5(b) is horizontal since, as stated, I, G and X are assumed to be autonomous.

An explanation of injections and leakages was given in **3** and **4** and changes in any of these variables will have an effect on aggregate demand and employment in the economy, if there are unemployed resources. Using Figure 11.5(b), in terms of injections (J), an increase in either I, G, or X will shift the injections line upwards and this will lead to an increase in equilibrium national income. A reduction in injections will have the opposite effect, with the J line shifting downwards, resulting in a lower equilibrium national income. In terms of leakages, a reduction in S, T or M will lead to a shift in the leakages/withdrawals line (W) downwards and this will result in an increase in equilibrium national income. Alternatively, an increase in leakages can be represented by a shift in the W line upwards. This will lead to a lower equilibrium level of national income, with a reduced aggregate demand and increased unemployment. You may find it useful at this point to consider how a change in each of the injections and leakages is likely to affect the equilibrium level of national income, using Figures 11.5(a) and 11.5(b)

13. The multiplier in a 4 sector economy

In section 8 the simple investment multiplier was introduced. We now have an open economy with a government and the value of the

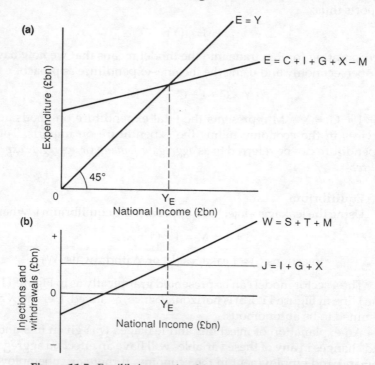

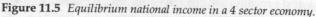

Figure 11.5 *Equilibrium national income in a 4 sector economy.*

multiplier will not only be affected by the MPS but also the *marginal propensity to tax* (MPT) and the *marginal propensity to import* (MPM). The *marginal propensity to withdraw* (MPW) or the *marginal propensity to leak* (MPL) is therefore:

$$MPW = MPS + MPT + MPM$$

Hence the multiplier (K) can be written as:

$$K = \frac{1}{MPS + MPT + MPM} \quad \text{or} \quad \frac{1}{MPW}$$

Thus, if the MPS was 0.15, the MPT 0.25 and the MPM 0.10, then the multiplier would be:

$$K = \frac{1}{0.15 + 0.25 + 0.10} \quad \text{or} \quad \frac{1}{0.5} = 2$$

So an increase in investment of £40bn would increase national income by £80bn.

14. The paradox of thrift

At a time of recession and unemployment in the economy it is normal for individuals to become more thrifty. It is, however, the case that at the macro level an increase in savings by all individuals in the economy may actually lead to a fall in savings. Hence the *paradox of thrift*.

Figure 11.6 can be used to illustrate the paradox of thrift.

The figure relates to a 2 sector economy and the investment function is slightly different in that it is not simply autonomous investment, hence the positive slope of the investment line (I). The economy is initially in equilibrium at Y_1 where savings (S) equal investment (I) at point A. If all individuals then seek to increase their saving, the savings curve will shift from S to S_1. The increased thriftiness on the part of the individual will cause planned saving to exceed planned investment by AB at the initial equilibrium level of national income Y_1. This being the case, national income will fall and thus planned saving will decline. Income will continue to fall until saving once more equals investment (point C) and this occurs at national income Y_2, which is the new equilibrium. Saving is now lower than the initial level — hence the paradox of thrift, where an attempt to save more has actually resulted in a reduction in saving.

15. The deflationary gap

There is only one level of aggregate demand or aggregate expen-

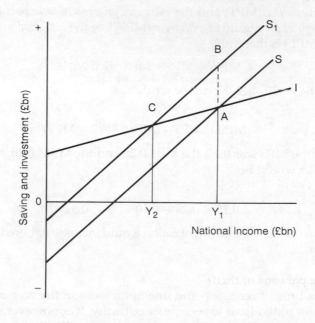

Figure 11.6 *The paradox of thrift.*

diture which achieves an equilibrium level of national income and this can be seen as Y_1 in Figure 11.7. At any other level of national income the economy will be unstable and will move towards the equilibrium.

The equilibrium level of national income in Figure 11.7 is not necessarily the full employment level and in fact Keynesian analysis argued that the economy could be in equilibrium with a high percentage of the workforce unemployed. In Figure 11.7 the full employment level of national income could be Y_F. At that level of national income, however, expenditure in the economy, i.e. C + I + G + X – M, could be insufficient to maintain full employment. The distance AB is referred to as the *deflationary gap* and, with leakages being greater than injections, national income would reduce until the equilibrium of Y_1 was reached. Thus to eliminate the deflationary gap and obtain full employment, the aggregate expenditure function should be shifted up. This could be achieved by an increase in government expenditure or a reduction in taxation.

The policy options aimed at managing the level of aggregate expenditure are discussed in more detail in Chapter 18.

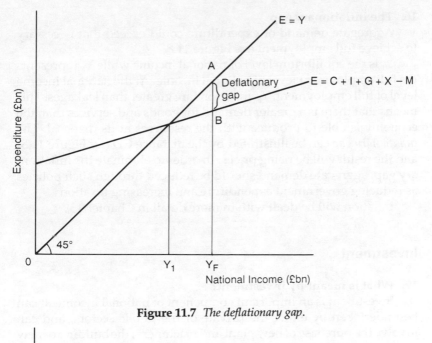

Figure 11.7 *The deflationary gap.*

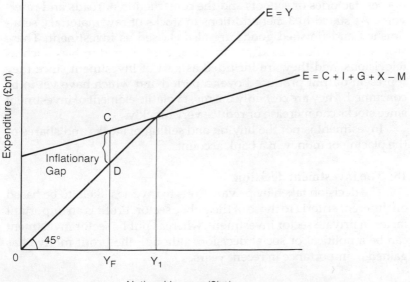

Figure 11.8 *The inflationary gap.*

16. The inflationary gap

Aggregate demand or expenditure could exceed that necessary to achieve full employment (*see* Figure 11.8).

Y_1 is the equilibrium level of national income while Y_F represents the full employment level of national income. At the national income level of full employment, Y_F, injections are greater than leakages. This means that there is a greater demand for goods and services than the economy is able to produce with the resources at its disposal. The *inflationary gap* can be illustrated by the distance CD (*see* Figure 11.8) and the result will be rising prices. In order to eliminate the inflationary gap, aggregate demand should be reduced through such policies as reducing government expenditure and increasing taxation.

Inflation will be dealt with in more detail in Chapter 13.

Investment

17. What is meant by investment?

Investment is an important component of national income. It can be undertaken by either the private or the public sectors, and can involve the purchase of new plant and machinery, the building of new houses, factories or schools and the construction of roads and reservoirs. As stated in **3**, net additions to stocks of raw materials, semi-finished and finished goods are also classed as investment. These stocks may include food produced or consumer durables such as televisions, and they are included as part of investment since they represent output produced over a period and which have yet to be consumed. They are certainly the most volatile element of investment since stocks can increase or reduce very quickly.

Investment is not the buying and selling of stocks and shares or the placing of money in a bank account.

18. The investment decision

The decision taken by private firms to invest is likely to be based on different criteria to those of the public sector. Profit is an important factor in private sector investment, whereas public sector investment can be a political or social decision, although the profit motive has gained in importance in recent years.

19. The determinants of investment

There are a number of factors which determine the level of investment, namely:

(a) the rate of interest;
(b) business expectations;
(c) the rate of change of consumer demand.

(a) *The rate of interest.* The rate of interest exerts an influence on the level of investment. When a firm purchases a new machine the expectation is that the *yield* from the investment will be greater than the *cost* of buying the machine. The expected yield is difficult to calculate since it will occur over a number of years. It is also the case that a given sum of money received next year will be worth less than the same sum received now.

One method of dealing with this is to calculate the *present value* (PV) of the investment and to compare the PV with the actual cost of the new machine. If the present value of the future stream of returns is greater than the current cost of the machine, the investment is worth undertaking. The process of presenting future values at a PV involves *discounting*. For example, if a machine which cost £2,000 has a life of 3 years and the estimated yield is £1,000 in each of the 3 years, then on the face of it the investment would seem profitable. Calculating the PV would, however, give us a clear picture as to whether the investment is, in fact, profitable. In order to calculate the PV the following equation is used:

$$PV = \sum \frac{A_t}{(1 + r)^t}$$

where
PV equals present value
A_t is the expected amount to be earned from the investment in year t
r is the rate of discount which we will assume to be 10 per cent expressed in the form 10 per cent equals 0.1
t is the number of years involved
Σ is the abbreviation for the sum of each of the years discounted earnings.
    Given the hypothetical data we have:

$$PV = \overset{\text{year 1}}{\frac{1,000}{(1 + 0.1)}} + \overset{\text{year 2}}{\frac{1,000}{(1 + 0.1)^2}} + \overset{\text{year 3}}{\frac{1,000}{(1 + 0.1)^3}}$$

This would give a PV of future returns of £2,486.85 which is greater than the present cost of the machine, which is £2,000 — thus the investment is profitable.

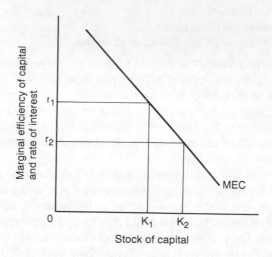

Figure 11.9 *The marginal efficiency of capital.*

A second method is to calculate the rate of return at which the future yield from the investment must be discounted in order that the PV is equal to the current cost of the machine. The rate of return is then compared with the current rate of interest and, if it is greater, the investment is profitable. The rate is called the *internal rate of return* (IRR) or the *marginal efficiency of capital* (MEC), thus if the MEC is greater than the current rate of interest the investment should proceed. The MEC is illustrated in Figure 11.9.

By investing, a firm can build up a stock of capital goods and, as with labour, capital is subject to the law of diminishing returns so the MEC will fall. So long as the MEC is greater than the rate of interest, the investment is worthwhile. The MEC curve shows the demand for capital at various interest rates and, in Figure 11.9, investment should cease once K_1 is reached at an interest rate r_1. The size of the capital stock, therefore, varies with the rate of interest. If the rate of interest falls to r_2 this will lead to a rise in the capital stock from K_1 to K_2. The increase in capital stock, $K_2 - K_1$, will require new investment to take place.

(b) *Business expectations.* Investment in new plant and machinery or a new factory are made by firms in order to produce output which is intended for sale in the future. This being the case, one of the determinants of investment is the firm's expectations of the future economic climate. Business confidence can be influenced by such things as a change of government or rumours of an increase in the rate of interest.

(c) *Changes in consumer demand*. If consumer demand increases then this can have an effect on investment. The rate of change of national income will bring about changes in the level of net investment through what is called the *accelerator principle*.

In the preceding analysis we assumed that investment was autonomous. This is an assumption which we now relax, with investment being partly *induced*. This means that investment is related to national income.

It is important to note that gross investment consists of replacement investment, used to take the place of worn out machinery, and net investment which adds to the productive capacity of the economy.

Table 11.3 The accelerator principle

Year	Aggregate demand (£m)	Changes in aggregate demand (£m)	Required capital stock (£m)	Replace-ment investment (£m)	Net invest-ment (£m)	Gross invest-ment (£m)
1	1,000	0	3,000	500	0	500
2	1,000	0	3,000	500	0	500
3	1,100	100	3,300	500	300	800
4	1,200	100	3,600	500	300	800
5	1,250	50	3,750	500	150	650
6	1,250	0	3,750	500	0	500

When aggregate demand increases there will be a need for an increase in net investment in order to expand the productive capacity. The accelerator principle is illustrated in Table 11.3. Certain assumptions are made:

    (*i*) The capital–output ratio is 3:1. This means that £3 of capital is required to produce £1 of output per annum.

    (*ii*) Capital has a life of 5 years and will, therefore, need replacing.

    (*iii*) In order for the capital stock to be maintained an investment of £500m per annum is required.

Relating to Table 11.3, in year 1 and 2 there is no desire by firms to increase the capital stock since there is no change in aggregate demand. This being so, the only investment which takes place is the replacement of worn out machinery valued at £500m and thus gross investment is £500m.

In year 3, however, there is a 10 per cent increase in aggregate demand and in order to meet this increased demand a capital stock of £3,300m is required. This being the case, net investment of £300m is needed, given a capital–output ratio of 3:1. Thus, through the accelerator principle, an increase in demand of £100m has led to an increase in net investment of £300m.

In year 4 the increase in demand is the same as the previous year, in which case the net investment required is £300m, and both net and gross investment are constant.

In year 5 net investment is less than the previous year, even though aggregate demand is still increasing. This is because the rate of growth of aggregate demand is slowing down. The £50m increase in aggregate demand leads to an increase in net investment of £150m.

In year 6 aggregate demand is constant at £1,250m, which means gross investment simply comprises replacement investment.

20. Problems in predicting the accelerator

In practice, the accelerator is difficult to predict. The reasons for this are:

(a) Firms may have spare capacity and excess stocks, thus they will not need to increase their investment as aggregate demand increases.
(b) Net investment depends on how confident firms are about the future. They may see the increase in aggregate demand as temporary and they may respond to the increase in demand in the short run by getting the labour force to work overtime.
(c) Firms may be restricted in their investment in new machinery by the limited capacity of the capital goods industry. There is a time lag in obtaining new capacity since new machinery cannot be manufactured immediately to meet the increase in demand. In other words, there are supply constraints.
(d) Firms may have a lack of space in the factory in which to install new machinery.

Although there are limitations with the accelerator principle, changes in aggregate demand do affect the level of new investment, particularly in the long run.

Progress test 11

1. What are meant by injections and leakages and how do they affect the circular flow of income? **(2, 3, 4)**

2. Outline the meaning of the term 'the consumption function'. **(5)**

3. Distinguish between the average and marginal propensities to consume and save. **(6)**

4. With the aid of diagrams, outline how the equilibrium level of national income is determined in a closed economy with no government. **(7)**

5. What is meant by the term 'the multiplier'? If the UK government spent an extra £10bn on the road transport network, calculate the probable effect of such a policy on aggregate demand assuming that the marginal propensity to leak is 0.6. **(8, 13)**

6. By what means could a government deal with a deflationary gap? **(15)**

7. Define investment and outline the factors which determine the level of investment. **(17–19)**

8. What is meant by the accelerator principle? **(19)**

12

Unemployment

1. Introduction

High unemployment has been a feature of the UK economy throughout the 1980s, rising to over 3 million during that period. The early 1990s has also seen an increase in unemployment.

The aim of this chapter is to outline the nature of the unemployment problem, and to analyse the possible causes of and cures for unemployment.

2. Definition of unemployment

Unemployment can be defined as those individuals who are willing and able to work but have not been able to find employment. Unemployment can be expressed as a number such as 2.7 million or a percentage, such as 9.7 per cent, of the labour force.

The labour force is made up of those who have employment and those who are registered as unemployed. The unemployment rate (U) is the percentage of the labour force without work but who are registered as being willing and able to work. Thus:

$$U = \frac{\text{Number unemployed and claiming benefit}}{\text{Labour force}} \times 100$$

Unemployment is a *stock concept*, which means that it is measured at a point in time and there are inflows and outflows from the stock (*see* Figure 12.1).

For example, individuals may be sacked or made redundant and, though they are still part of the labour force, they represent an inflow into the unemployment total. An outflow can take the form of unemployed individuals emigrating.

There are a number of problems encountered when attempting to measure the unemployment rate. One such problem is that there may be individuals who are out of work and looking for employment but have not registered as unemployed. These individuals will not appear in the official statistics, although from an economic point of view they are part of the labour force and should be included as part of the unemployed.

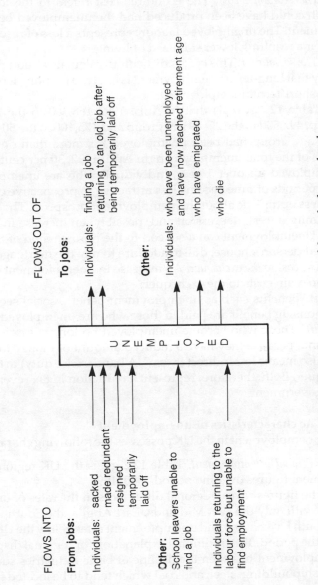

FLOWS INTO

From jobs:

Individuals: sacked
made redundant
resigned
temporarily
laid off

Other:

School leavers unable to
find a job

Individuals returning to the
labour force but unable to
find employment

FLOWS OUT OF

To jobs:

Individuals: finding a job
returning to an old job after
being temporarily laid off

Other:

Individuals: who have been unemployed
and have now reached retirement age

who have emigrated

who die

Figure 12.1 *Flows into and out of the stock of unemployed.*

3.   The cost of unemployment
The costs of unemployment can be seen as:

(a)   *The economic cost.* The economic cost refers to the lost output which could have been produced had the unemployed been in employment. The unemployed labour represents a loss of resources and with it a resulting lower standard of living.

(b)   *The social cost.* This cost is difficult to calculate although it is true to say that long-term unemployment is likely to be more demoralising than short-term unemployment.

Table 12.1 reveals that in April 1992 168,300 in the 18–24 age group, 497,500 in the 25–49 age group and 175,100 in the 50 years and over age group had been unemployed for more than one year. In terms of the total unemployment in April 1992, 30 per cent had been unemployed for over 1 year. Individuals who are unemployed for long periods of time become less attractive to prospective employers and less optimistic about their employment prospects. The result can be family unrest, depression and, possibly, an increase in the crime rate. Unemployment can also lead to the repossession of the unemployed person's house, due to a failure to pay the mortgage.

(c)   *The cost to the exchequer.* An increase in unemployment can result in two main costs to the exchequer:

(i)   Benefits such as unemployment benefit, social security and housing benefit are paid to those who are unemployed.

(ii)   Those who become unemployed no longer pay income tax and, because they have a reduced amount of money to spend, it also means less indirect taxes (VAT and excise duty) to the exchequer. Both, therefore, represent a reduction in tax revenue to the government.

4.   The characteristics of unemployment
Unemployment in the UK possesses the following characteristics:

(a)   *Regional unemployment.* Table 12.2 gives the UK regional unemployment figures over the period 1980–1992.

The figures reveal regional differences in the rates of unemployment with only the East Midlands, East Anglia, the South West, and the South East having had unemployment rates below the UK average over the period. The traditional explanation for regional disparities in unemployment has been the decline of basic industries such as textiles, shipbuilding, steel, and coal which tend to be located in specific regions.

It is not possible to raise aggregate demand as a means of dealing

Table 12.1 UK unemployment by age and duration—male and female (in 100s)

Age	Duration	April 1990	April 1991	April 1992
18-24	Up to 26 weeks	288.7	430.5	431.9
	Over 26 weeks and up to 52 weeks	92.0	134.5	189.9
	Over 52 weeks	84.5	94.0	168.3
	All	465.2	659.0	790.0
25-49	Up to 26 weeks	413.6	646.7	684.5
	Over 26 weeks and up to 52 weeks	147.9	221.1	320.0
	Over 52 weeks	283.0	309.2	497.5
	All	844.4	1,177.0	1,502.0
50-over	Up to 26 weeks	99.3	151.4	171.6
	Over 26 weeks and up to 52 weeks	43.7	56.1	87.5
	Over 52 weeks	172.3	151.8	175.1
	All	315.3	359.3	434.1

Table 12.2 Regional rates of unemployment (%)

Annual averages	1980	1982	1984	1986	1988	1990	1992*
United Kingdom	5.1	9.5	10.7	11.2	8.1	5.8	9.7
North	8.0	13.3	15.3	15.4	12.1	8.7	11.3
Yorkshire and							
Humberside	5.3	10.4	11.7	12.6	9.6	6.7	9.8
East Midlands	4.5	8.4	9.9	10.1	7.4	5.1	8.8
East Anglia	3.8	7.4	7.9	8.5	5.2	3.7	7.6
South East	3.1	6.7	7.8	8.3	5.3	4.0	9.1
South West	4.5	7.8	9.0	9.5	6.2	4.4	9.0
West Midlands	5.5	11.9	12.7	12.9	8.9	6.0	10.5
North West	6.5	12.1	13.6	13.8	10.4	7.7	10.6
Wales	6.9	12.1	13.2	13.6	10.0	6.6	9.7
Scotland	7.0	11.3	12.6	13.4	11.3	8.1	9.4
N. Ireland	9.4	14.4	15.9	17.4	16.0	13.4	14.3

*1992 figures are for April, from *Employment Gazette*, June 1992
Source: *Annual Abstract of Statistics*, 1992

with regional unemployment since the result is likely to be inflation-ary pressures elsewhere in the economy. Regional policy has been used as a remedy for regional disparities in unemployment (*see* **6**).

(b) *Female unemployment.* Table 12.3 reveals that female unemploy-ment as a percentage of the labour force was lower than that of males over the period 1986–1992.

One reason for this could be the fact that unemployed women are less likely to register as unemployed. If this is the case, the true picture with regard to female unemployment is likely to be underestimated.

(c) *Age-related unemployment.* In terms of the long-term unemployed,

Table 12.3 Male and female unemployment

UK unemployment	(Percentage of the workforce)	
	Male	Female
1986	13.7	9.1
1987	12.5	7.8
1988	10.1	6.1
1989	7.9	4.2
1990	7.6	3.2
1991	10.7	4.6
1992*	13.0	5.3

*9 April 1992
Source: *Employment Gazette*, June 1992

Table 12.1 reveals that in April 1992 40 per cent of the 50 years and over age group had been out of work for over 52 weeks, whereas for the 18–24 age group the figure was 21 per cent. This would seem to suggest that those individuals who are over 50 years of age and out of work are more likely to remain unemployed for longer periods than those in the younger age group. Table 12.1 also reveals that 29 per cent of the total unemployed are in the 18–24 age group. One of the possible reasons for this is that as a recession occurs employers are likely to cut back first on those who have not accumulated skills and experience.

The causes and remedies of unemployment

5. Frictional unemployment

(a) *Causes*. This type of unemployment comprises those individuals who are between jobs. Workers who leave one job in order to look for another need time to search because of the lack of information on all the possible jobs available. There are 'search' costs involved, in terms of lost earnings and travel expenses for such things as interviews, but they can be viewed as an investment.

(b) *Remedies*. There will always be individuals between jobs but measures to cut the search time involved will invariably reduce frictional unemployment. Improving the flow of information with regards to the availability of particular employment is one such measure, as is a reduction in unemployment benefit, although this is a controversial method. It could be argued that by reducing unemployment benefit individuals will spend less time searching for another job.

6. Structural unemployment

(a) *Causes*. The pattern of demand and methods of production are continually changing. There could be a change in the comparative costs of an industry, technological change may mean that an industry's labour requirements are somewhat less or demand for a particular product may simply decline. Any of these changes could lead to structural unemployment. Examples in the UK include unemployment resulting from a decline in the production of textiles, ship building, coal and steel. Those workers who become structurally unemployed are available for work but they have either the wrong skills for the jobs available or they are in the wrong location. There is

a *mismatch* between the skills, the location and the unfilled vacancies.
(b) *Remedies*. The remedy for structural unemployment involves retraining those made redundant in the skills required by the developing industry and possible relocation to other areas of the UK. Such government schemes include the Travel to Interview scheme, which offers help to those who are unemployed and who have to travel beyond daily travelling distance for a job interview. The scheme involves paying travelling expenses and the cost of overnight stays where necessary. Regional policy can be used to attract industry into those areas suffering from structural unemployment.

Regional policy has been used as a means of dealing with structural unemployment. It has taken a number of different forms:

(i) Capital subsidies for manufacturing firms locating in Assisted Areas have been offered. One of the major forms of capital subsidy has been the Regional Development Grant (RDG) which was introduced by the 1972 Industry Act. This was automatically available for business wishing to invest in plant, machinery and buildings, and was one of the main components of regional policy during the 1970s and early 1980s. The 1972 Act also saw the introduction of Regional Selective Assistance (RSA), available on a discretionary basis to firms in Assisted Areas.

(ii) Labour subsidies, mainly in the form of the Regional Employment Premium, were in operation between 1967 and 1977. This was a subsidy available in Assisted Areas and paid to manufacturing industry, with different rates being automatically paid for males, females and juveniles.

(iii) Restraint on the location of industry, through the use of the Industrial Development Certificate (IDC), was operated by British governments between 1947 and 1981. Any proposed new industrial development above a certain floor-space limit had to obtain an IDC before planning permission could be granted. The aim was to restrict expansion in certain parts of the country and encourage those firms not given planning permission to develop in Assisted Areas, many of which were suffering from structural unemployment.

(iv) Current regional policy. In January 1988 the government White Paper, *DTI — the Department for Enterprise*, was published. The RDG, for so long a major part of regional policy, was to cease. This meant an end to the automatic grant which had been available to firms irrespective of their size and without any assessment of the likely benefits from such a grant. Now companies in Assisted Areas who seek government assistance have to show that

their projects need regional aid in order to proceed, and that they are both viable and of benefit to the community. Companies which were previously eligible for the RDG are now able to apply for the RSA.

The 1988 White Paper also introduced a new scheme whereby small companies in Development Areas were eligible for what has become known as the Regional Enterprise Grant. The RSA is available in Development Areas and Intermediate Areas, collectively known as Assisted Areas, and is primarily available for manufacturing firms although certain service sector projects are eligible. The grants are discretionary, being based on whether the project is: regarded as being viable; unlikely to proceed, or to proceed on a much smaller scale if the grant was not available; seen to benefit the regional and national economy; and likely to create new jobs or protect existing ones.

7. Demand deficient unemployment

(a) *Causes.* This is often referred to as *Keynesian unemployment* or *cyclical unemployment.* It occurs when aggregate demand is too small, there being a deficiency of demand for goods and services. Since labour is a derived demand, the lack of demand for goods and services will also lead to a deficiency of demand for labour. This is the type of unemployment Keynes was concerned with in his *General Theory* (1936).

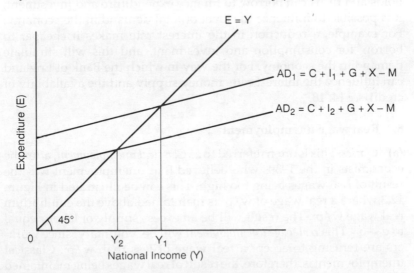

Figure 12.2 *Demand deficient unemployment.*

Demand deficient unemployment can be outlined by reference to Figure 12.2. The assumption is made that the economy is initially at full employment when aggregate demand — comprising consumer expenditure, investment, government expenditure, exports minus imports — is AD_1 and national income is Y_1. (If you are unsure about this Figure, refer back to Chapter 11.) There may then be a reduction in investment, perhaps because of a fall in business confidence (*see* 11: **19**). Aggregate demand will then fall to AD_2 resulting in a reduction in national income to Y_2. This being the case, the result is an increase in the numbers unemployed, i.e. demand deficient unemployment.

(b) *Remedies*. It is possible to use *fiscal policy* and *monetary policy* in order to reduce demand deficient unemployment. Their use is referred to as *demand management* and the aim is to influence the total demand for goods and services in the economy. Fiscal policy can increase aggregate demand, either through the increase in total government expenditure or by the reduction of taxes. Referring back to Figure 12.2, assuming the economy is in equilibrium at a level of income Y_2, but that the full employment level of income is Y_1, then an increase in government expenditure would shift aggregate demand from AD_2 to AD_1 and alleviate the demand deficient unemployment.

Monetary policy can influence the level of aggregate demand by means of the money supply, the interest rate and the level of credit available. By influencing the amount and the terms on which households and firms can borrow to finance expenditure and investment, it is possible to influence the level of total demand in the economy. For example, a reduction in the interest rate makes it cheaper to borrow for consumption and investment, and this will stimulate demand in the economy. For the way in which the Bank of England can influence the interest rate, money supply and the availability of credit, *see* 14: **18**.

8. Real wage unemployment

(a) *Causes*. This is often referred to as *Classical unemployment*, after the economists in the 1930s who believed that unemployment was the result of real wages being too high. This can be illustrated in Figure 12.3 where a real wage of w/p^2 is maintained above the equilibrium real wage w/p^1. The result will be an excess supply of labour equal to $q_{L3}-q_{L2}$ This *real wage unemployment* will be 'voluntary' since workers are refusing to accept a real wage of less than w/p^2. Classical unemployment is, therefore, the result of real wages being maintained above an equilibrium real wage w/p^1.

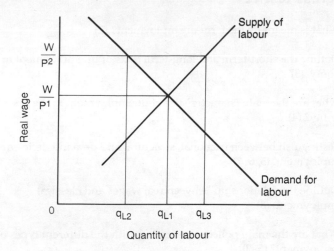

Figure 12.3 *Real wage unemployment.*

(b) *Remedy*. It is not easy to cure this type of unemployment for it involves the reduction of real wages which could require agreement between the government, trade unions and employers. An added problem is that a cut in real wages would reduce aggregate demand since real wages influence consumers' expenditure. A reduction in aggregate demand would lead to a reduction in the equilibrium national income and, therefore, create unemployment.

9. Supply-side policies

Supply-side policies, together with fiscal and monetary policies, will be covered in more detail in Chapter 18, although it is important to mention them here as a remedy for unemployment.

Supply-side policies are based on the belief that output, economic growth and *employment* can be increased by raising aggregate supply. The view is that by allowing competitive market forces to operate, both households and firms will be motivated by financial rewards to supply their services. Thus, supply-side policies include a reduction in income tax, improvements in government training and retraining schemes, and the reform of both trade unions and the benefit system.

Progress test 12

1.   What is meant by the term unemployment? **(2)**

2.   Outline the short-term and long-term costs of unemployment to the economy. **(3)**

3.   What are the main characteristics of unemployment in the UK economy? **(4)**

4.   Distinguish between frictional, structural and demand deficient unemployment. **(5, 6, 7)**

5.   Outline the relationship between real wages and classical unemployment. **(8)**

6.   What are the main policies for dealing with the different types of unemployment? **(5–9)**

13

Inflation

1. Introduction

Inflation is something which affects all of our lives and certainly throughout the 1980s and early 1990s the UK government has had as its number one priority the control of inflation.

This chapter examines how inflation is measured, the effects of inflation and the main theories of inflation.

2. Definition of inflation

Inflation cannot be viewed simply as an increase in the general level of prices since an increase one month can be followed by a decrease the next. Inflation, therefore, is a *persistent* tendency for the general level of prices to increase. Inflation represents a change in the purchasing power of money.

In extreme circumstances an economy may suffer *hyperinflation* where there is a rapidly accelerating rise in prices. In a situation of hyperinflation, members of society tend to lose confidence in the ability of currency to fulfil its functions (*see* 14: **2-5**) and there can follow a breakdown in the country's monetary system.

Figure 13.1 shows the rate of inflation in the UK over the period 1970–1991. It can be seen that UK inflation reached a peak of approximately 25 per cent in 1975.

The measurement of inflation

3. Calculating the Retail Price Index

The most commonly quoted measure of inflation is the *Retail Price Index* (RPI). It is calculated by the Central Statistical Office and measures the monthly change in the cost of a 'basket' of goods and services bought by a typical household.

The first stage in calculating the RPI is to establish which items are to be included in the index. The Family Expenditure Survey is all important in calculating the RPI, with approximately 7,000 households keeping a careful record of their day-to-day expenditure over a

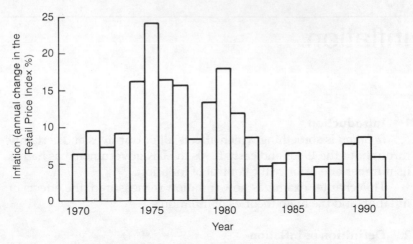

Figure 13.1 *The UK rate of inflation, 1970–1991.*

period of two weeks. From this it is possible to obtain a clear picture of which goods and services most households spend their income on. Weights are then attached to the items the 'typical' family purchases, with the larger weights given to those goods and services on which the household spends the most. For example, a family is likely to spend more on electricity than it does on eggs so, in calculating the 1992 RPI, the weights used were 24 and 2 respectively. These are part of an 'all items weight of 1,000', and the weights change annually to reflect the change in consumer expenditure patterns. The 1992 weights for the general RPI are given in Table 13.1. They exclude pensioners and the top 1 per cent of the income distribution, since they have a very different pattern of spending from most households.

It can be seen from Table 13.1 that housing, which includes among other things, rent, mortgage interest payments, the community charge, insurance and DIY materials, has the biggest weight.

The second stage in calculating the RPI is to collect price data — obtained from retail outlets in different areas of the country. Given this information, the average prices are calculated for the items in the index. It is then possible to calculate the weighted average. Finally, all index numbers must relate to a base year, which for the current RPI is January 1987=100.

Table 13.2 can be used to explain how the RPI is calculated. To simplify the situation only 4 items are included and the weights are out of 10 rather than 1,000. The base year is given as Year 1 and the

Table 13.1 Weights used for the RPI in 1992

Food	152
Catering	47
Alcoholic drink	80
Tobacco	36
Housing	172
Fuel and light	47
Household goods	77
Household services	48
Clothing and footwear	59
Personal goods and services	40
Motoring expenditure	143
Fares and other travel costs	20
Leisure goods	47
Leisure services	32
All items	**1,000**

Source: *Employment Gazette*, June 1992

Table 13.2 Calculation of the Retail Price Index

Year 1

Item	Average price (£)	Weight	Index	Weighted index
W	2.00	4	100	400
X	1.50	1	100	100
Y	3.00	3	100	300
Z	4.00	2	100	200

The price index = $\dfrac{1,000}{10}$ = 100

Year 2

Item	Average price (£)	Weight	Index	Weighted index
W	3.00	4	150	600
X	1.50	1	100	100
Y	6.00	3	200	600
Z	5.00	2	125	250

The price index = $\dfrac{1,550}{10}$ = 155

price index is obtained by adding together the weighted index and dividing by the sum of the weights. In Year 1, the base year, the price index is 100. This will always be the case with the base year. In Year 2 the index is the average price in Year 2 expressed as a percentage of the price in Year 1. Following the same procedure as in Year 1, by summing the weighted index and dividing by the sum of the weights, we obtain a price index of 155. This means that the average household has experienced an increase in their cost of living of 55 per cent between Years 1 and 2.

Since the index is an average, it hides the fact that the prices of some products will have risen by more than 55 per cent whereas others will have risen by less than 55 per cent. It may also be the case that the prices of some products could have fallen.

4. Pensioners and a price index

An index can also be calculated for 1 person and 2 person pensioner households, although there is a difference in the weights attached to their items of expenditure from those used for the average household. For example, for a one-person pensioner household the weights in 1992 for food and fuel and light are much higher, i.e. 311 and 170 respectively, while the weights for alcoholic drink and motoring are much lower than for the average family, i.e. 26 and 27 respectively. The reason for this is that pensioners have a different pattern of spending to most other households.

The effects of inflation

5. Introduction

The effects of inflation can be identified as arising from either *perfectly anticipated* or *unexpected inflation*. With perfectly anticipated inflation the rate of inflation has been expected by the various decision-making agents in the economy, such as households and firms, whereas unexpected inflation is a situation where the economy may under or over predict the actual rate of inflation.

6. Perfectly anticipated inflation

If inflation is perfectly anticipated then everybody knows what the rate of inflation is going to be — say, 5 per cent. This means that the various agents in the economy have adjusted their decision making accordingly. The main costs of perfectly anticipated inflation can be seen as follows:

(a) *Shoe-leather costs.* If there is a high, perfectly anticipated rate of inflation then it is likely that the rate of interest offered to savers will increase. Since there is an opportunity cost to holding money, individuals will place their money in interest-bearing assets. Thus, shoe-leather costs will arise since individual members of society, holding more of their wealth in, say, bank accounts, will require frequent visits to the bank to withdraw their money.

(b) *Menu costs.* Even though inflation may be perfectly anticipated there is still the cost of frequently changing price labels, vending machine prices and so on. Obviously the faster the rate of change of inflation, then the higher the menu costs will be.

7. Unexpected inflation

There are a number of effects from unexpected inflation.

(a) *Redistributional effects.* Different income groups are likely to be affected in different ways. For example, those on fixed incomes will see their purchasing power reduced by inflation, as too will those workers who belong to weak trade unions, unable to obtain wage increases for their members in line with the increase in inflation. Those workers, on the other hand who belong to powerful trade unions with effective bargaining power are likely to be able to cushion their members against the effects of inflation.

Retired members of society who saved throughout their working lives to provide for their old age will find that their savings are worth less as a result of unexpected inflation.

In times of inflation there is also likely to be a *redistribution* of income away from the income earner to the government. The reason for this is that money incomes normally rise when inflation occurs and income earners, therefore, move into higher tax brackets. This means that the taxpayer will pay a higher proportion of their income in tax, hence a redistribution from the tax payer to the government. This is called *fiscal drag.*

Redistributional effects will also occur, involving movement away from lenders (creditors) to borrowers (debtors). In times of unexpected inflation repaid loans will be worth less than they were when the loans were initially obtained, hence the borrower is set to gain while the lender is set to lose.

Example

If the rate of interest is 12 per cent but the rate of inflation is 18 per cent, then the *real rate of interest* is in fact negative, at minus 6 per cent.

(b) *The effect on business.* Unexpected inflation may make it difficult for business to enter into long-term contracts because of the uncertainty of the inflation rate.

Inflation may be the result of rising costs of production, particularly wages. If the increased costs cannot be matched by price increases then business will see its profits reduced, which could eventually lead to bankruptcy.

In the previous section it was stated that one of the costs of perfectly anticipated inflation are menu costs. Menu costs can also be a cost of unexpected inflation, as businesses have to adjust their prices and possibly revise their advertising in line with the price increases.

Businesses may also suffer if their unionised workforce take industrial action in support of a wage claim to offset the unexpected inflation.

(c) *The effect on the balance of payments.* Inflation can cause balance-of-payments problems. For example, if the UK inflation rate is higher than that of its major competitors, the goods and services produced in the UK will be less competitive abroad, while goods and services produced abroad will become more competitive in the UK. Depending on the price elasticity of demand, under a fixed exchange rate, the cumulative effect could be a deficit on the balance of payments (*see* Chapter 17).

Theories of inflation

Essentially the theory of inflation can be divided into monetarist and non-monetarist theories.

8.   The monetarist theory of inflation

The monetarist view of inflation is based on the premise that it is changes in the money supply which bring about changes in the price level. If this view of inflation is to be believed, then in order to control inflation it is necessary to control the growth of the money supply. Central to the monetarist view of inflation is the *quantity theory of money* and the *expectations-augmented Phillips curve*.

9.   The quantity theory of money

The simplest form of the quantity theory of money is that based on the work of Irving Fisher, the Fisher equation for exchange being:

$$MV \equiv PT$$

The equation can be analysed in terms of the money supply in circulation determined by the monetary authorities (M), multiplied by the average number of times money changes hands, that is the velocity of circulation (V), being identical to the average price level of all transactions (P) multiplied by the total number of transactions (T). The equation for exchange is an identity (denoted by $\equiv$) since both sides of the equation must be equal.

In terms of the Fisher equation, the argument is that in the long run the velocity of circulation (V) and the number of transactions (T) are constant. The velocity of circulation is assumed constant since it depends on institutional factors such as the pattern of payments. The total number of transactions are assumed constant since it is the view of the classical economist that the economy will always return to full employment in the long run. The importance of making these two assumptions is that, if both V and T are constant, a change in the money supply will cause a proportionate change in the price level.

10. The Cambridge version of the quantity theory of money

This theory is an adaptation of the Fisher equation and it argues that the aggregate demand for money (Md) depends on national income (Y). Thus:

$$Md = kY$$

where k is a constant and Y represents the total spending on all final goods and services in the economy. In fact, Y is money national income and as such can be viewed as the national output (Q) multiplied by the general price level (P). Therefore:

$$Md = kPQ$$

In the above equation k is in fact the reciprocal of the income velocity of circulation of money (1/V).

If we assume that the money market is in equilibrium then the demand for money will be equal to the supply of money. Thus:

$$Md = Ms$$

This, therefore, means that:

$$Ms = kPQ$$

and with the Cambridge economists believing that both k and Q are constant (Q representing actual output at full employment), then an increase in the money supply will lead to an increase in the price level. In other words, an increase in the money supply will lead to inflation.

11. The Phillips curve

The relationship between unemployment and inflation can be analysed by reference to the *Phillips curve*. The traditional Phillips curve described the inverse relationship between unemployment and the rate of change of money wages (i.e. wage inflation).

The relationship illustrated in Figure 13.2 was presented by A W Phillips in 1958 and was based on empirical evidence from the UK over the period 1861 to 1957. What became known as the 'Phillips curve' appeared to indicate a stable relationship between unemployment and inflation, the view being that when the level of demand in the economy increased, unemployment would fall but at the expense of higher inflation. The reason put forward for this is that if there is excess demand in the labour market it will result in a reduction in unemployment. The excess demand for labour will cause an increase in the money wage rate and, since wages are a cost of production, this is likely to lead to an increase in prices, i.e. price inflation.

The Phillips curve relationship between unemployment and inflation behaved throughout the 1950s and most of the 1960s in the way it had for the previous 100 years and it appeared to offer policy makers a clear choice — a certain level of unemployment could be 'traded off' for a certain rate of inflation (*see* Figure 13.2). Thus, if the policy makers were unhappy with a particular level of unemployment, they could stimulate demand in the economy but the reduction in unem-

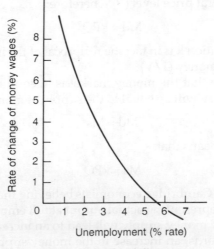

Figure 13.2 *The Phillips curve.*

ployment would be at the expense of higher inflation. Alternatively, lower inflation would imply higher unemployment.

12. The breakdown of the Phillips curve

From the late 1960s, however, the Phillips curve relationship between unemployment and inflation broke down. The rate of inflation associated with a particular level of unemployment was found to be much higher than the traditional Phillips curve predicted, and at various times both unemployment and inflation increased. In response to this the monetarists argued that there was no stable relationship between unemployment and inflation in the long run, and they explained this by the *expectations-augmented Phillips curve* developed by Friedman and Phelps.

13. The natural rate of unemployment (NRU)

Before outlining the expectations-augmented Phillips curve it is important to define a concept known as the *natural rate of unemployment* (NRU). The NRU is illustrated by use of Figure 13.3 with the equilibrium real wage (w/p) in a perfectly competitive labour market being determined by the interaction of the demand for labour D_L and the supply of labour S_L.

The equilibrium real wage is accompanied by a 'full employment' level of employment, N. At this 'full employment' level all those who wish to work at the real wage (w/p) are able to obtain work, although

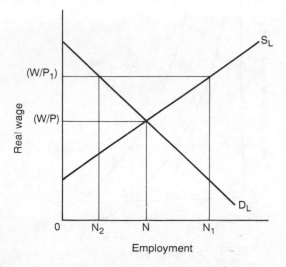

Figure 13.3 *The labour market.*

there will still be those who are not employed. For example, there will be frictional and structural unemployment, frictional unemployment relating to those individuals who are between jobs and structural unemployment relating to those who have been made redundant but are not prepared to take a lower paid job (*see* 12: **5, 6** for an explanation of frictional and structural unemployment). They are both deemed to be voluntary unemployment and as such are classed as part of the NRU.

The real wage rate could be (w/p_1) in Figure 13.3. At this wage rate the supply of labour would be N_1 and the demand for labour would be N_2. There would thus be an excess supply of labour equal to $N_1 - N_2$. At a real wage rate of (w/p_1), with there being an excess supply of labour the wage rate would be bid down until the equilibrium real wage (w/p) was restored. At this point the unemployment which existed would be the natural rate.

14. The expectations-augmented Phillips curve

The monetarists believe that although in the short run there is an inverse relationship between unemployment and the rate of inflation, in the long run there is no relationship. In fact, in the monetarist view, in the long run the Phillips curve is a vertical line through the NRU — at U_n in Figure 13.4.

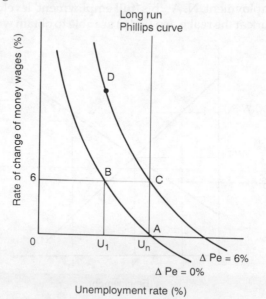

Figure 13.4 *The expectations-augmented Phillips curve.*

The monetarists claim that there will be a whole series of short run Phillips curves, each representing a different expected rate of inflation. This can be seen in Figure 13.4 which shows just two short run Phillips curves, one with an expected rate of inflation of zero and the other with a 6 per cent expected rate of inflation. We assume that the level of unemployment is initially at the natural rate, i.e. at point A in Figure 13.4, with a zero actual and expected rate of inflation.

The government may, however, be unhappy with a rate of unemployment, U_n and may take steps to reduce it by stimulating demand in the economy through an expansion of the money supply. As aggregate demand increases, the level of unemployment will fall to U_1 and firms, in attracting extra labour to meet the increase in demand, will have to increase the wage rate, say by 6 per cent. This increase in the wage rate will soon be followed by an increase in the level of prices. The economy is now at point B in Figure 13.4, moving up the short run Phillips curve from point A to B. As workers obtain the increase in money wages they will perceive themselves as being better off since they are expecting zero inflation ($\Delta Pe = 0\%$). The workers are, however, suffering from *money illusion* since their real wage has not changed.

This money illusion will not last long and, therefore, point B is only a short run position. This is because when the workers realise they are no better off, those who have recently obtained employment will no longer have the incentive to remain in employment and so unemployment will increase back to the NRU, U_n. The economy is now at point C in Figure 13.4 with the same level of unemployment as before, but with an actual rate of inflation of 6 per cent as opposed to 0 per cent initially. This rate of inflation is now the expected rate of inflation ($\Delta Pe = 6\%$).

If the government now wishes to reduce unemployment again (below U_n) by expanding the money supply, the economy will move along the short run Phillips curve ($\Delta Pe = 6\%$) to a point such as D and the process will repeat itself. This being the case, the long run Phillips curve can be viewed as a vertical line through the NRU, U_n joining points A, C and so on.

15. The non-monetarist theory of inflation

In the 1960s the Keynesian view of inflation was that it was caused by excess demand for goods and services in a fully employed economy. This was the *demand-pull* view of inflation which was illustrated by the inflationary gap, discussed in 11: **16**. The problem with the Keynesian 45° diagram covered in Chapter 11 was that it could only deal with inflation caused by excess demand and offered no explanation of inflation caused by rising costs not associated with excess demand. It was also the case that it provided no explanation of stagflation which occurred with the breakdown of the Phillips curve in the mid 1960s. *Stagflation* refers to an economy experiencing high levels of unemployment *and* rising prices. The following sections will deal with both demand-pull and cost-push inflation. The cost-push view of inflation is concerned with the factors which cause a firm's cost of production to increase. It emphasises the role of trade unions and the influence the cost of imported goods can have on the rate of inflation.

16. Aggregate demand and aggregate supply

Before outlining the non-monetary theory of inflation it is important to introduce the concepts of aggregate demand and supply which

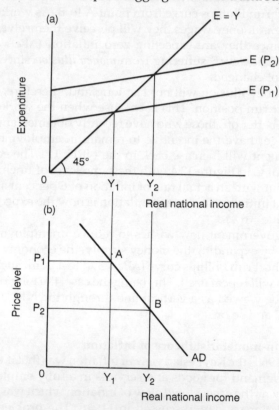

Figure 13.5 *The derivation of aggregate demand.*

will get around the problem of the Keynesian 45° diagram and also help us to understand the non-monetary view of inflation.

(a) *Aggregate demand (AD)*. Unlike the aggregate demand developed as part of the Keynesian model in Chapter 11, this section will derive an aggregate demand curve which more closely resembles the normal downward sloping demand curve with the price level on the vertical axis and the economy's real national income on the horizontal axis. Figure 13.5 shows the derivation of aggregate demand.

In Figure 13.5(a) the initial aggregate expenditure is $E(P_1)$ with an equilibrium level of national income Y_1. This equilibrium level of national income is associated with a particular price level P_1, thus giving point A in Figure 13.5(b). If there is then a fall in the price level to P_2 it is normal to expect an increase in the level of aggregate expenditure to, say, $E(P_2)$. The reason for this is that a fall in the price level will reduce the transactions and precautionary demand for money, which will reduce the rate of interest, and therefore increase investment and thus aggregate expenditure to $E(P_2)$. (For an explanation of the transactions and precautionary demand for money, *see* 9: **9, 10**.) A lower price level P_2 is therefore associated with a higher equilibrium level of national income, Y_2, thus giving point B in Figure 13.5b. The result is a downward sloping aggregate demand curve.

(b) *Aggregate supply (AS)*. The aggregate supply curve indicates the level of output firms are willing to supply in the economy at particular price levels.

The short run aggregate supply curve, assuming the stock of capital is fixed, is illustrated in Figure 13.6. It is positively sloped since

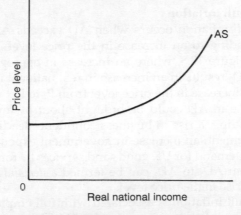

Figure 13.6 *The aggregate supply curve.*

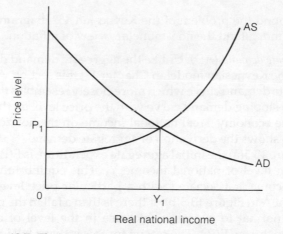

Figure 13.7 *The interaction of aggregate demand and aggregate supply.*

the higher the price level, the more willing firms are to supply extra output. However, as the economy reaches the limit of its productive capacity, the AS curve will become more inelastic since there is an upward pressure on costs, such as an increase in the amount of overtime worked and bottle-necks in the productive process.

17. Interaction of aggregate demand and aggregate supply

The interaction of AD and AS will result in an equilibrium price level P_1 and an equilibrium real national income Y_1 as seen in Figure 13.7.

18. Demand-pull inflation

Demand-pull inflation occurs when AD exceeds AS at current prices, thus leading to an increase in the price level. This can be illustrated in Figure 13.8, where an increase in aggregate demand from AD_1 to AD_2 results in an increase in real national income from Y_1 to Y_2 and an increase in the price level from P_1 to P_2.

The increase in AD could be brought about by an increase in consumer spending, a rise in business confidence leading to an increase in investment, an increase in government expenditure or an increase in the demand for UK goods and services by foreigners. The shift in AD from AD_1 to AD_2 can be termed a *demand shock* which causes a single rise in the price level.

Demand-pull inflation is associated with full employment and the concept of the inflationary gap (*see* 11: **16**). The reason for this is

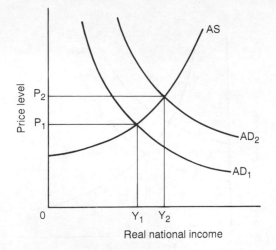

Figure 13.8 *Demand-pull inflation.*

that if the economy is at less than full employment, then an increase in AD can more easily be accommodated by an expansion in output with a limited effect on the price level.

In outlining demand-pull inflation it has been assumed that the increase in AD has been the result of an increase in aggregate expenditure, such as government expenditure. This is, in fact, a Keynesian explanation of inflation. However, the increase in AD could have been the result of an increase in the money supply, resulting in a monetary rather than a non-monetary explanation of inflation.

19. Cost-push inflation
Cost-push inflation occurs when there is an increase in the cost of production not associated with excess demand.

Cost-push inflation is associated with the supply side of the economy and is illustrated in Figure 13.9.

An increase in the costs can be represented by a shift in the AS curve to the left. If firms see an increase in their costs, they are likely to respond by rising their prices and cutting back on production — the result being a reduction in real national income from Y_1 to Y_2 and an increase in the price level from P_1 to P_2. The effect shown in Figure 13.9 can be termed a *supply shock*, bringing about a single rise in the price level. The situation in Figure 13.9 is one of stagflation where there has been an aggregate supply shock such as a rise in oil prices. Firms have passed on their increased costs in higher prices and

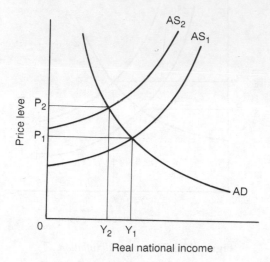

Figure 13.9 *Cost-push inflation.*

aggregate demand has fallen, thus leading to an increase in unemployment and, therefore, stagflation.

Cost-push inflation can be the result of an increase in any of the following.

(a) *Wage costs.* Trade unions may push up wages through their bargaining power, with the increase in wages not being matched by an increase in productivity. Wages tend to be the largest cost of production so an increase in wages is likely to have an important effect on a firm's overall costs and, therefore, the prices they charge. This increase in prices is likely to lead to further wage claims and this could result in what is known as the *wage-price spiral*.

(b) *Profits.* This is perhaps less important than an increase in wage costs. There could be a situation where firms use their monopoly power to increase prices in order to increase profit margins. In this situation the increase in the price of the product is not associated with an increase in consumer demand.

(c) *Import prices.* A rise in import prices can be an important contributor to inflation. World commodity prices rose in the early 1970s, as did oil prices, and both led to higher inflation in the UK. Although an increase in import prices can be seen as imported cost-push inflation in the UK, it could have initially been the result of demand-pull inflation in the country in which the product originated.

Counter-inflationary policies

The following are possible methods of dealing with inflation and they have all been used in the UK at various times.

20. Fiscal policy

Fiscal policy comprises changes in government expenditure and/or taxation. The aim is to affect the level of AD through a policy known as *demand management*. In the case of controlling inflation, this involves reducing government expenditure and/or increasing taxation in what is called a *deflationary fiscal policy*. Such policies are likely to be effective if inflation has been diagnosed as demand-pull since a reduction in government expenditure or an increase in income tax will reduce aggregate demand in the economy.

In the 1950s and 1960s, fiscal policy was viewed as the main means by which inflation could be controlled.

21. Monetary policy

Monetary policy is concerned with influencing the money supply and the interest rate. Up until the mid 1970s, monetary policy was viewed as a supplement to fiscal policy; however, it now plays a major role in economic policy in the UK. In terms of controlling inflation, the government can aim to reduce the money supply thus reducing spending and, therefore, the aggregate demand, or it can increase the interest rate so as to increase the cost of borrowing. Both policies can be seen as *deflationary monetary policy*. As stated earlier, monetarists view the growth of the money supply as being the main cause of inflation, therefore, any control of inflation from a monetarist view point must involve control of the money supply.

22. Prices and incomes policy

A prices and incomes policy can be seen as direct intervention in the economy. The aim is to limit and, in certain cases, freeze wage and price increases. In the past they have either been statutory or voluntary. Statutory prices and incomes policies have to be enforced by government legislation, such as that introduced in 1967. With a voluntary prices and incomes policy the government aims to control prices and incomes through voluntary restraint, possibly by obtaining the support of the TUC and the CBI.

If a prices and incomes policy is pursued, the general belief behind it is that inflation is caused by trade unions. Historically, governments have found it difficult to enforce prices and incomes policies since firms have always found ways of circumventing them and unions have often resorted to industrial action against them, particularly if wages have been more strictly controlled than prices.

Progress test 13

1. What is meant by inflation? **(2)**

2. Outline the way in which inflation is measured using the Retail Price Index. **(3–4)**

3. In terms of the effect of inflation, distinguish between perfectly anticipated and unexpected inflation. **(5–7)**

4. Outline the quantity theory of money. **(9, 10)**

5. Explain what is meant by the 'natural rate of unemployment'. **(13)**

6. According to the monetarists, if the government attempts to reduce unemployment below the 'natural rate', what will be the effect on the rate of inflation? **(14)**

7. Define stagflation. **(15)**

8. With the use of aggregate demand and supply diagrams, distinguish between demand-pull and cost-push inflation. **(18, 19)**

9. Outline the various methods of controlling inflation. **(20–22)**

14

Money and banking

1. Introduction

The aim of this chapter is to consider what is meant by the term 'money'. To this end the functions of money are outlined and the official measures of the money supply, as used by the Bank of England, are defined. The chapter also deals with the main business of banks, the role of the Bank of England and the instruments used by the Bank of England to control the money supply.

The functions of money

2. A medium of exchange

When considering money it is useful to consider the four functions of money; the first being its function as a medium of exchange. This can be viewed as the main function of money. Money allows us to specialise in the production of certain goods and services. Without money the economy would revert to a system of *barter*, where goods and services would be exchanged directly for each other. This is an inefficient system of exchange not least because of the need for *double-coincidence of wants*. This means that if I want a particular good, not only must I find someone who has that good but that person must also want what I have. There is also the problem of what exchange value to attach to the goods concerned. Barter is a time-consuming process and leads individuals to produce for themselves the majority of products they require. It is inappropriate for a modern economy, producing a wide range of goods and services.

For money to perform the function of a medium of exchange it does not necessarily have to have any *intrinsic value* (i.e. it need not, in itself, be valuable) but it must be generally acceptable as a medium of exchange, i.e. have a claim on the goods and services with intrinsic value.

3. A unit of account

Where money is used as a unit of account every good and service is valued against a common standard, namely money, rather than against each other. Money as a unit of account allows a quick comparison to be made between the value of different goods and services.

4. A store of value

Money is not perishable and so it has yet another advantage over barter in that it allows us to delay the purchase of a good or service. In other words money makes *saving* possible, i.e. assets can be built up. However, it is important to note that if the economy is experiencing inflation this will reduce the value of money and affect people's preparedness to hold it as a store of value.

5. A standard of deferred payment

Money allows for the existence of credit, for it makes it possible for contracts to be agreed involving payment in the future. But, as with a store of value, inflation will affect the willingness of people to accept a set sum of money in future settlement of a debt.

The definitions of money and measures of the money supply

6. What is money?

Money can be defined as any item which is readily acceptable as a means of settling a debt. The item must enjoy the confidence of those using it. In saying this there is still the question of what exactly constitutes money in a modern economy. Banknotes and coins are generally acceptable as money, as are current accounts (also known as sight deposits) on which cheques are drawn. In terms of the functions of money, notes and coins and sight deposits act as a medium of exchange.

7. Liquidity

Liquidity is all important when defining money. An asset can be defined as liquid and, therefore, part of the money supply if it can be quickly turned into cash without a financial loss. Deposit accounts (called *time deposits*) can therefore be considered as part of the money supply, even though they can not immediately be withdrawn from a bank. They are liquid since only seven days' notice of withdrawal is normally required. If the time deposits of a bank are to be included in a definition of the money supply then building society deposits should also be included.

8. Measures of the money supply

A number of official definitions of the money supply have been used in the UK in recent times although at present there are only three, namely MO, M2 and M4. These current official measures of the money supply as used by the Bank of England differ in terms of their levels of liquidity.

(a) *MO*. MO is the narrowest definition. It consists of the notes and coins in circulation outside the Bank of England, that is notes and coins in the hands of the general public and the till money of banks, plus balances the commercial banks hold at the Bank of England. MO is the *monetary base*, the central stock of cash on which all money supply expansion is based. Since April 1984, the government has had target rates of growth for MO and the Bank of England has been reasonably successful in keeping the growth of MO close to the target range. In March 1992 the seasonally adjusted total for MO was £18,879m.

(b) *M2*. M2 consists of all the notes and coins in circulation with the general public, plus non-interest bearing sight deposits with the banks (current accounts), and retail deposits which bear interest with the banks and the building societies. The M2 definition of money aims to cover cash and all the deposits which are likely to be available at any one time for the purchase of goods and services. M2 is a measure of the money supply that the public can readily obtain in order to spend. In March 1992 the seasonally adjusted total for M2 was £279,600m.

(c) *M4*. M4 is a broad definition of the money supply, including not only money held as transactions balances but also for savings. It includes all notes and coins in circulation with the private sector plus non-interest and interest bearing sterling bank deposits, as well as sterling certificates of deposit (*see* **14** for a definition). It also includes the private sector holdings of building society shares and deposits, and certificates of deposit. M4 was introduced in 1987 as a measure of the money supply in order to account for the increased importance of building societies. Building society deposits are being used more and more in transactions through the use of cheques and credit cards. In March 1992 the seasonally adjusted total for M4 was £505,779m.

At the present time MO is the only monetary aggregate which has its growth rate targeted by the government. The main reason for defining and controlling the rate of growth of the money supply is the belief by the monetarists that it is the money supply which determines the level of prices and the rate of inflation.

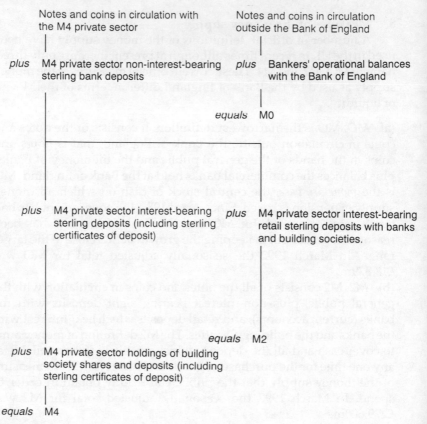

Figure 14.1 *UK monetary aggregates. (Source: Bank of England Quarterly Bulletin, February 1992.)*

Figure 14.1 shows schematically the different official definitions of money.

Credit creation

9.   Credit creation in a single bank system

In the previous section it was illustrated how bank deposits form part of the money supply. Banks are able to create new deposits through a process known as *credit creation*. Credit creation can be illustrated by the use of Figure 14.2.

It is necessary to make a number of simplifying assumptions when considering the concept of credit creation.

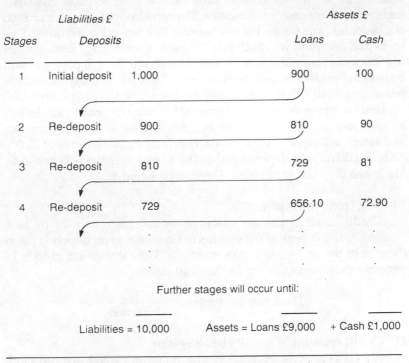

Stages	Liabilities £ Deposits		Assets £ Loans	Cash
1	Initial deposit	1,000	900	100
2	Re-deposit	900	810	90
3	Re-deposit	810	729	81
4	Re-deposit	729	656.10	72.90

Further stages will occur until:

Liabilities = 10,000   Assets = Loans £9,000   + Cash £1,000

Note: Only deposits resulting from lending are newly created money.

Figure 14.2 *Credit creation in a single bank system.*

(a) The economy has a single commercial bank, a monopoly bank, which has a number of branches.
(b) The bank has found from experience that it needs to hold 10 per cent of its assets in the form of cash to meet the normal demand for cash withdrawals from its customers.
(c) All the loans made by the bank are re-deposited with it. In practice this is unlikely to be the case.
(d) There are sufficient borrowers willing to take up the loans issued by the bank.

Suppose a customer deposits an extra £1,000 cash in the bank, illustrated by stage 1 in Figure 14.2. The new deposit is classed as a liability since the bank owes that money to its account holder and must pay it back whenever the holder demands it. The deposit is in fact a claim against the bank. Having obtained the initial deposit of £1,000 the bank, given assumption (b), needs to maintain a 10 per cent cash ratio. Thus, on the asset side, £100 cash is held to meet customer requirements for cash withdrawals. The remaining 90 per cent or £900 can be loaned out. Given the assumption that assets loaned out will be spent and find their way back into the bank, then in stage 2 re-deposits of £900 will occur. Of this re-deposited amount £90 (10 per cent) will be held in the form of cash in order to meet claims on the bank and the remaining £810 (90 per cent) will be loaned out. This process will continue with the amount available for lending continually declining, as with stages 3 and 4 in Figure 14.2, until eventually total liabilities and assets will equal £10,000. Thus, from an original deposit of £1,000 cash, £10,000 of new deposits and £9,000 of new loans have been made. There has thus been a multiple expansion of credit.

10. The credit multiplier

Credit creation can be analysed by use of the *credit* or *bank multiplier*. The extent of the creation of new deposits depends upon the size of the cash ratio banks maintain. Thus if the cash ratio is 10 per cent, then the credit multiplier is 10 since:

$$\text{The credit multiplier} = \frac{1}{\text{cash ratio}}$$

11. Credit creation in a multi-bank system

The concept of credit creation is more complicated in a multi-bank system. The reason is that when a bank makes a loan to a customer, say to buy a new car, then the garage from which the car is purchased will not necessarily deposit the money in the same bank which initially gave the loan. Even though this is the case, the end result in terms of credit creation is exactly the same provided all the banks in the economy create deposits to the limit of the cash ratio.

The banking sector

12. What is the banking sector?

The main business of banks can be outlined by reference to their balance sheet. Table 14.1 shows the balance sheet of the banks in the UK for March 1992. The Banking Act 1979 laid down certain criteria whereby institutions wishing to call themselves banks had to satisfy the Bank of England as to their range of services, financial status and reputation. The banking sector includes:

(a) *Retail banks.* The retail banks include the High Street banks such as Barclays, Lloyds and National Westminster Bank plc, the TSB Bank plc, Girobank plc, The Royal Bank of Scotland plc, the Ulster Bank Ltd, and the former building society, Abbey National plc.

Table 14.1 Balance sheet of banks in the UK, March 1992

	£ million		£ million	£ million
Liabilities		**Assets**		
Notes outstanding	1,630	*Sterling assets*		
Sterling deposits	513, 066	Notes and coin		2, 917
		Balances with Bank of		
Other currency		England:		
deposits	618, 338	Cash ratio deposits	1, 378	
		Special deposits	0	
Items in suspense		Other	12	
and transmission	26, 790			1, 390
		Market loans:		
Capital and other		Discount houses	8, 883	
funds	86, 182	Other	124, 981	
				133, 864
		Bills:		
		Treasury bills	3, 633	
		Other	9, 980	
				13, 613
		Advances	379, 719	
		Banking Department		
		lending to central		
		Government	1, 114	
		Investments	31, 594	
		Miscellaneous	33, 828	
				446, 255
				598, 039
		Other currency assets		
		Market loans	419, 914	
		Advances	146, 194	
		Bills	9, 237	
		Investments	58, 905	
		Miscellaneous	13, 717	
				647, 967
Total liabilities:	1, 246, 006	Total assets:		1, 246, 006

Source: *Bank of England Quarterly Bulletin,* May 1992.

(b) *British merchant banks* such as Hill Samuel Bank and Kleinwort Benson Ltd.

(c) *Other British banks* such as the Bank of Wales plc.

(d) *American, Japanese and other overseas banks.*

(e) *Discount Houses* such as S G Warburg Discount Ltd.

The banks' balance sheet can be split into liabilities and assets.

13. Banks' liabilities

The banks' liabilities consist mainly of the deposits they have accepted. Sterling deposits comprise customers' accounts both *sight deposits* and *time deposits.*

Sight deposits can be transferred or withdrawn on demand without any interest penalty. Time deposits on the other hand normally require notice of withdrawal if the depositor is not to lose interest. This has usually been seven days for small 'retail' deposits. The longer the period of notice required, then the greater the interest received. Sight deposits are, therefore, more liquid.

A large proportion of liabilities (and also assets) are in non-sterling currencies. These are predominantly deposits of non-residents and in March 1992 they comprised approximately 50 per cent of total liabilities.

14. Banks' assets

Banks have a whole range of assets ranging from cash, which is the most liquid, to advances comprising overdrafts and loans (the so-called *earning assets*). Banks face the dilemma of *liquidity and profitability.* On the one hand they need to keep a certain amount of their assets in a liquid form in order to meet the demands of their customers for money. They are however in the business of making profits and this is what their shareholders expect them to do. The most liquid assets tend to be the least profitable while the less liquid tend to be the most profitable but involve more risk; therefore, banks need to strike a balance between liquidity and profitability.

In examining the balance sheet in Table 14.1, it is found that there are a spectrum of assets with different levels of liquidity.

(a) *Notes and coins.* It is necessary for banks to hold notes and coins in order to meet cash withdrawals from their customers. Banks will aim to keep the amounts held to a minimum since they earn no interest and are, therefore, the least profitable asset.

(b) *Balances with the Bank of England.* As seen in Table 14.1 balances with the Bank of England can be divided into three main deposits:

(i) Cash ratio deposits. Banks with eligible liabilities of £10m or more are required to hold cash ratio deposits at the Bank of England. The amount they currently have to lodge is 0.35 per cent of their eligible liabilities for which they receive no interest. *Eligible liabilities* are essentially sterling deposit liabilities with less than 2 years to maturity. These deposits can not be drawn upon by the banks.

(ii) Special deposits. Banks with eligible liabilities of £10m or more may be requested by the Bank of England to make special deposits at the Bank. These are 'frozen' assets in that banks cannot use them to loan out to customers. Interest is paid on these special deposits based on the average Treasury Bill rate. These special deposits form part of monetary policy and can be used to control the money supply (*see* **18**).

(iii) Other deposits. Banks keep what are known as *operational balances* at the Bank in order to allow for the settling of debts between banks. They are essentially the banks' own current accounts.

(c) *Market loans to discount houses.* Market loans consist of funds lent for a short period of time.

Money is loaned by banks to the members of the London Discount Market Association (LDMA) at *call* and *short notice*. Money lent at call to the discount houses means that it can be called upon immediately if required, whereas money at short notice is for periods of up to 14 days. The rate of interest banks earn on these loans will depend upon the duration of the loan.

These loans are a liquid part of the banks' balance sheet since they can be called upon quickly if they are short of cash.

(d) *Other market loans.* These include:

(i) Other UK banks. Banks make and obtain loans from other UK banks on a short-term basis.

(ii) Certificates of Deposit (CDs). Banks issue CDs to those customers who are willing to deposit money for a certain period of time at a fixed rate of interest. This forms part of a banks' liabilities. However, these CDs are marketable and banks hold CDs issued by other banks as part of their asset structure.

(iii) Local authorities. Local authorities borrow short term in order to finance their commitments. This does not include the money lent by banks to local authorities as part of their normal business which is included in banks' advances.

(e) *Bills.* Banks hold a number of bills, one of the most important being *Treasury Bills*. These are issued by the Bank of England on behalf of the government to finance their current expenditure. They are sold weekly, have a life of three months and they are initially purchased by discount houses. Banks may subsequently purchase the bills from the discount houses. Discount houses and Treasury bills are dealt with in more detail in **15**.

(f) *Investments.* Investments comprise British government stock, termed gilt-edged securities, with a maturity of 1 year or more. Banks will hold government stock with a range of maturity dates, and as well as being profitable they are an extremely safe form of asset.

(g) *Advances.* These are the banks most profitable asset. They consist of overdrafts and loans made to customers.

15. The discount market

The discount market is concerned with short-term loans and centres around the discount houses, who act as intermediaries between the Bank of England and the commercial banks. Discount houses borrow money on a very short-term basis and, as seen in **14**, some of it is repayable to the banks 'at call and short notice'. These funds are used to *discount bills* such as Treasury bills.

Each week the Bank of England issues Treasury bills on behalf of the government. A Treasury bill has a life of three months, at the end of which the government promises to pay a certain amount, e.g. £50,000. They are purchased by discount houses for, say, £48,500 which means that they are buying the bill for less than its face value, i.e. *at a discount*. In this example it costs the government £1,500 to borrow £48,500 which is an annual rate of interest of over 12 per cent. This is calculated as follows:

$$\frac{1500}{48,500} \times \frac{100}{1} \times \frac{365}{91} = 12.4\%$$

The rate of interest discount houses pay on money borrowed short term is less than the amount they receive for the money loaned out for 91 days. The difference between the two represents the discount houses' profit. Discount houses do not normally hold all the bills until they mature — they may sell a quantity to commercial banks. The commercial banks will then hold the Treasury bills as part of their liquid assets (*see* **14**).

The Bank of England

16. What is the Bank of England?

The Bank of England is the Central Bank of the UK and can be referred to as 'the Bank'. As seen in Table 14.2, it is divided into 2 departments, namely the *Issue Department* and the *Banking Department*.

(a) *The Issue Department* is responsible for the note issue. The liabilities consist of notes in circulation and those held in the Banking Department ready for issue to the banking sector. The assets consist of securities, with the note issue being a *fiduciary issue* in that it is not backed by gold.

(b) *The Banking Department* is concerned with the business of the Bank, which consists of:

(i) *Public deposits* which are held by the central government.

(ii) *Special deposits* which are called from the banking sector on occasions in order to reduce the banks' liquidity (*see* **14** and **18**).

(iii) *Bankers' deposits*, which consist of operational deposits held by the clearing banks and the non-operational cash ratio deposits (both are dealt with in **14**).

(iv) *Reserves and other accounts* consist of the deposits of overseas central banks and the accounts of local authorities and public corporations. There are also a number of private sector accounts.

The *asset side* of the Banking Department consists of government securities, advances, premises, equipment, securities, and notes and coins ready for issue to the clearing banks, which they can obtain through their operational balances.

Table 14.2 Bank of England Balance Sheet (£ millions), 18 March 1992

Issue Department

Liabilities		Assets	
Notes in circulation	15,512	Government securities	9,227
Notes in Banking Department	8	Other securities	6,293
	15,520		15,520

Banking Department

Liabilities*		Assets	
Public deposits	128	Government securities	1,333
Special deposits	0	Advances and other accounts	2,130
Bankers' deposits	1,570	Premises, equipment, etc	1,766
Reserves and other accounts	3,525	Notes and coin	8
	5,237		5,237

*The Bank's capital of £14.6 million is not shown on the Balance Sheet since it is held by the Treasury.

Source: *Bank of England Quarterly Bulletin*, May 1992.

17. Functions of the Bank of England

The functions of the Bank can be seen as:

(a) *Banker to the banking sector.* The Bank of England holds accounts of other banks. These operational balances are used for inter-bank settlements at the end of each banking day.

(b) *Banker to the government.* The Bank acts as the government's bank, responsible for their finances. Taxation revenue is paid into, and government expenditure is taken out of, the Exchequer Account at the Bank of England.

(c) *Banker to other customers.* The Bank holds accounts for a number of overseas central banks, as well as for a few private individuals.

(d) *Manager of the national debt.* The Bank has the responsibility for the issue of new national debt, such as the weekly issue of Treasury bills, and for the interest payments and final redemption on maturity of existing national debt. The national debt is dealt with in more detail in 15: 12.

(e) *Manager of the Exchange Equalisation Account.* This is an account managed by the Bank which is composed of sterling and foreign currency and is used to intervene in foreign exchange markets in order to influence the value of sterling.

(f) *Note issue.* The Bank is the sole issuer of notes in England and Wales. This function includes the printing, issue and withdrawal of banknotes.

(g) *Supervision of the banking sector.* In order to maintain the international reputation of the UK banking sector, the Bank has a statutory obligation to supervise the banking sector. This stems from the 1987 Banking Act.

(h) *Implementation of monetary policy.* The Bank is responsible for the implementation of the government's monetary policy. This includes control of the money supply and the rate of interest and will be covered in more detail in 18.

18. Control of the money supply

There are a number of policy instruments the Bank of England has at its disposal in order to control the money supply.

(a) *Open market operations.* Open market operations refers to the sale or purchase of securities on the open market by the Bank of England. If, for example, the Bank wishes to reduce the money supply it will sell government debt, i.e. sell gilts on the open market — to the non-banking private sector. The individuals or institutions who purchase these securities will use cheques drawn on their accounts at commercial banks. The Bank will present these cheques for payment to the relevant commercial banks and the result will be a transfer of money to the Bank from the commercial bank's operational balances at the Bank (*see* **14**). The effect of this will be a reduction in the commercial banks' cash reserves and, since this represents a fall in the banks' liquidity, they will reduce their lending so as to avoid the risk of being unable to meet claims for cash withdrawals. The sale of securities on the open market will thus lead to a multiple contraction of deposits and, therefore, a reduction in the money supply.

If on the other hand the Bank wishes to *increase* the money supply, it will purchase securities on the open market using cheques drawn on itself. The individuals or institutions concerned will deposit these cheques in their bank accounts and the banks will present the cheques for payment to the Bank. The result will be an increase in their operational balances and the extra liquidity will allow the commercial bank to increase their lending. There will thus be a multiple expansion of deposits, i.e. credit creation, and an expansion of the money supply.

(b) *Interest rate policy.* Interest rate policy can be linked to that of open market operations. If the Bank sells securities on the open market it will have the effect of reducing banks' operational balances at the Bank of England. In response to this, banks may recall their loans to the discount houses thus making them short of money. The discount houses may then be forced to borrow from the Bank as *lender of last resort*. The Bank can alter the rate of interest it charges. If it requires the rate of interest to increase they will offer a lower price to the discount houses for the bills it is purchasing. This will then influence the whole structure of interest rates in the economy.

If the demand for loans in the economy is assumed to be responsive to a change in the interest rate, then a rise in the interest rate will reduce the demand for loans, so affecting the banks' ability to create credit and, therefore, restricting the growth of the money supply.

(c) *Special deposits.* Special deposits are not currently being used as a method of controlling the money supply. The Bank can, if it so wishes, call for special deposits from the institutions in the banking sector which have average eligible liabilities of £10m or more. These deposits are placed in an account at the Bank and, although they receive a rate of interest, they are frozen until the Bank sees it as the correct time to return them to the banks.

If the Bank calls for special deposits it has the effect of reducing bank liquidity. This leads the banks to reduce their lending and, therefore, results in a contraction of the money supply. A release of special deposits on the other hand has the effect of leading to an expansion of the money supply. Although special deposits are a policy instrument, it can be seen from Table 14.1 that the Bank of England were not holding special deposits as at March 1992.

(d) *Funding.* Funding involves altering the composition of government borrowing. By the issue of more long-term debt, such as gilts, and less short-term debt, such as Treasury bills, the maturity of the government debt is effectively lengthened. Longer-term debt is likely to be bought by the non-banking sector, unlike short-term debt. The effect of this is to reduce the liquidity of the banks' assets, which restricts the banks' ability to engage in the multiple expansion of credit.

Funding is not actively used at present as a means of controlling the money supply.

(e) *Ceilings.* From time to time ceilings have been placed on the growth of deposits, allowing banks to increase them by say 6 per cent. This type of *quantitative control* could be supplemented with *qualitative controls*, whereby the Bank instructed or offered guidance as to the composition of bank lending — such as discouraging personal lending and the borrowing for property deals. Ceilings were used in the 1950s and 1960s.

(f) *Changing the reserve ratio.* The banks could be required to keep a certain proportion of their assets in a particular form, the proportion being some percentage of their liabilities. The effect of this would be a reduction in the banks' ability to create credit.

Progress test 14

1. Outline the four main function of money. **(2–5)**

2. Distinguish between the various official definitions of the money supply. **(8)**

3. What is meant by credit creation? **(9–11)**

4. Outline the problem faced by the banking sector in achieving an acceptable balance between liquidity and profitability. **(14)**

5. What are special deposits? **(14, 18)**

6. What are the functions of the Bank of England? **(17)**

7. Outline the process of open market operations as a means of controlling the money supply. **(18)**

8. Explain what is meant by the 'lender of last resort' in relation to the Bank of England. **(18)**

15
Public expenditure and finance

1. Introduction

The main aim of this chapter is to outline 3 main issues, namely public expenditure, taxation and the government's budget deficit or surplus. The public sector, which comprises central government, local government and public corporations, is an important sector in the economy. In fact in 1991–92 General government expenditure (which comprises central government and the local authority sector) was 41.5 per cent of GDP.

2. Rationale for a public sector

It is possible to identify a number of reasons for the involvement of the public sector in the economy.

(a) *Provision of goods and services.* There are certain goods and services which would be under-provided if left to the market mechanism. Examples include *public goods* such as defence, law and order and flood control schemes, and *merit goods* such as education and health.

Public goods have two main characteristics:

(i) If they are provided to one individual then they are provided to all, which means there is *non-excludability.*

(ii) Consumption by one individual does not impede its consumption by others, which means there is *non-rivalry.*

Public goods are consumed *collectively* and so it is difficult to finance their supply through the market. Thus there is the need for them to be provided either by the state or by the private sector stimulated or enabled by the state.

Merit goods are viewed as being desirable by the government and, therefore, their consumption should be encouraged. Merit goods are likely to be provided through the market mechanism, but not in the quantity deemed necessary by the government.

(b) *The control of externalities.* In producing goods and services the private sector tends to take account only of their private costs, i.e. the costs of raw materials, labour and energy. They often fail to take account of the costs incurred on *society*, such as pollution, noise and congestion. These costs are called 'externalities'. State involvement can make sure that the private sector accounts for the externalities, either through the imposition of taxes or by the use of legislation to impose minimum standards.

(c) *The redistribution of income and wealth.* The aim of the public sector may be to obtain a more equitable distribution of income and wealth. This can be achieved through a progressive tax structure (*see* 8) and the use of transfer payments, such as the retirement pension, sickness benefit, child benefit and unemployment benefit. Transfer payments are an important part of public expenditure as can be seen by the amount devoted to social security in Table 15.1.

In the UK since 1979 it has been the policy of the Conservative Government to reduce the progressive nature of taxation and to scale down the eligibility for transfer payments. The basis for this is to offer a greater incentive to work and to reduce the number of individuals dependent upon the state.

(d) *To encourage competition.* The allocation of resources through the market mechanism requires competition both in the factor and product market. Over time, an unrestrained free market could lead to the creation of monopolies which operate against the public interest. There is a need, therefore, for public sector involvement in the economy in order to ensure competition through the agency of bodies like the *Monopolies and Mergers Commission* (MMC), which investigates mergers and acquisitions which might produce monopolies. A company can be referred to the MMC if it supplies 25 per cent and over of the market, and the investigation examines whether or not the monopoly is acting 'contrary to the public interest'.

It could, however, be argued that throughout the twentieth century the state has restricted competition via a policy of nationalisation. This is something the Conservative Government has sought to redress in the 1980s, through large scale privatisation (*see* 18: **12**).

(e) *To regulate the level of economic activity.* Chapter 11 outlined how the public sector influence the level of economic activity through changes in government expenditure and taxation. Fiscal policy has been used extensively to achieve the objective of full employment, price stability, economic growth and a balance-of-payments equilibrium. These objectives are dealt with in more detail in 18: **2**.

Government expenditure

3. What is government expenditure?
The Public Expenditure Plans up to 1994–95 were published in

Table 15.1 General government expenditure

	1991–92 estimated outturn	1992–93 plans	1993–94 plans	£ billion 1994–95 plans
Ministry of Defence	22.9	24.2	24.5	24.8
Foreign and Commonwealth Office	3.0	3.3	3.4	3.5
Ministry of Agriculture, Fisheries and Food	2.3	2.3	2.4	2.4
Trade and Industry	1.3	1.1	1.0	1.0
Energy	0.5	0.5	0.5	0.5
Department of Employment	3.2	3.5	3.5	3.5
Department of Transport	2.5	2.6	2.7	2.8
DOE – Housing	3.1	2.8	3.1	3.1
DOE – Other environmental services	0.9	0.7	0.6	0.6
DOE – Local government	0.3	0.3	0.2	0.2
Home Office (including Charity Commission)	2.2	2.2	2.4	2.5
Lord Chancellor's and Law Officers' Departments	1.7	1.8	1.8	1.9
Department of Education and Science	4.6	4.9	5.1	5.3
Office of Arts and Libraries	0.6	0.6	0.6	0.6
Department of Health and Office of Population Censuses and Surveys	25.5	27.9	29.8	31.5
Department of Social Security	61.3	66.0	71.2	74.5
Scotland	6.0	6.4	6.7	6.9
Wales	2.5	2.8	3.0	3.1
Northern Ireland	6.4	7.0	7.4	7.7
Chancellor of the Exchequer's Departments	4.8	5.0	5.2	5.4
Cabinet Office, Privy Council Office and Parliament	0.4	0.5	0.5	0.5
European Communities	0.9	2.5	2.6	2.9
Total central government expenditure	156.7	168.7	178.1	185.4
Central government support for local authorities	53.3	58.5	61.0	64.0
Financing requirements of nationalised industries	2.7	3.4	2.9	2.1
Reserve		4.0	8.0	12.0
Privatisation proceeds	–8.0	–8.0	–5.5	–5.5
Adjustment	0.3			
Planning total	205.0	226.6	244.5	258.0
Local authority self-financed expenditure	10.5	8.5	9.0	9.0
Central government debt interest	16.7	16.5	17.5	18.5
Accounting adjustments	4.3	4.5	5.0	5.5
General government expenditure	236.4	256.4	276.6	291.2

* In this table the items may not add up to totals because of rounding.
Source: *Public Expenditure Analysis to 1994–95*, H M Treasury, January 1992.

January 1992 and Table 15.1 gives an outline of general government expenditure. It can be seen that in 1992–93 general government expenditure was planned to be £256,400 million.

The main areas of central government expenditure are defence, health, and social security which together, in 1991–92, comprised 70 per cent of total central government planned expenditure.

4. Reasons for the control of public expenditure

Since 1979 one of the main aims of the Conservative Government has been to reduce public expenditure, taxation and government borrowing. Both taxation and government borrowing will be discussed later in this chapter but, in terms of public expenditure, a number of possible reasons can be outlined as to why the control of public expenditure is seen as so important.

(a) *To control the money supply.* Growth in public expenditure and a resulting increase in the Public Sector Borrowing Requirement (PSBR) can, depending on how it is funded, lead to an increase in the money supply and hence inflation. The link between the PSBR and the money supply is outlined below (*see* 11). According to the monetarists it is necessary to restrict public expenditure in order to control the growth in the money supply and, therefore, inflation.

(b) *Crowding out.* It is possible that an excessive growth in public expenditure can lead to what has become known as the *crowding out effect.* The growth in public expenditure could be financed by an increase in the PSBR through the sale of government securities. An increase in the number of securities on the market requires the interest rate to rise in order to encourage their sale. The result of this is that the cost of private sector investment increases and thus *crowding out* occurs. The increase in public expenditure could be the result of the government purchasing productive resources which could have been more effectively used in the private sector.

If the notion of crowding out is accepted, then the control of public expenditure will allow the private sector to use the resources, possibly in a more efficient way than the public sector.

(c) *Incentive to work.* The control of public expenditure should make it possible for there to be a reduction in taxation, in particular in income tax, which could act as an incentive to work. The evidence as to the effect a reduction in income tax has on the incentive to work is, however, inconclusive.

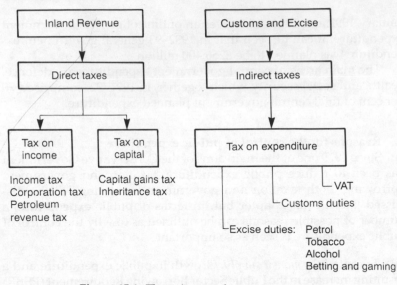

Figure 15.1 *The main central government receipts.*

Government receipts (taxation)

5. What are taxes?

Taxes can be defined as the compulsory transfer of money from individuals or institutions to the government. They can take the form of either *direct* or *indirect taxes*, as shown in Figure 15.1.

Direct taxes are levied on income and capital and they are paid directly to the Inland Revenue. In the case of personal income tax this is mainly through Pay As You Earn (PAYE). Indirect taxes are essentially a tax on expenditure, for example Value Added Tax. Indirect taxes are so called because they are paid by the consumer of goods and services to the retailer, who in effect acts as a collecting agent for the Customs and Excise Department. This form of tax therefore reaches the exchequer *indirectly*.

The latest estimates and forecasts of government receipts can be seen in Table 15.2, where it can be noted that general government receipts are forecast to be £229.8bn in 1992–93.

6. Direct taxes

The following can be viewed as the main direct taxes.

(a) *Personal income tax*. As seen in Table 15.2, income tax is the major source of revenue for the government. Personal income tax is not paid

Table 15.2 General government receipts

	£ billion 1991–92 Latest estimate	£ billion 1992–93 Forecast
Inland Revenue:		
Income tax	58.0	59.6
Corporation tax	18.4	16.8
Petroleum revenue tax	−0.2	0.1
Capital gains tax	1.2	1.1
Inheritance tax	1.3	1.3
Stamp duties	1.7	1.5
Total Inland Revenue	**80.4**	**80.4**
Customs and excise:		
Value added tax	35.5	40.0
Petrol, derv duties etc.	10.9	11.8
Tobacco duties	6.1	6.6
Alcohol duties	5.0	5.3
Betting and gaming duties	1.1	1.1
Car tax	1.2	0.7
Customs duties	1.8	1.9
Agricultural levies	0.2	0.0
Total Customs and Excise	**61.8**	**67.4**
Vehicle excise duties	3.0	3.2
Oil royalties	0.5	0.5
Rates	14.4	14.1
Other taxes and royalties	3.9	4.1
Total tax and royalty receipts	**164.0**	**169.8**
Social security receipts	36.3	38.7
Community charge receipts	7.1	8.0
Interest and dividends	6.1	5.5
Gross trading surpluses and rent	3.8	3.7
Other receipts	4.8	4.0
General government receipts	**222.1**	**229.8**

Source: *Financial Statement and Budget Report 1992–93*, H M Treasury, March 1992.

on all income, with each individual being given a tax-free allowance. In 1992–93 the single personal allowance was £3,445, while a married couple under the age of 65 were given an additional allowance of £1,720. The rate of tax is given in Table 15.3 and reveals the progressive nature of income tax, which means that the *marginal rate of tax is greater than the average rate of tax.*

Table 15.3 UK income tax schedules, 1992–1993

Taxable income	Rate of tax %
0–2,000	20
2,000–23,700	25
Over 23,700	40

It is important to remember when referring to Table 15.3 that the higher rates of tax only apply to the increments above the various tax bands. So an individual will only pay 40 per cent tax on taxable income above £23,700. The basic rate limit is up to £23,700.

(b) *Corporation tax.* This is a tax which is levied on company profits after taking account of interest payments and an allowance for depreciation. The main rate of corporation tax is currently 33 per cent, although for small companies the rate is 25 per cent. This represents those companies with a profit limit of £250,000.

(c) *Capital gains tax.* This is a tax which applies to gains made from the sale of assets. In other words it is the difference between the buying price and the selling price of an asset. In 1992–93 the annual exemption rate for individuals was £5,800, with gains above this amount being taxed at the income tax rate. Certain assets are exempt from capital gains tax, assets such as an individual's principal residence, winnings on the pools, motor cars and so on.

(d) *Inheritance tax.* This tax is levied on gifts made during an individual's life or when that individual dies. Inheritance tax is paid on transfers of over £150,000 and is subject to a single rate of tax, i.e. 40 per cent.

7. Indirect taxes

The three main indirect taxes are value added tax, customs duty and excise duty.

(a) *Value added tax (VAT).* VAT is the most important indirect tax, comprising 15 per cent of the total public money in 1991–92 (*see* Table 15.2). VAT is a tax levied at each stage of the production and distribution of goods and services, and the rate is currently set at 17½ per cent. This tax is called an *ad valorem tax* in that it is set at a fixed percentage of the value of the product.

Certain goods and services are *zero rated* or *exempt* from VAT. Zero rated goods and services currently include children's clothing, books, newspapers, basic food items, domestic fuel and power, public transport fares, medicines on prescription, the construction of new building, and water and sewage services. In the case of zero rating, the trader does not charge the customer VAT and can reclaim VAT on the inputs used.

VAT exempt means that the trader does not charge VAT to its customers but at the same time cannot reclaim VAT from the Customs and Excise Department. VAT exempt goods and services include, among other things, postal services, insurance, rent and betting.

(b) *Customs duties.* Customs duties are charged on imported goods and services although products imported from other EC member countries are exempt.

(c) *Excise duties.* Excise duty raised 9.5 pence in every £1 of public money raised in 1991–92. Excise duty is placed on those goods and services which have a relatively inelastic demand or which are viewed as being detrimental to the public interest — or both. Excise duty is levied principally on tobacco, beer, wine and spirits, betting and gaming, and petrol.

8. Progressive, regressive and proportional taxation

Taxes can be classified as progressive, regressive or proportional. This can be illustrated by Table 15.4 which uses income tax as an example.

With a progressive tax the percentage of income paid in tax increases as income increases, whereas with a regressive tax the percentage of income paid in tax reduces as income increases. With a proportional tax the percentage of income paid in tax remains constant as income increases.

It is important to remember when differentiating between the 3 types of taxation that it is not sufficient to discuss them in terms of the *amount* of tax paid, for in all three examples in Table 15.4 the amount

Table 15.4 Progressive, regressive and proportional tax

Income	Progressive tax		Regressive tax		Proportional tax	
£	Income tax	% of income paid in	Income tax	% of income paid in tax	Income tax	% of income paid in tax
100	10	10	10	10	10	10
1,000	200	20	80	8	100	10
10,000	3,000	30	600	6	1,000	10
100,000	40,000	40	4,000	4	10,000	10

paid actually increases as income increases. It is the *percentage* of income paid in tax which is the distinguishing feature.

The government budget — deficit or surplus

9.   The Budget

The Budget occurs annually, usually in March, when the Chancellor of the Exchequer makes a financial statement both to Parliament and the nation. In the Budget the Chancellor reviews economic policy and proposes taxation changes for the coming year. This is published in the *Financial Statement and Budget Report* (known as the Red Book).

On certain occasions the government has viewed it necessary to have an extra budget, a mini budget, which usually takes place in the autumn or winter.

Changes in government expenditure are announced by the Chancellor in October in what is known as the *Autumn Statement*, although there are moves to bring the taxation and expenditure plans together so they can be announced in one budget in December of each year.

The budget can be in deficit or surplus. If in deficit, then planned government expenditure will be greater than the government's estimated revenue and there will be a need to finance the deficit through borrowing, hence the need for the Public Sector Borrowing Requirement (PSBR) (*see* **10**). If the budget is in surplus, then estimated revenue is greater than planned government expenditure and the surplus can be used to repay previous years' borrowing. It could also be the case that there is a balanced budget. In this situation estimated revenue would be equal to planned government expenditure. During the 1950s and up to the early 1970s, when the UK government tended to be Keynesian in its thinking, a budget deficit became an important part of macroeconomic policy. A budget deficit was used as part of fiscal policy in order to stimulate demand in the economy as a means of achieving full employment (*see* Chapter 11). In recent years, however, the aim has been to reduce the budget deficit in line with monetarist thinking.

10.   The Public Sector Borrowing Requirement (PSBR)

In Table 15.5 it can be seen that general government expenditure is likely to be greater than receipts in 1991–92 and 1992–93. This shortfall needs financing and forms part of the PSBR.

The PSBR comprises the borrowing of central government (CGBR) and local government (LGBR), which together is called the

Table 15.5 The public sector borrowing requirement

	£ billion 1991–92 Latest estimate	£ billion 1992–93 Forecast
General government expenditure	236.5	258.5
General government receipts	222.1	229.8
General government borrowing requirement	14.3	28.7
Public corporations' market and overseas borrowing	−0.5	−0.6
Public sector borrowing requirement	**13.8**	**28.1**

Source: *Financial Statement and Budget Report 1992–93*, H M Treasury, March 1992.

general government borrowing requirement (GGBR), and the borrowing of public corporations (PCBR). So:

$$PSBR = CGBR + LGBR + PCBR$$

A budget deficit will require a positive PSBR whereas a budget surplus allows the government to repay part of the previous borrowing, there being a negative PSBR. This is known as the Public Sector Debt Repayment (PSDR).

The forecast for 1991–92 was a PSBR of £13.8bn, which is equivalent to 2¼ per cent of GDP. In the previous four years there had been debt repayments totalling £26½bn. Over this period a PSDR had been achieved through strict control on public expenditure and the sale of public assets, i.e. the revenue from privatisation.

The PSBR can be used, as part of macroeconomic policy, as a means of manipulating aggregate demand. The monetarists have, however, stressed the adverse effects which the growth in the PSBR has had on the rate of inflation. Hence the Conservative Government has since 1979 aimed at controlling the PSBR, with varying degrees of success (*see* 4).

11. The PSBR and the money supply
The PSBR can be financed by a number of means:

(a) *The issue of notes and coins.* This method of financing the PSBR involves the government borrowing directly from the Bank of England. The government will sell securities to the Bank of England in return for an issue of notes and coins from the Bank, which the government can then spend. This new currency in circulation will find its way into the banking sector, and will lead to an expansion of bank deposits and, therefore, an expansion of the money supply.

(b) *Borrowing from the banking sector*. This method involves the government in selling short-term or long-term debt to the banking sector, which includes the clearing banks, building societies and discount houses. For example, the government may sell short-term debt, namely Treasury bills (*see* 14: **15**) to the banking sector and this will affect the money supply. The sale of Treasury bills to the banking sector will result initially in a reduction in commercial banks' deposits at the Bank of England since they have been used to pay for the Treasury bills. When the government spends these deposits they will find their way into accounts held at commercial banks and, with the increase in such deposits, there will be an increase in the money supply.

(c) *Borrowing from the general public outside the banking sector*. This involves the sale of gilt-edged securities or national savings securities to the non-monetary banking sector, such as insurance companies, pension funds, manufacturing companies and individuals. This will have no effect on the money supply since all that has occurred is the bank deposits of the general public have been transferred to the government in exchange for securities. It is the government who spends these deposits and, with there being no new deposits created, there is no change in the money supply.

(d) *Borrowing from abroad*. If the government borrows from abroad in order to spend, that money will eventually be deposited in the bank accounts of individuals in the economy. Through credit creation, this will lead to a further increase in the money supply.

The national debt

12. What is the national debt?

The national debt is the accumulated central government debt from successive years of budget deficits. In recent times the national debt has fallen as a proportion of GDP due to a number of years of Public Sector Debt Repayment (PSDR). The national debt is primarily held by the citizens and institutions in the UK, although a small percentage is held overseas. Table 15.6 gives a summary of the distribution of the sterling national debt. At 31 March 1991 overseas residents held approximately 11 per cent of the total sterling debt.

13. Arguments against the national debt

The question could be asked, should the national debt be viewed as a burden?

Table 15.6 Summary of the distribution of the sterling national debt

Amounts outstanding at 31 March 1991
£ billions

MARKET HOLDINGS	
Public corporations and local authorities	1.2
Banking sector	7.0
Building societies	5.2
Institutional investors:	
Insurance companies and pension funds	67.3
Other	0.8
Overseas residents	21.6
Individuals and private trusts	39.1
Other (including residual)	13.3
Total market holdings	155.6
OFFICIAL HOLDINGS	34.6
Total sterling debt	190.2

Source: *Bank of England Quarterly Bulletin*, November 1991.

(a) The debt incurred by the present generation will have to be repaid by future generations, including the interest on the debt. This could be viewed as an unacceptable burden on future generations.

(b) The national debt can be viewed primarily as an internal debt in that we owe the debt to ourselves. This means that there is a redistribution of income from the taxpayer to the government debt holder, which can in fact be one in the same person. Although this is true for internal debt, 11 per cent of the national debt is held externally (overseas) which can be viewed as a real burden on the economy in terms of an outflow from the UK of the final redemption and interest payments.

(c) The existence of the national debt means that the level of taxation is higher than it would be if the national debt did not exist. It can be argued that higher income tax has a disincentive effect on effort and, therefore, on the levels of production. It is also the case that taxation is taken out of hard earned income whereas interest paid to holders of the national debt is purely a transfer payment with no effort involved.

(d) There are costs incurred in administering the national debt and, although these costs are only a small proportion of GDP, these resources could have been used elsewhere in the economy.

14. The national debt in a wider context

Although a case can be made against the national debt equally it is important not to consider the debt in isolation. The reasons for this are:

(a) The national debt and successive PSBRs should be viewed as a useful instrument of fiscal policy. It is not meaningful to consider the size of the national debt in isolation and, perhaps, it is more relevant to consider its size in relation to GDP. For example, on 31 March 1991 the net public sector debt as a percentage of GDP was 27.3 per cent. This had reduced from a percentage of 46.2 per cent on 31 March 1980.

(b) As stated in **13**, we owe the debt to ourselves. Hence the debt simply represents a *redistribution* of income from the taxpayer to the debt holder.

(c) Although the national debt is placing a burden on future generations, it should be remembered that future generations will also inherit the benefits — both tangible (schools, hospitals, roads and so on) and intangible (human knowledge and technical know-how) — which derive from current investment.

(d) A small national debt could suggest an adherence to the principle of a balanced budget. The economy, however, may be experiencing high levels of unemployment and low growth. This may require an increase in public expenditure. If there is no compensating increase in taxation, there would be an increase in the PSBR and hence an increased national debt. It is possible to argue, therefore, that the national debt is a justifiable part of macroeconomic policy.

Progress test 15

1. Outline the reasons for the existence of the public sector. **(2)**

2. What is meant by the 'crowding out effect'? **(4)**

3. Distinguish between direct and indirect taxation. **(5)**

4. What are the differences between progressive, regressive and proportional taxation? **(8)**

5. Define the PSBR and the PSDR. **(10)**

6. Outline the effect an increase in the PSBR has on the money supply. **(11)**

7. What is meant by the national debt? **(12)**

8. Is the national debt a burden? **(13, 14)**

16

International trade and protection

1. Introduction

In the previous chapters we have concentrated on national trade, but trade also takes place across international boundaries. For example, in terms of the UK, in 1990 £10.4bn worth of agricultural produce was imported, of which 29 per cent comprised vegetables and fruit and 18 per cent dairy products. £47.3bn of machinery and transport equipment were also imported in 1990, 27 per cent of which were road vehicles. In terms of exports, £4.3bn worth of agricultural produce were exported in 1990, 24 per cent of which were cereals and cereal preparations. With regard to machinery and transport equipment, £42.2bn were exported with road vehicles comprising only 17 per cent of that total.

In terms of the country of origin of UK imports, Figure 16.1(a) reveals that in 1991 52 per cent of UK imports were from the EC and similarly, in terms of UK exports, Figure 16.1(b) reveals that over half went to members of the EC. It might be surprising to note that Japan, which in Figures 16.1(a) and 16.1(b) is included as part of 'other OECD countries', accounted for only 6 per cent of UK imports and 2 per cent of UK exports.

International trade has the potential to lead to increased living standards for the participating countries. The first part of this chapter examines the theory of the gains from trade, namely comparative advantage. It may be the case, however, that unrestricted free trade can have adverse effects on certain countries or on particular groups of people, thus leading to the argument for trade restrictions. In the second part of this chapter the various types of import control are examined and their possible benefits and disadvantages discussed.

The gains from trade

2. Why trade internationally?

International trade takes place for a number of reasons. Countries have different factor endowments whether it be plentiful supplies of

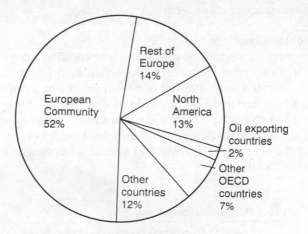

Figure 16.1(a) *UK imports by country of origin, 1991.*

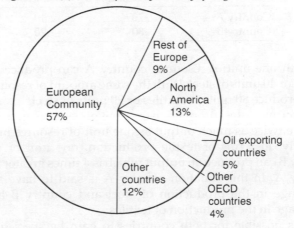

Figure 16.1 (b) *UK exports by country of destination, 1991.*

raw materials, such as copper and zinc, or climatic conditions which allow them to produce items such as bananas, coffee and cotton that many other countries would find too costly to produce. It is easy to see why trade in these products takes place across international boundaries but there is also a large amount of world trade in products which could be produced in the importing countries.

David Ricardo in the early nineteenth century developed the *theory of comparative advantage*, which showed the possible gains to be made from trade. Before outlining the theory of comparative advantage it is necessary to consider *absolute advantage*.

3. Absolute advantage

A country is said to have an *absolute advantage* over another country if it can produce more of a particular product than other countries, with the same amount of resources. If 2 countries have an absolute advantage in different products it is possible for specialisation to lead to an increase in world output and, therefore, via world trade, to an increase in the welfare of the countries involved. This can be outlined by reference to Table 16.1 which is hypothetical data for countries A and B.

Table 16.1 Absolute advantage

	Output from one unit of resource:	
	Textiles	*Steel*
Country A	20	40
Country B	80	20

With one unit of resource, country A can produce 20 units of textiles or 40 units of steel. With the same amount of resource country B can produce 80 units of textiles or 20 units of steel.

In terms of steel production one unit of resource in country A can produce twice as much output as one unit of resource in country B. Similarly, in terms of textile production, one unit of resource in country B can produce an output which is 4 times greater than that in country A. In this situation country A is said to have an absolute advantage in the production of steel and country B an absolute advantage in the production of textiles.

It is possible for both countries to gain by specialising in the production of the commodity in which they have an absolute advan-

Table 16.2 The gains made from the movement of one unit of resource

	Textiles	*Steel*	*Movement of one unit of resource from:*
Country A	−20	+40	textiles to steel
Country B	+80	−20	steel to textiles
World output	+60	+20	

tage. This can be seen in Table 16.2, where, by reallocating one unit of resource from textiles to steel in country A and one unit of resource from steel to textiles in country B, world output of both products can be increased. There are gains to be made, therefore, from specialisation and trade.

4. Comparative advantage

It is obvious that given the situation of absolute advantage outlined above (3) there are gains to be made from trade. It is not so obvious that there are gains to be made when a country has an absolute advantage in *both* products. This example is illustrated in Table 16.3 where country A is more efficient in the production of both textiles and steel.

Table 16.3   Comparative advantage

| | *Output from one unit of resource:* | |
	Textiles	*Steel*
Country A	320	40
Country B	80	20

The difference between Tables 16.3 and 16.1 is that country A has improved its output of textiles per unit of resource, possibly through technological change in the textile industry. Although country A is better at producing both products, there are still gains to be made through specialisation for, despite the fact that country A has an absolute advantage in both products, country A is *relatively* more efficient in the production of textiles. This can be seen by referring to Table 16.3 which shows country A is 4 times better at producing textiles than country B and only 2 times better at producing steel. In this situation country A is said to have a *comparative advantage* in the production of textiles and country B a *comparative advantage* in the production of steel.

By reallocating resources within the 2 countries it is possible to increase world output, and so there are gains to be made from specialisation and trade. By reallocating one unit of resource from steel to textiles in country A and three units of resource from textiles to steel in country B, it is possible to increase world output by 80 units of textiles and 20 units of steel.

The result of specialisation in the 2 countries means there are gains to be made through trade which will benefit both countries.

Table 16.4 Gains made from the reallocation of resources in a comparative advantage situation

	Textiles	Steel	Movement of resources:
Country A	+320	−40	1 unit of resource from steel to textiles
Country B	−240	+60	3 units of resource from textiles to steel
World output	+80	+20	

5. Comparative advantage and opportunity cost

In developing the theory of comparative advantage it is possible to use the concept of opportunity cost, first introduced in 1: 4. Referring back to Table 16.3, if it is assumed that all resources are fully employed it is only possible to produce one more unit of one commodity if resources are reallocated from the production of the other commodity. In terms of country A, the production of one more unit of textiles requires 1/8 units of steel to be sacrificed, thus giving an opportunity cost ratio of 1 : 1/8. In terms of country B, the production of one more unit of textiles requires 1/4 units of steel to be sacrificed, the opportunity cost ratio therefore being 1 : 1/4. In terms of steel, in country A one extra unit of production requires 8 units of textiles to be foregone, whereas in country B for 1 extra unit of steel only 4 units of textiles have to be sacrificed. The opportunity cost ratios are summarised in Table 16.5.

The opportunity cost of producing textiles is higher in country B than in country A, whereas for steel it is higher in country A than B. The difference in the opportunity cost ratios means that there are benefits to be obtained from specialisation and trade, with country A specialising in textiles and country B in steel production.

A country therefore has a comparative advantage in the production of the commodities whose opportunity cost is lower. There is no advantage and, therefore, no gain to be made from trade if the opportunity costs are identical.

Table 16.5 Opportunity cost

	Opportunity cost of producing textiles: (one unit of textiles in terms of units of steel)	Opportunity cost of producing steel: (one unit of steel in terms of units of textiles)
Country A	1/8	8
Country B	1/4	4

6. Limitations of the theory of comparative advantage
Limitations of the theory can be seen as:

(a) *Reciprocal demand*. The theory assumes what is known as *double coincidence of wants*. This means that in the example we have used, following specialisation, country A should demand steel from country B, and country B textiles from country A.

(b) *Transport costs*. Transport costs are not included in the theory of comparative advantage. Transport costs, however, increase production costs and therefore offset the gains made through specialisation.

(c) *Factor mobility*. The theory assumes that resources can be reallocated from the production of one product to another. In the real world, however, resources are likely to be immobile. In the example used in **3** and **4**, it is unlikely that resources can be freely moved from steel to textile production or from textile to steel production.

(d) *Returns to scale*. The theory assumes constant costs, thus ignoring the possibility that economies or diseconomies of scale can be obtained as output increases.

(e) *Full employment*. The assumption is made that there is full employment of the factors of production. Thus, as specialisation takes place, those resources freed by one sector are automatically transferred to the sector the country is specialising in. This assumption means that it is possible to calculate the opportunity cost.

(f) *Free trade*. Free trade is an obvious assumption of the theory of comparative advantage. There are no trade barriers such as tariffs and quotas, for these would limit the scope for specialisation in the 2 countries. This is unlikely to be the case in the real world. (For a discussion of tariffs and quotas *see* **9** and **10**.)

7. The terms of trade
The preceding sections have outlined how countries specialise in the production of particular goods in which they have a comparative advantage. In order to obtain the goods they are *not* producing it is necessary to trade. Referring to the previous analysis, suppose country B exports 60 units of the steel it produces to country A in exchange for 320 units of textiles. The ratio at which steel is externally traded for textiles is 1 unit of steel for $5\frac{1}{3}$ units of textiles. The ratio $1:5\frac{1}{3}$ can be taken to be the physical *terms of trade*. If country B set out to produce 320 units of textiles from within its own economy it would have to sacrifice 80 units of steel. Country B, therefore, faces a domestic opportunity cost ratio for steel of 1:4 (*see* Table 16.5), which is less favourable than the terms of trade $1:5\frac{1}{3}$. When considering country

A, it gains 60 units of steel from country B by exporting 320 units of textiles. If country A had produced the 60 units of steel itself it would have been at the expense of 480 units of textiles. Specialisation and trade are, therefore, of mutual benefit to both countries, although there is no reason why the benefits are necessarily split equally between the two countries.

So far we have assumed 2 countries and 2 products, namely textiles and steel. There are, however, many countries and many products, and the terms of trade are calculated by taking the indexed price of exports and dividing by the indexed price of imports:

$$\text{Terms of trade index} = \frac{\text{Index of export prices}}{\text{Index of import prices}} \times \frac{100}{1}$$

The concept of index numbers is outlined in chapter 13: **3** and **4**. In relation to the terms of trade, the index number incorporates weights which are attached to each good and service based on their relative importance in total exports and total imports. The terms of trade for the period 1985–1990 can be seen in Table 16.6.

Table 16.6 The UK terms of trade (1988=100)

Year	Index price of exports	Index price of imports	Terms of trade
1985	100.0	100.0	100.0
1986	90.1	95.4	94.4
1987	93.5	98.0	95.4
1988	93.4	97.0	96.3
1989	100.8	104.2	96.7
1990	106.2	108.1	98.2

Source: *Economic Trends, Annual Supplement*, HMSO, 1992

The base year is 1985 where the indexed price of exports and imports are made equal to 100, thus giving a terms of trade of 100. In 1986 the UK terms of trade was 94.4 which was obtained by dividing 90.1 by 95.4 multiplied by 100.

Between 1985 and 1986 there was thus a fall in the terms of trade index, with the indexed price of imports rising relative to the indexed price of exports. Between 1986 and 1990 the indexed price of exports rose relative to the indexed price of imports, thus the terms of trade index increased. A rise in the terms of trade is called a *favourable movement* whereas a fall is called an *unfavourable* movement.

Care must be taken when interpreting the terms of trade. A favourable movement does not necessarily imply a value of over 100, but simply an improvement on the previous year's value. Although a rise in the relative price of exports in relation to imports, i.e. a favourable terms of trade, means that more imports can be obtained per unit of exports, this may still have a detrimental effect on the balance of trade. The reason for this is that a rise in the relative price of exports will, depending on the price elasticity of demand, lead to a reduction in the total value of export sales, whereas imports will appear relatively more attractive and so the total value of imports may increase.

Protectionism

8.   What is protectionism?
Government intervention or *protection* in international trade can occur for a number of reasons (*see* **15**), can take a variety of forms and can have both positive and negative effects. Some of the forms of protectionist policy are discussed below.

9.   Tariffs
A tariff is a tax placed on imported commodities with the aim of raising their price and, therefore, discouraging their purchase. A tariff can take the form of a *specific tax*, i.e. a *lump sum tax*, where the tariff is based on a fixed amount on an imported item. Alternatively, it can be *ad valorem*, in which case it is based on a percentage of the price of the product.

As well as raising the price of imports relative to domestic products, tariffs can also act as a source of revenue for the government.

With the aid of Figure 16.2 it is possible to examine the effect of a tariff on a particular imported product. The assumption is made that the world supply, S_w, is *perfectly elastic* at a price of P_w, and that D_d and S_d are domestic demand and supply of the good. Before the imposition of a tariff the domestic price would be set at the world price P_w. At this price domestic demand would be Oq_4 and domestic producers would be willing to supply Oq_1. The result of this would be that the excess demand of $q_4 - q_1$ would be satisfied by importing the product.

If the government then imposes a tariff equal to $P_1 - P_w$, it has the effect of shifting the world supply curve to $S_w +$ tariff. The domestic price will now be P_1 and this will have the dual effect of reducing domestic demand to Oq_3 and increasing the amount domestic firms

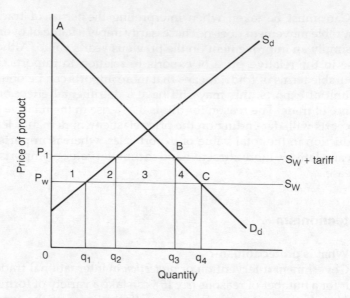

Figure 16.2 *The effect of the imposition of a tariff.*

are willing to supply to Oq_2. The desired outcome of the tariff will have been achieved, since imports of the product are now only q_3-q_2.

As well as reducing imports, the imposition of the tariff will have other implications. Before the tariff, consumer surplus (*see* 6: **13**) was ACP_w, while after the tariff the consumer surplus was reduced to ABP_1. Part of this reduction in consumer surplus will go to the government in the form of tariff revenue and this can be represented by area 3 in Figure 16.2, being the amount of the tariff P_1-P_w multiplied by the imported quantity q_3-q_2. The domestic producers of the product will obtain an increase in their producer surplus of area 1. This then leaves areas 2 and 4 which no party benefits from; they are a *cost to society* and are called *net welfare losses*.

10. Quotas

A quota is a physical limit placed on the amount of a commodity that can be imported over a certain period of time. This works on the basis that once a specified quantity has been imported no more of that commodity will be allowed into the country.

11. Exchange controls

The use of exchange controls places limits on the amount of foreign currency domestic residents can obtain. Such controls were in operation in the UK until 1979 and acted as a control over the import of commodities, on investment abroad and on the amount of foreign currency available to citizens travelling abroad.

12. Subsidies

Subsidising exported commodities is designed to improve the competitiveness of domestic producers both in the home and foreign markets.

13. Administrative barriers

These can take a number of different forms, ranging from time-consuming formalities such as official form filling on commodities imported into a particular country to strict health and safety standards such as those regarding the ingredients of imported food.

14. Voluntary export restraints

These represent agreements between 2 countries to limit the export of a particular commodity from 1 country to the other. *Voluntary export restraints* act as do quotas and have become increasingly popular in recent years.

15. Arguments for protection

There are several arguments put forward in favour of protection and these can be outlined in general terms, ignoring the distinction between tariffs and quotas.

(a) *To protect infant industry.* This is possibly the best known argument for protection. A newly established or *infant industry* is likely to have relatively high costs and, without protection, it might find it difficult to compete with established producers in other countries who are possibly benefiting from economies of scale (*see* 5: **21**).

It may be difficult, however, for a government to identify the potential infant industries which are likely to be successful. Also, if the infant industry will ultimately be profitable, obtaining a comparative advantage, the question needs to be asked: why is private business not willing to invest, relying instead on government assistance? An added problem is that it is often difficult for the government to remove the protection once in place, since the infant industry may have grown accustomed to it. The infant industry may never become efficient because of the protection and this means that resources are not being used most efficiently in the economy.

(b) *To prevent dumping.* Protectionist measures may be used to counter the threat of *dumping*. Dumping relates to a situation in which a company sells its product in an overseas market at a price lower than it is sold in its domestic market. It may be that the firm in question is practising price discrimination (*see* 6: **14**), selling at one price in its domestic market and at a lower price in an overseas market where the price elasticity of demand may be different. However, the aim of the dumping may be to drive an overseas competitor out of business, in which case it is known as *predatory dumping*. This may involve the predatory firm selling its product in another country at a loss in the short run.

(c) *To protect strategic industry*. Particular industries may be regarded as strategic in times of war. It may, therefore, be viewed as necessary to maintain these industries through protection rather than rely on foreign suppliers. Aerospace, shipbuilding, agriculture and armaments could be classed as strategic industries, and the decision about whether or not to protect them is essentially political.

(d) *To reduce structural unemployment*. A particular industry could have lost its comparative advantage and may be finding it hard to compete with foreign companies. Since the result of this may be structural unemployment and the human costs which go with it, the government may offer temporary protection.

(e) *To aid economic recovery*. This concerns the wider macroeconomic objective of stimulating the economy. It is a view associated with the Cambridge Economic Policy Group in the 1980s, who argued that general import controls would lead to a switch in demand from imported to domestically produced products, and with it an increase in output and employment.

16. Arguments against protection

There are a number of arguments put forward against protectionism:

(a) *Retaliation*. If the UK imposes import controls, for example on Japanese electrical goods, then Japan may impose import controls on UK products. If this is the case, any gain to UK companies competing with Japanese companies would be offset by the losses made by UK exporters to Japan. The overall result could be a trade war.

(b) *A cost on society*. Protectionist measures, particularly tariffs, impose a cost on society. This has already been discussed in **9**, where with the aid of Figure 16.2 it was shown that following the introduction of a tariff, there would be an increase in the price of commodities paid by the domestic consumer, a subsequent fall in consumer surplus and the resulting loss of welfare.

(c) *Companies may remain inefficient.* Since import controls protect particular industries from foreign competition, it means that they have less incentive to reduce their costs and increase their efficiency.

17. General Agreement on Tariffs and Trade (GATT)

In 1947 the *General Agreement on Tariffs and Trade* (GATT) was established, with the primary aim of liberalising trade world-wide. With this in mind the member countries have met periodically in order to negotiate reductions in tariffs and other barriers to trade. A number of 'rounds' of negotiations have taken place since 1947, the most notable being the Kennedy round (1964–67), the Tokyo round (1973–79) and the Uruguay round which started in 1986. The Kennedy round led to a reduction in tariffs of approximately one third as did the Tokyo round in the 1970s. With the Uruguay round, negotiations have been slow due to the conflicting interests of the member countries of GATT.

GATT is also concerned with the provision of the *most favoured nation* clause which requires that any tariff reduction made available by one country to another has to be made available to all the other members.

The main problem with GATT is that it relies on a voluntary code of compliance.

18. Free trade area

Members of a *free trade area* agree to remove tariffs and quotas between the member states. Such restrictions, however, are maintained against non-member countries. A free trade area (FTA) is, therefore, a tariff free area, but with individual members being free to set their own tariff levels against *non member* countries.

A problem with this is that imports from outside the free trade area can enter the area through the country with the lowest external tariff. This is called *trade deflection* because trade is deflected from high to low tariff countries within the free trade area.

19. Customs union

A *customs union* is similar to a FTA in that there is tariff free trade between member countries. There is, however, one important difference: members of the customs union adopt a *common external tariff* on imports from non-member countries and customs revenues are distributed among member countries according to an agreed formula.

20. Common market

A *common market* is the same as a customs union (*see* 19) with the addition of the free movement of labour and capital between member countries, common taxes, and common laws on employment, production and trade. In terms of degrees of integration, the ultimate form would be *economic union* where there would be an integration of member countries' economic policies.

21. European Community

The EC (formerly the European Economic Community or EEC) was formed in 1957 with the aim of encouraging free trade between the member states. It started as a customs union but has developed into a common market. The implementation of a Single European Market in December 1992 following the Single European Act of 1987 sees the removal of all trade barriers and the free movement of all the factors of production.

Progress test 16

1. Outline what is meant by absolute advantage? **(3)**

2. Distinguish between absolute and comparative advantage. **(3–5)**

3. What are the principal limitations of the theory of comparative advantage? **(6)**

4. What is meant by the terms of trade? **(7)**

5. Distinguish between a tariff and a quota. **(9, 10)**

6. With the aid of a diagram outline who gains and who loses from the imposition of a tariff. **(9)**

7. Briefly describe the arguments for and against the imposition of import controls. **(15, 16)**

17

The balance of payments and exchange rates

1. Introduction

This chapter examines the structure of the UK's balance of payments and the measures a government can use to correct a balance-of-payments deficit. It also deals with the various exchange rate regimes which have existed throughout the world this century, ranging from the fixed to the floating exchange rate. There is also a section on the Exchange Rate Mechanism (ERM).

The UK balance of payments

2. What are the UK balance of payments?

The UK balance of payments are a set of official accounts published annually by the Central Statistical Office in what is known as 'The Pink Book'. The accounts are a record of the transactions that have occurred between the residents of the UK and the rest of the world over a 1 year period. For example, if a UK company produces cars which it sells abroad this will lead to an inflow (+) of money into the UK which will be recorded as a credit item in the balance-of-payments accounts. On the other hand if, for example, a UK resident buys a German car this will lead to an outflow (−) of money from the UK and be recorded as a debit item in the balance of payments accounts. These are just two of the many transactions which occur annually. Table 17.1 gives a summary of the UK balance of payments accounts for 1990.

The accounts are divided into two main sections, namely the *current account* and the *capital account*, which is known as the transactions in UK assets and liabilities.

3. The current account

The current account can be divided into visible and invisible trade (*see* Table 17.1).

(a) *Visible trade* refers to the export and import of physical items,

Table 17.1 Summary of the balance of payments, 1990

	£ million
Current account	
Visible trade	
Exports	102,038
Imports	−120,713
Visible balance (1)	−18,675
Invisible trade	
Exports	117,350
Imports	−113,055
Invisible balance (2)	4,295
Current balance (1)+(2)	−14,380
Transactions in UK assets and liabilities	
UK external assets	−72,301
UK external liabilities	84,381
Net transactions	12,081
Balancing item	2,299

Source: *United Kingdom Balance of Payments*, CSO, 1991.

namely goods such as cars, electrical products, textiles and chemicals. As seen in Table 17.1 the UK is a net importer of physical items with a visible balance (or balance of trade) deficit of −£18,675m in 1990.

(b) *Invisible trade* is concerned with the trade in services. It includes:

(i)   Banking, such as the charges, fees and commission paid on current accounts held by foreign residents in UK banks.

(ii)   Insurance earnings, such as when foreign firms take out insurance cover with a UK insurance company.

(iii)   Civil aviation and sea transport, with the carriage of foreign passengers and freight on UK airlines and ships.

(iv)   Tourism, with foreign residents taking holidays in the UK.

These are all classed as invisible exports but there will also be invisible imports such as a UK resident taking a holiday in Greece, leading to an outflow of money from the UK. Other items which are included in the invisible balance are military expenditure on UK bases abroad and US expenditure on bases in the UK; the provision of UK embassies; interest profit and dividends either earned on UK investments abroad or paid to foreigners on their investments in the UK; and the private transfer of money into the UK from groups such as UK nationals temporarily working abroad. In 1990 there was a surplus of £4,295m on invisibles.

Taking the visible and invisible balance together the UK experienced a current account deficit of –£14,380m in 1990.

4. Transactions in UK assets and liabilities

This section of the balance of payments (the capital account) includes the movement of short-term and long-term capital between the UK and other countries, such as UK investment abroad and overseas investment in the UK, as well as borrowing and lending overseas by UK banks and the drawings on and additions to official reserves in terms of gold and foreign currency held by the Bank of England in the Exchange Equalisation Account.

5. Short term capital flows

Short term capital flows refer to liquid funds held in bank accounts or short term government securities such as Treasury bills (*see* 14: **15**). For example, US residents may purchase sterling and deposit it in a UK bank. This can be viewed as a short-term investment in the UK and is recorded as a credit item in the UK external liabilities section of the balance of payments. Short-term capital flows can be referred to as 'hot money' since the owners of these liquid funds can transfer them from one country to another very quickly in order to take advantage of a rise in the rate of interest in a particular country or the appreciation of a particular currency.

6. Long-term capital flows

Long-term capital flows refer to items such as private overseas investment in the UK – as with a Japanese car company investing in a new car assembly plant in Derbyshire. This would represent a credit item in the balance-of-payments account. Alternatively, private investment overseas, although an asset, represents an outflow of funds and is therefore a debit item in the accounts.

Long-term capital flows can be divided into direct investment and portfolio investment.

(a) *Direct investment* refers to investment such as a UK company taking ownership of an existing foreign subsidiary. This would be classified as outward direct investment, whereas investment in the UK by overseas companies would be inward direct investment.

(b) *Portfolio investment* refers only to investment in securities with an original maturity of more than 1 year, namely long-term government securities, and those with no fixed maturity such as ordinary shares.

The transactions in UK assets and liabilities also include transac-

tions which are required to deal with a deficit or surplus on the
balance of payments after taking account of the visible and invisible
trade and capital flows.

Transactions in visible and invisible trade and capital flows can
be termed *autonomous transactions* and if the outward flow of autonomous transactions (debit items) is greater than the inward flow of
autonomous transactions (credit items) then a balance-of-payments
deficit exists. Since, however, the balance-of-payments accounts *must*
balance, then if the autonomous transactions have produced a deficit
they must be matched by *accommodating transactions* to offset the
deficit. This is achieved by an outflow of foreign currency from the
Bank of England official reserves or by official borrowing from foreign
banks or the International Monetary Fund (IMF). If there is a surplus
on autonomous transactions then additions can be made to the official
reserves or previous borrowing can be repaid.

7. The balancing item

The balance of payments is compiled from a large number of
different sources and invariably there will be inaccuracies in some of
the data used. For this reason a balancing item is included to account
for all the errors and omissions, and to ensure that the balance-of-
payments accounts sum to zero. Thus, by reference to Table 17.1, net
transactions plus the balancing item equal the current balance.

Measures to correct a balance-of-payments deficit and their effects

8. Policies to correct a balance-of-payments deficit

Although the balance of payments always balance this does not
mean that there is necessarily a balance of payments equilibrium. It
could be that a country has a balance of payments deficit or surplus.
If there is a deficit which is only short term then it can be financed by
either running down official reserves or by official borrowing. There
may, however, be what is called a *fundamental disequilibrium in the
balance of payments*, with a persistent deficit. If this is the case then
other measures have to be pursued. These policies include:

(a) *Deflation*. Deflationary fiscal and monetary policy could be used
to reduce the level of aggregate demand in the economy. As well as
reducing the demand for imports this policy could limit the inflationary pressure in the economy, thus reducing the relative prices of

exports. This policy would make exports more competitive abroad and imports less competitive in the UK.

The problem with the use of a deflationary policy to alleviate a persistent balance-of-payments deficit is that it could conflict with other government objectives, namely the achievement of full employment and economic growth.

(b) *Import controls.* Tariffs place a tax on imports, raising their price, while quotas limit the quantity of particular products which can be brought into the country. Import controls can be used as a means of dealing with a balance-of-payments deficit, although they fail to deal with the root cause of the deficit.

Import controls were explained in more detail in 16: **8–14**.

(c) *Devaluation.* If an economy is operating under a fixed exchange rate regime then a devaluation of its currency will make the country's exports cheaper in terms of foreign currency and its imports dearer in terms of domestic currency, (*see* **18** for a more detailed explanation of devaluation). If an economy is operating under a floating exchange rate regime then a depreciation of its currency will have the same effect. Whether a devaluation is successful in remedying a balance-of-payments deficit depends on the price elasticity of demand for its exports and imports.

9. The Marshall-Lerner condition

The Marshall-Lerner condition relating to the devaluation of a particular currency, states that an improvement in an economy's balance of payments following a devaluation will only occur if the

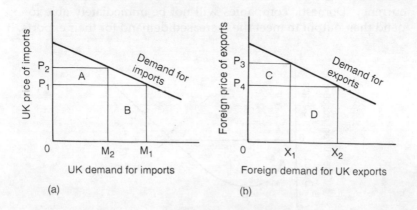

Figure 17.1 *Elastic demand for UK imports and exports.*

sum of the price elasticity of demand for its exports and imports is greater than unity (i.e. elastic). This can be outlined by reference to Figure 17.1 where, following a devaluation of the pound, the price of imports increases and the price of exports decreases.

In Figure 17.1(a) a devaluation of the pound has increased the price of imports from P_1 to P_2 and reduced their demand from M_1 to M_2. This leads to an increase in expenditure on imports of area A but a reduction in expenditure of area B, thus there is an overall reduction in expenditure on imports of $(A - B)$ since the demand for imports is elastic. In Figure 17.1(b) the devaluation of the pound has resulted in a reduction in the foreign price of exports from P_3 to P_4 and an increase in the demand for exports from X_1 to X_2. Given the elastic demand for exports, this will lead to a reduction in expenditure by foreigners on UK exports by area C, but at the same time there will be an increase in expenditure by foreigners of area D. Overall there will have been an increase in expenditure on UK exports of $(D - C)$.

In terms of the balance of payments, the effect will have been an improvement of $(A - B) + (D - C)$, since the outflow of currency from the economy has reduced and the inflow of currency has increased.

10. The J-curve

In Figure 17.2 the economy is initially assumed to be at point A, experiencing a current account deficit.

In response to the deficit, the economy's currency may be devalued. Initially this will cause the deficit to worsen, noted by a movement to point B in Figure 17.2. The reason for this is that it takes time for the economy to adjust to the change in the external value of its currency. Domestic companies will not be immediately able to expand their output to meet the increased demand for their exports. It

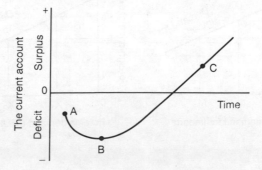

Figure 17.2 *The J-curve.*

will also take time for importers to adjust their consumption patterns and find cheaper substitutes for the imported products. After a period of time, however, the current account will begin to improve, eventually moving into a situation of surplus such as point C in Figure 17.2.

Exchange rate regimes

11. The exchange rate

Countries throughout the world have their own currencies and if international trade is to operate smoothly then it has to be possible for currencies to be readily convertible. The *foreign exchange market* (FEM) is the market where international currencies are traded. The FEM is not, however, a physical place but simply consists of traders who buy and sell world currencies on behalf of private individuals, firms, banks and other institutions.

The exchange rate is determined on the foreign exchange market and represents the rate at which one currency can be exchanged for another currency. The rate of exchange is essentially the *price* of the currency.

In outlining the determination of the exchange rate of a particular currency we will make the assumption that 2 countries are involved, namely the UK and the US. The exchange rate is, therefore, the pound in terms of the dollar. There are a number of different exchange rate regimes which have operated throughout the world this century and the following sections will deal with four such regimes: the floating exchange rate, the fixed exchange rate, the managed exchange rate and the system currently operating within the EC, namely the Exchange Rate Mechanism (ERM).

12. The floating exchange rate

The floating exchange rate system is where the exchange rate is determined by market forces with no government intervention. The external value of the pound against the dollar is, therefore, determined by demand and supply as illustrated in Figure 17.3.

In the absence of speculation and investment, the demand for sterling is mainly determined by the US demand for UK exports. For example, if US tourists visit the UK they need to convert dollars into pounds to pay for the UK hotel they are staying in, for gifts, for spending money and so on. The demand for sterling is illustrated in Figure 17.3 as a negatively sloped curve (D£). The reason for the negative slope is that if the external value of sterling increased from

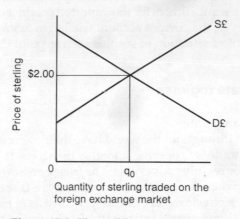

Figure 17.3 *The equilibrium exchange rate.*

$2 to $4, Americans would now only receive 25 pence for each dollar exchanged whereas previously they received 50 pence. The result would be less UK exports demanded by the US.

The supply of sterling to the foreign exchange market (S£) in Figure 17.3 is mainly the result of the demand for US goods and services by UK importers. If, for example, a UK importer demanded US goods he or she would need to sell sterling on the FEM and purchase dollars in order to pay the US for their goods. The supply of sterling in Figure 17.3 can be seen as positively sloped since if the external value of sterling were to increase from say $2 to $4, a good in the US with a price of $10 would initially cost the UK importer £5. However, when the value of sterling increased to $4 the UK importer would only have to pay £2.50. The assumption is, therefore, that when the external value of sterling increases there will be an increase in its supply to the FEM in order to buy the cheaper imported goods and services.

Given the demand for and the supply of sterling it is possible to determine the exchange rate as in Figure 17.3. The interaction of demand and supply gives the rate of exchange of £1 equal to $2 (or $1 = 50p)

13. Terminology

At this point it is worth elaborating on certain terms used when discussing exchange rate regimes. In a floating exchange rate system an increase in the external value of sterling on the FEM is termed an *appreciation* of sterling, whereas a decrease in the value is called a *depreciation*. In a fixed exchange rate regime (*see* **17–20**), when a decision is taken to increase the external value of sterling it is called a *revaluation* whereas a decision to lower the value is termed a *devaluation*.

14. Changes in the exchange rate

There are a number of factors which will lead to a change in the exchange rate, such as:

(a) *An increase in the demand for UK exports*. If this occurs the effect will be an increase in the demand for sterling on the FEM. The result of this will be a shift in the demand curve to the right and, therefore, an appreciation of sterling. A decrease in the demand for UK exports would cause the demand curve for sterling to shift to the left and this would have resulted in a depreciation.

(b) *An increased demand for imports*. This will have the effect of shifting the supply curve for sterling to the right and will result in a depreciation of sterling on the FEM.

(c) *A change in the rate of inflation*. A rise in the UK rate of inflation relative to that of the US will, other things being equal, reduce the demand for UK products in the US and increase the demand for US products in the UK. There will thus be a reduction in the demand for sterling and an increase in the supply of sterling on the FEM. The result will be a depreciation of the pound on the FEM.

(d) *A change in the rate of interest*. A rise in the UK rate of interest is likely to attract short-term capital flows into UK financial institutions. This inflow of hot money (*see* 5) will increase the demand for sterling on the FEM and, therefore, lead to an appreciation.

(e) *North Sea oil*. The first North Sea oil came ashore in 1976 with the result that there was a reduction in the demand for imported oil (shifting the supply curve for sterling to the left) and a demand for North Sea oil from abroad (shifting the demand curve for sterling to the right). The result was an appreciation of sterling on the FEM.

15. Advantages of a floating exchange rate

The advantages can be viewed as:

(a) A floating exchange rate should automatically correct a balance-of-payments disequilibrium. For example, a country with a balance-of-payments deficit will experience an outflow of currency and with it an exchange rate depreciation. A depreciation of the currency will make the country's exports cheaper and imports dearer and this should correct the country's balance-of-payments deficit — provided the price elasticity of demand for the country's exports and imports summed together is greater than 1 (*see* 9).

(b) If a floating exchange rate automatically corrects a balance-of-payments deficit, the balance of payments will cease to be a constraint on the government's internal economic policy. This means that the government can pursue objectives such as full employment and economic growth without having to tailor its fiscal and monetary policy to alleviating a balance-of-payments deficit.

(c) With a floating exchange rate there is less need to keep large 'official reserves' in order to support the exchange rate.

16. Disadvantages of a floating exchange rate

The disadvantages can be viewed as:

(a) A floating exchange rate regime can lead to uncertainty in international trade both for the trader and the investor, since they are unsure about the future exchange rate. To a certain extent this can be overcome by use of the 'forward market', where the trader can 'hedge' against the risk of a change in the exchange rate by agreeing with a bank the current exchange rate for a particular date in the future. Banks make a charge for such a service.

(b) A floating exchange rate can give rise to speculation and, in fact, speculation can lead to wide fluctuations in the exchange rate. An example of speculation could involve the expectation of an appreciation of sterling. If an appreciation of sterling is expected, speculators will purchase sterling and this will lead to an inflow of hot money into the UK — the result being an appreciation in the exchange rate, possibly greater than the one which was expected.

(c) A floating exchange rate can lead to a lack of discipline in the government's internal economic policy. For example, a government may pursue a policy aimed at full employment which could prove inflationary. The government may consider this as an acceptable trade-off since it will not lead to a loss of export markets. The reason for this is that a depreciation in the external value of the currency will occur as a result of the inflation, and this will reduce the price of exports and so offset the inflationary pressure on export prices. There will, however, be added inflationary pressure in the domestic market since there will be an increase in import prices following depreciation.

17. The fixed exchange rate

With a fixed exchange rate, governments agree to maintain their particular exchange rate at a predetermined level. The rate of exchange is maintained through intervention in the FEM by each

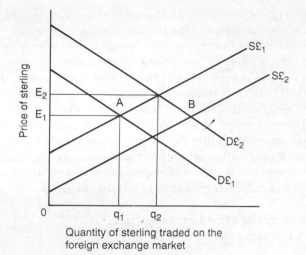

Figure 17.4 *The fixed exchange rate.*

country's central bank. The fixed exchange rate regime can be illustrated by reference to Figure 17.4.

We could assume that E_1 is the fixed exchange rate, this being the rate which would be the free market equilibrium rate if $D£_1$ and $S£_1$ were the respective demand for and the supply of sterling on the FEM. Suppose now there is an increase in the demand for sterling, represented by a shift in the demand curve to the right, to $D£_2$ in Figure 17.4. This could be the result of an increase in the demand for UK exports. The exchange rate would now rise to E_2, which is above the predetermined rate E_1. In this situation the government would be forced (through its central bank) to supply sterling, equal to AB, through the purchase of foreign currency, thus shifting the supply curve to $S£_2$ and restoring the predetermined exchange rate E_1.

If the price of sterling had fallen below E_1 then the central bank would have purchased sterling using its foreign currency reserves in order to maintain its value at E_1.

If the central bank found difficulty in maintaining the exchange rate at E_1, then it would be possible for a revaluation or a devaluation of the external value of the currency to take place.

18. Revaluation and devaluation

If the exchange rate was *consistently* above or below E_1, being associated with either a balance-of-payments surplus or deficit, then a revaluation or a devaluation of the currency could take place. A revaluation raises the external value of the currency against all other currencies which are part of the fixed exchange rate regime. Alternatively, a devaluation lowers the external value of a country's currency. A revaluation is likely to be resisted by the country concerned since it makes exports dearer and imports cheaper and could, therefore, worsen their balance of payments. A devaluation would, on the other hand, be welcomed since it makes exports cheaper and imports dearer. There is, however, the problem in that countries holding the devalued currency will find their reserves are worth less overnight.

Before a revaluation or a devaluation occurs, the country concerned is expected to undertake measures aimed at alleviating a surplus or a deficit on the balance of payments.

19. Advantages of a fixed exchange rate

The advantages can be viewed as:

(a) There is more certainty in foreign trade with a fixed exchange rate regime. For example, a company will find it easier to calculate its profit from selling goods in foreign markets since the profit will not be eroded by exchange rate fluctuations.

(b) A fixed exchange rate encourages a government to be disciplined in its internal economic policy. If a country has a rate of inflation which is higher than that of its competitors it will lead to a balance-of-payments deficit and, therefore, a need for deflationary measures.

(c) There is a belief that fixed exchange rates reduce speculation. This, however, is only likely to be the case if the exchange rate is viewed as being fixed in the long run, otherwise speculation is still a possibility.

20. Disadvantages of a fixed exchange rate

(a) With a fixed exchange rate, the government's internal economic policy may be constrained by both the exchange rate and the balance of payments. For example, if a government seeks to reflate the economy and reduce unemployment it could lead to an increase in imports, and result in a balance-of-payments deficit and pressure on sterling. In this situation the government would be forced to 'deflate the economy'.

(b) Unlike 19 (c), speculators may believe that a fixed exchange rate is not sustainable at a particular rate and that devaluation is likely. In this situation the speculator cannot lose. They will sell the currency on the FEM, which will in fact make the balance-of-payments deficit worse and make a devaluation more likely.

(c) Under a fixed exchange rate regime countries have to hold large reserves of gold and foreign currency so that if their currency comes under pressure on the FEM the central bank can enter the market and restore the currency to the fixed rate.

21. Managed flexibility

Since 1972 a system of managed flexibility has been in operation in the world currency markets. This means that the exchange rate has been determined by market forces but it has not been allowed to float *cleanly*, since the central bank has on occasions interfered in the market. In other words, it has been a *dirty float*, since the exchange rate has been influenced by direct government intervention in the FEM through the buying and selling of currency.

22. The European Monetary System (EMS)

The EMS came into existence in 1979 with the main aim of promoting monetary stability in Europe. Central to the EMS is the Exchange Rate Mechanism (ERM) which is designed to keep the member country's exchange rates within agreed limits (or bands). The other important part of the EMS is the European Currency Unit (ECU).

23. The Exchange Rate Mechanism (ERM)

The UK entered the ERM in October 1990 at an agreed central rate of £1 = DM2.95. At the time the UK entered the ERM, individual currencies, that is the deutschmark, the French franc, the guilder, the Belgium and Luxembourg franc, the Danish krone, the Irish punt and the lira, were allowed to move (or float) within a predetermined band ± 2.25 per cent either side an agreed central rate against the other member currencies in the mechanism. Sterling, the escudo and the peseta were allowed to fluctuate within a wider band of 6 per cent, although eventually they were expected to move to the 2.25 per cent margin operated by the other ERM currencies. The ERM currencies also had central rates against the ECU.

24. The European Currency Unit (ECU)

The ECU is an artificially created currency. The ECU comprises certain amounts of EC currencies, the amounts being based on the relative economic weight of each of the countries. Thus the German D-Mark has a weight of 30 per cent in the ECU, whereas UK sterling has a weight of 13 per cent. The weights are revised every 5 years. The ECU is, therefore, a weighted average exchange rate and it means that each individual currency can be compared against a *currency basket*.

One of the main functions of the ECU is as a *divergence indicator*, providing a means whereby those currencies in the ERM whose exchange rates are diverging from other member currencies can be identified and the appropriate action taken. Intervention in the FEM by the appropriate central banks is required when the *divergence threshold* is reached, the divergence threshold being 75 per cent of the maximum deviation of a particular currency in the ERM against the ECU.

25. Intervention in the Foreign Exchange Market (FEM)

The way in which the ERM operates is that if a currency within the ERM reaches its limit against another member currency either side of the agreed central rate, or if it reaches its divergence threshold, then intervention in the FEM is required by the central banks of the 2 currencies concerned. If, for example, a currency falls to its minimum level against the German D-Mark, then the central banks must buy that currency on the FEM and sell D-Marks. In practice, intervention is likely to occur before the maximum or minimum limits are reached and this is called *intra-marginal intervention*.

As well as buying and selling currency central bank action could take the form of an increase or decrease in the rate of interest. As with the fixed exchange rate regime (*see* 17), currencies in the ERM can be formally devalued or revalued, although this should be viewed as a final resort after all other possible policy options have been used. If a devaluation or revaluation takes place, it requires the agreement of all the member countries of the ERM.

Intervention in the FEM by a particular member country requires substantial foreign exchange reserves and the EMS has a facility called the *very short-term financing facility* (VSTF) which makes funds available for intervention deemed necessary to protect a currency. Unlimited credit is available and this is automatic if a currency has reached its limit against another currency. The credit requires repayment within a short period of time.

This section has outlined how the mechanism is intended to operate. However, in the period up to and including 16 September 1992 it came under increasing pressure, culminating in the suspension of the pound and the lira as members of the ERM.

26. The suspension of sterling within the ERM (16 September 1992)

Over a period of time the financial markets had become increasingly convinced that the UK government would be unable to maintain sterling at its pegged rate of DM2.95 within the ERM. There were a number of reasons as to why sterling had come under pressure within the ERM:

(a) There had been reductions in US interest rates and, as the value of the dollar fell on the foreign exchange market, investors moved into D-Marks. This strengthened the value of the D-Mark on the FEM and weakened the value of other currencies, including the pound against the D-Mark.

(b) There were few signs of recovery in the UK economy and this placed the pound under further pressure on the FEM as investors sold pounds. The general belief was that the UK would be forced, eventually, into lowering the sterling central rate in order to make its industries more competitive. By selling pounds *before* the anticipated devaluation of sterling, a profit could be made by repurchasing sterling at a lower price after the anticipated devaluation.

(c) German interest rates were at historically high levels, adding to the attractiveness of D-Marks as a currency in which to invest. This was the case even after the Bundesbank had reduced German interest rates by 0.25 per cent on 14 September 1992.

(d) There was growing uncertainty surrounding the outcome of the French referendum on the Maastricht Treaty. This had cast doubt on the likelihood of Monetary Union and increased the possibility of a realignment of currencies within the ERM.

As a result of all these factors, the value of sterling had fallen close to its floor within the ERM of DM2.7780. The anticipation was, therefore, that sterling would have to be devalued within the ERM in much the same way that the lira had been devalued on 13 September 1992.

The pound came under increasing pressure on the FEM on 16 September 1992 and this resulted in the Bank of England intervening to buy pounds in an effort to maintain its value within the permitted bands. The intervention of the Bank of England failed to improve the value of sterling, as did the efforts of the Bundesbank and the Bank of France in supporting sterling. In response to this the UK government announced an increase in interest rates from 10 per cent to 12 per cent. This was followed by further spending by the Bank of England in support of sterling. Both measures failed, however, to stop the pound falling below its ERM floor as speculators were not convinced that the value of the pound could be maintained above a value of DM2.7780.

Since the maintenance of sterling's parity within the ERM remained the main strand of the UK government's macroeconomic policy, they announced a further rise in interest rates on the afternoon of 16 September — to 15 per cent. Even this failed to halt the fall in the value of sterling, and eventually the UK government suspended its membership of the Exchange Rate Mechanism and the second rise in interest rates was cancelled. The pound was thus allowed to float on the foreign exchange market. The Italian lira was also suspended from ERM membership and the Spanish peseta was devalued by 5 per cent.

Progress test 17

1. Outline the difference between the visible balance and the invisible balance. **(3)**

2. Explain what is meant by short-term and long-term capital flows. **(5, 6)**

3. What does the balancing item balance? **(7)**

4. What measures are at a government's disposal for dealing with a balance-of-payments deficit? **(8)**

5. Explain the Marshall-Lerner condition. **(9)**

6. What is meant by the J-curve? **(10)**

7. Outline the advantages and disadvantages of a floating exchange rate. **(15, 16)**

8. In a fixed exchange rate regime, when may a revaluation or devaluation take place? **(18)**

9. What is the difference between a clean float and a dirty float? **(21)**

10. Outline the factors which led to the suspension of sterling as a member of the ERM on 16 September 1992. **(26)**

18
Managing the economy

1. Introduction

The aim of this chapter is to outline the macroeconomic objectives and the instruments that a government can use in order to achieve those objectives.

The objectives and instruments of economic policy

2. What are the objectives of economic policy?

The main macroeconomic objectives can be seen as the achievement of full employment, price stability, economic growth and a balance-of-payments equilibrium, although not all governments will share these objectives. It is also true that there will be trade-offs and potential conflicts between the objectives, and different governments will attach differing priorities to them.

In Table 18.1 the performance of the UK government in terms of the four main objectives is given over the period 1981 to 1991.

(a) *Full employment.* Full employment is difficult to define. There will always be individuals between jobs, termed frictional unemployment (*see* 12: **5**) and those who are unemployed because of the constantly changing demand for goods and services, termed structural unemployment (*see* 12: **6**). For these reasons full employment cannot mean zero unemployment. The Beveridge Report on *Social Insurance and Allied Services* in 1942 defined a workable and acceptable level of full employment as being no more than 3 per cent of the working population unemployed and this figure became a benchmark for governments in the UK throughout the 1950s and 1960s. As seen from Table 18.1, this is not a level which as been achieved in the UK during the 1980s.

There are certainly economic, social and political reasons why full employment should be a major macroeconomic objective. These reasons are explained in detail in 12: **3**.

(b) *Stable prices.* This has been the major aim of the UK government throughout the 1980s and early 1990s. It is, however, unrealistic to talk about zero inflation since changing demand conditions will always mean that there is an element of inflationary pressure in the economy. In the post-war period an 'acceptable' target for inflation was in the region of 2.5 per cent. In recent times however, the UK rate of inflation *compared* to that of its major competitors has been viewed as more important than the absolute rate of inflation. The annual UK rate of inflation in the 1980s did not fall below 3.4 per cent and, in fact, was as high as 18 per cent in 1980 (*see* Table 18.1).

(c) *Economic growth.* Economic growth is all important because it affects the economy's standard of living. Economic growth can be measured in terms of the growth in Gross Domestic Product (GDP). As seen in Table 18.1, there have been years throughout the 1980s when a growth in GDP above 4 per cent was achieved, whereas in other years the growth in GDP was negative.

There is increasing criticism of economic growth as an objective since it creates social costs, such as pollution, and these costs could outweigh the benefits.

(d) *Balance-of-payments equilibrium.* This objective does not mean that there should be neither a balance-of-payments surplus nor deficit, but that the government should aim at a surplus in the long run, avoiding a large change or a disequilibrium in the balance of payments.

Table 18.1 The four main objectives of government policy

Year	Unemployment as a % of total workforce	Annual change in the RPI (%)	Annual change in GDP at factor cost (%)	Balance of payments (current balance) (£ million)
1981	8.1	11.9	−1.1	6,748
1982	9.5	8.6	1.8	4,649
1983	10.5	4.6	3.6	3,765
1984	10.7	5.0	1.7	1,811
1985	10.9	6.1	3.8	2,878
1986	11.1	3.4	3.6	187
1987	10.0	4.2	4.5	−4,159
1988	8.1	4.9	4.1	−15,520
1989	6.3	7.8	2.1	−20,404
1990	5.8	9.5	0.9	−15,446
1991	8.1	5.9	−2.3	−4,399

Source: Central Statistical Office

3. Instruments of economic policy

The government has a number of instruments at its disposal as a means of achieving its objectives. These instruments have been discussed in detail in previous chapters so this section will act as a summary.

(a) *Fiscal policy.* Fiscal policy is concerned with government expenditure and taxation as a means of influencing the level of aggregate demand in the economy. In the post-war period up until the mid 1970s, fiscal policy was aimed at stimulating demand and little importance was given to the size of the PSBR. In the late 1970s and 1980s, however, more attention was given to the PSBR mainly because of its implications for the growth of the money supply and inflation (*see* Chapter 15).

(b) *Monetary policy.* Monetary policy, and in particular the use of interest rates, has been the main policy instrument used by the Conservative Government throughout the 1980s and early 1990s. The rate of interest is seen to be important since it affects the cost of borrowing and, therefore, consumer spending and company investment. The interest rate also has an influence on the balance of payments through the exchange rate, with an increase leading to an inflow of currency into the country.

Control of the money supply is also part of monetary policy and is interlinked with the rate of interest (*see* 14: **18**). The control of the money supply has been seen as important in order to achieve a lower rate of inflation.

(c) *Prices and incomes policy.* Prices and incomes policies (*see* 13: **22**) have been used in an attempt to influence the rate of increase in prices and wages in a more direct way. When the policy has been used in the UK the impact has been felt most in the public sector where the government directly control the 'purse strings' and use the public sector to give a 'lead' to the private sector. A prices and incomes policy was last used formally in 1979.

(d) *The exchange rate policy.* The exchange rate has been used as an instrument in order to influence the balance of payments and the rate of inflation. For example, an increase in the value of sterling on the foreign exchange market will make imported goods and services cheaper in the UK and this will have beneficial implications for the inflation rate, especially if the imports are basic raw materials.

(e) *Import controls.* Like exchange rate policy, import controls are a way of affecting the balance of payments. They have not, however, been used to any great extent in recent times.

Managing the economy

4. The problems of managing the economy

From the mid 1940s up until the mid 1970s the main method used by UK governments to achieve their objectives was to stimulate demand in the economy through a process known as *demand management* (*see* Chapter 11). The difficulty faced by successive governments, however, was that they could not simultaneously achieve all of the objectives. For example, a stimulation of demand to achieve full employment often led to an increase in inflation. It also led to pressure on the balance of payments since stimulating the economy increased the demand for imports and diverted products to the domestic market which would have otherwise have been exported. There is therefore a *trade-off* of objectives against each other and this is still a problem (*see* Table 18.1).

Certainly throughout the 1950s, 1960s and the early 1970s full employment was viewed as the main objective of government policy, although since then the control of inflation has been the number 1 priority.

5. The Medium Term Financial Strategy (MTFS)

Following the election of the Conservative Government in 1979 the main aim of macroeconomic policy became the control of inflation. With this in mind the MTFS was introduced in 1980, the aim of which was to constrain the growth of the money supply and to decrease the size of the PSBR through the control of public expenditure. If inflation was to be reduced, it was viewed as necessary to control the growth of the money supply, and in terms of fiscal policy to reduce the PSBR, since there was seen to be a direct link between the money supply and the PSBR (*see* 15: **11**). An increase in the PSBR also resulted in an increase in the rate of interest so that funds would be attracted to the public sector and this could result in the 'crowding out' of the private sector.

Since 1980 the MTFS has set targets for the growth of the money supply and the PSBR over the medium term.

Supply-side policies

6. What are supply-side policies?

As stated earlier in the chapter, from the late 1940s until the 1970s the main macroeconomic aim was to stimulate demand in the econ-

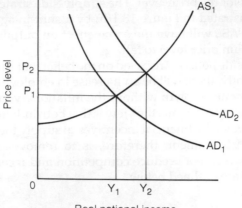

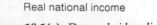

Figure 18.1(a) *Demand-side policy.*

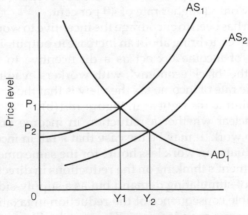

Figure 18.1 (b) *Supply-side policy.*

omy through a policy of demand management. In the early 1980s, however, the emphasis shifted from the demand-side, with the supply-side of the economy becoming more important. These two approaches can be represented by the use of aggregate demand and aggregate supply curves (*see* 13: **16–17**).

In Figure 18.1(a) a shift in aggregate demand from AD_1 to AD_2 will stimulate output (real national income) but will also have implications for the price level. The supply-side strategy on the other hand, as illustrated in Figure 18.1(b) by a shift in aggregate supply from AS_1 to AS_2, will have the same effect on output but will cause the equilibrium price level to fall.

Supply-side policies are based on the belief that if markets operate more efficiently, there will be an increase in employment opportunities and economic growth without the inflationary pressure. If markets are allowed to operate, the view is that both individuals and firms will be motivated by financial incentives to supply their services. The role of the government, therefore, is to remove the market imperfections which both reduce competition and incentives. Supply-side policies are outlined below.

7. Taxation

Since 1979 the basic rate of income tax has been reduced from 33 per cent to 25 per cent, and in the 1992 Budget it was reduced further to 20 per cent on the first £2,000 of taxable income. Nine higher rates of income tax up to 83 per cent have also been replaced since 1979 and there is now only 1 higher rate of 40 per cent.

The aim has been to encourage the incentive to work and, through these incentives, to bring about an increase in output. The belief is that high levels of income tax act as a disincentive to work and also encourage the 'black economy', with workers evading taxation. By lowering the rate of income tax the view is that the aggregate supply curve will shift to the right as in Figure 18.1(b).

It is unclear whether a reduction in income tax increases the incentive to work. It may be the case that a fall in income tax means that individuals can work less hours for the same amount of income. The government's thinking on the reductions in direct taxation is not as a means of stimulating demand but as a supply-side measure.

A possible consequence of the reduction in taxation is that total taxation revenue may increase. This can be illustrated by what is known as the *Laffer curve*, named after the American economist Professor A. Laffer.

With reference to Figure 18.2, if there is a zero tax rate there will be zero tax revenue. If, on the other hand, there is a tax rate of 100 per cent this will also yield zero tax revenue since a rate of 100 per cent will discourage individuals from working simply to provide the government with revenue. Government revenue will be at a maximum at a particular tax rate (T) and if the tax rate is higher than T there will be a fall in tax revenue. If the tax rate, is above T then a reduction can result in an increase in tax revenue. The problem the

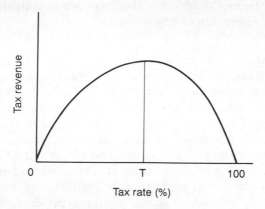

Figure 18.2 *The Laffer curve.*

government has is estimating the correct tax rate which minimises the disincentive to work and maximises the tax revenue. The reduction in the top rate of income tax to 40 per cent in 1988–89 was based on supply-side economics and the Laffer curve.

8. Trade union reform

The view of supply-side economists is that trade unions use their monopoly power in order to restrict entry into the labour market, with a resulting decrease in the numbers employed and an increase in the wage rate. Industrial action and restrictive practices are also seen as reducing industry's competitiveness. Through the Trade Union Act 1984, the Wages Act 1986 and a series of Employment Acts 1980, 1982, 1988, 1989, the government have sought among other things to:

(a)   restrict secondary industrial action;
(b)   make secondary picketing unlawful;
(c)   make unions liable for unlawful industrial action;
(d)   restrict the enforcement of the closed shop;
(e)   require secret ballots for union elections;
(f)   make industrial action called without a ballot illegal;
(g)   restrict the functions of wage councils;
(h)   prohibit disciplinary action by unions against members who refuse to take industrial action.

The effect of the legislation has been to reduce the power of the trade unions with the aim of producing a more flexible labour market.

In terms of Figure 18.1(b), the aim has been to shift the aggregate supply curve from AS_1 to AS_2.

9. Training

Training can be viewed as all important in lowering unemployment, increasing productivity, reducing skills shortages and producing a more flexible, mobile workforce. With this in mind, there have been a series of training initiatives particularly aimed at the unemployed. In 1991 a network of 82 Training and Enterprise Councils (TECs) were introduced in England and Wales and 22 Local Enterprise Companies (LECs) in Scotland. These are independent employer-led bodies with responsibility for planning and delivering training, enterprise and vocational education provision locally. Their aim is to make sure that business plays a central role in the local planning and delivery of training. TECs are expected to develop the Employment Department's (ED) main training programmes in order to meet local needs.

The ED training programmes are contracted to TECs and a number of the Department's provisions include:

(a) *Youth Training (YT)*. The aim of YT is to provide young people with, in the words of the Department of Employment, 'the broad based skills necessary for a flexible and self-reliant work-force' and 'with training leading to National Vocational Qualifications'. YT is guaranteed to all those between the age of 16 and 17 years who are not in full-time education or training and who do not have a job. It is the responsibility of TECs to choose the YT providers and to ensure that all the trainees on YT receive at least the minimum weekly allowance.

(b) *Training credits*. The White Paper entitled *Education and Training for the 21st Century* saw the extension of training credits. They allow young people to choose and buy training to meet their requirements. It is the responsibility of each TEC to develop their own approach to training credits in terms of, among other things, giving guidance to young people as to how to use their credits, guaranteeing suitable training places and making sure that credits are aimed at NVQ level 2 and above.

(c) *Employment Training (ET)*. ET is aimed at the long-term unemployed, i.e. those people who have been unemployed for between 6 and 12 months in the 18–24 age group and those who have been unemployed for over 2 years in the 18–50 age group. ET assists the TECs and Employment Service by offering places on a publicly-funded training or employment scheme.

(d) *National Council for Vocational Qualifications (NCVQ).* The NCVQ aims to rationalise the vocational qualifications system. National Vocational Qualifications (NVQ) are based on standards of workplace competence relating to the needs of each industry. Once an industry satisfies the NCVQ as to the quality and relevance to industry of the qualification, they are given NCVQ accreditation.

(e) *Employment Action (EA).* Introduced in October 1991, EA is available to those who have been unemployed for over 26 weeks in a period when jobs are relatively scarce. The aim is to provide temporary work opportunities for those who are long-term unemployed but who do not need or want training, to ensure that they remain ready to re-enter the labour market and to provide participants with job search support.

In terms of Employment Services the main objective is to provide help for the unemployed through such programmes as Restart courses, Jobclubs and personal advice and counselling, to help them get back to work.

10. Welfare payments

It is argued that welfare benefits to the unemployed may be too high relative to the wage rate in the lower paid labour markets. Unemployment benefit and social security may discourage individuals from working. It may also encourage those who are unemployed to spend more time searching for the 'ideal' job. Also, because of the tax system, certain individuals may receive more in benefits while unemployed than they would after income tax if they were working In this situation the marginal rate of tax is over 100 per cent and it is obviously a disincentive to work. This is called the *unemployment trap*.

If the gap between the wage received from working and the welfare payments individuals receive while unemployed was greater (and in favour of working), then the unemployed would be more willing to take up employment and the aggregate supply curve in Figure 18.1(b) would shift from AS_1 to AS_2.

11. Deregulation

Deregulation involves the removal of government regulations that are seen to restrict competition. Examples of deregulation include the bus industry following the Transport Act 1985, through which Road Service Licence requirements were abolished outside London, and the Big Bang in 1986 which deregulated the capital market by removing Stock Exchange restrictions. The aim is to improve the working of the market and, by so doing, shift the aggregate supply curve in Figure 18.1(b) to the right.

12. Privatisation

Privatisation can also be viewed as a supply-side policy, the belief being that companies in the private sector will make better use of resources than if they were under government control.

The move to privatisation followed the election in 1979 of a Conservative Government with a free market philosophy. Privatisation is normally defined as the transfer of assets from the public sector to the private sector and it can take a number of different forms. For example, it can involve the complete sale of the state-owned company as with the National Freight Corporation, or it can involve the sale of the profitable parts of the nationalised industry as with BR hotels.

Privatisation can also take the form of putting public sector activities *out to tender* as with BR catering, hospital cleaning and refuse collection, these all being services which have been contracted out. The sale of council houses is another example of privatisation. Table 18.2 gives a list of the major privatisations since 1979 and there are proposals for the privatisation of the coal industry and BR.

Many arguments both economic and political have been advanced for and against the privatisation programme but it is important to remember that the arguments put forward do not apply equally to all industries.

Table 18.2 The main privatisations

British Petroleum	1979, 1983 & 1987
British Aerospace	1981
Cable and Wireless	1981
Amersham International	1982
National Freight Corporation	1982
Britoil	1982
Associated British Ports	1983
Enterprise Oil	1984
Jaguar	1984
British Telecom	1984
British Gas	1986
British Airways	1987
Royal Ordnance	1987
Rolls-Royce	1987
BAA	1987
Rover Group	1988
British Steel	1988
Water	1989
Electricity	1990

13. The arguments for privatisation
The following case can be made for privatisation:

(a) A common view is that nationalised industries are inefficient, state controlled monopolies and that resources are allocated more efficiently through the price mechanism. If this view is accepted then a case can be made for privatisation in order to promote competition. Increased competition, as well as leading to a more efficient allocation of resources, should also make business more responsive to changing patterns of consumer demand.

(b) Efficiency can be encouraged through less government involvement in the firms' pricing and investment decisions. It could be argued that government officials are not the best individuals to be involved in commercial decision taking.

(c) The revenue from privatisation has allowed the PSBR to be reduced. In fact privatisation proceeds made an important contribution to the Budget surpluses of the late 1980s. It has been estimated that privatisation revenue will be £32.3bn over the period 1990–91 to 1994–95 and this will help to maintain a lower PSBR for the foreseeable future.

(d) Privatisation has promoted a wider share ownership both for individuals and employers.

14. The arguments against privatisation
The following arguments can be put forward against privatisation:

(a) Privatisation has not necessarily brought about competition. In fact in a number of instances, notably BT and British Gas, privatisation has simply meant the transfer of ownership from the public sector to the private sector.

(b) Opposition to privatisation has also been based on the belief that state-owned assets have been sold off too cheaply. This can be seen by the fact that public share offers have been over-subscribed and large profits have been made on the increased price of the shares of newly privatised companies.

(c) Privatisation can be viewed as simply the 'selling of the family silver' in order to finance current government expenditure and reduce the size of the PSBR.

(d) When the sales of shares through privatisation have taken place there has been a large outflow of funds from financial institutions, particularly building societies. This raises the possibility of 'crowding out'.

Progress test 18

1. With the aid of Table 18.1 outline the performance of the UK government during the 1980s in terms of the 4 main economic objectives. **(2)**

2. What is the difference between fiscal policy and monetary policy? **(3)**

3. What is meant by the Medium Term Financial Strategy? **(5)**

4. Distinguish between demand-side and supply-side economic policies. **(6)**

5. What does the Laffer curve attempt to show? **(7)**

6. What is meant by the unemployment trap? **(10)**

7. Outline the arguments for and against privatisation. **(12–14)**

Index